Eliminating Poverty through Development in China

In recent years China has achieved impressive economic growth, and also made remarkable progress in human development. However, contemporary China is still faced with the great challenge of widespread poverty. This not only constitutes a barrier against China's pursuit of sustainable economic growth, but also poses a potential threat to China's attempts to construct a harmonious society in the future. The report, directed by the China Development Research Foundation, one of China's leading think-tanks – and drawing on the research of over twenty of China's top scholars in this field, including chief authors Wang Xiaolu, Li Shi and Wang Sangui – three renowned poverty-reduction experts – examines China's efforts to eliminate poverty through development. It analyses all of the key issues, providing a review of China's past record in poverty alleviation, comparing this with the experiences of other countries, identifying the new characteristics and trends in poverty in recent years, and discussing the factors responsible. It assesses the objectives and success of the poverty alleviation policies adopted by the Chinese government in a comprehensive way, and puts forward suggestions for policy makers. Overall, this report is a valuable account of China's own thinking on its problems of poverty, and the best ways to tackle it and achieve sustainable economic development.

China Development Research Foundation (CDRF) is a nation-wide non-profit organization founded on the initiative of the Development Research Center (DRC) of the State Council. CDRF's mission is to advance good governance and public policy to promote economic development and social progress in China.

Routledge Studies on the Chinese Economy

Series Editor

Peter Nolan, *University of Cambridge*

Founding Series Editors

Peter Nolan, *University of Cambridge and*
Dong Fureng, *Beijing University*

The aim of this series is to publish original, high-quality, research-level work by both new and established scholars in the West and the East, on all aspects of the Chinese economy, including studies of business and economic history.

Eliminating Poverty through Development in China

China Development Research Foundation

Routledge
Taylor & Francis Group

LONDON AND NEW YORK

中国发展研究基金会
China Development Research
Foundation

First published 2009
by Routledge
2 Park Square, Milton Park, Abingdon, Oxon OX14 4RN

Simultaneously published in the USA and Canada
by Routledge
711 Third Avenue, New York, NY 10017

*Routledge is an imprint of the Taylor & Francis Group,
an informa business*

Typeset in Times New Roman by
RefineCatch Limited, Bungay, Suffolk

British Library Cataloguing in Publication Data
A catalogue record for this book is available from the British Library

Library of Congress Cataloging in Publication Data
A catalogue record has been requested for this book

ISBN 978–0–415–46277–8 (hbk)
ISBN 978–0–415–55134–2 (pbk)
ISBN 978–0–203–88772–1 (ebk)

MIX
Paper from
responsible sources
FSC
www.fsc.org   FSC® C013056

Printed and bound in Great Britain by
TJ International Ltd, Padstow, Cornwall

Contents

Figures

Tables

Boxes

Foreword

Over the last three decades, China has made historic progress in poverty alleviation. The number of rural poor has dropped from 250 million people in 1978 to about 20 million today, with the poverty incidence rate declining from 31 percent to 2.5 percent in that period. Culture, education and medical care have developed differently across China. By and large the productivity and living conditions of the rural poor have improved, while poor urban residents have mostly had their subsistence guaranteed. China's accomplishments in poverty elimination are immensely laudable.

China is a developing country, and her economic situation today is well off, but still at a low level with some inconsistencies and imbalances. Since the start of the twenty-first century, when China entered a development stage featuring concerted efforts to build a well-off society, anti-poverty initiatives have confronted changing new circumstances and, consequently, have involved new tasks. Tens of millions of Chinese people in rural and urban areas remain in poverty, even as China's economic growth and social advancement mean the yardstick for identifying poverty is undergoing corresponding changes. Today, emerging from poverty is not just dependent on having enough food and clothing. Instead, people need the capabilities to embrace development on their own, eliminating both the causes and the effects of poverty.

China's burgeoning economic strength today allows it to exert more efforts to support poverty-stricken populations and regions to escape poverty and cultivate wealth. New socioeconomic circumstances require better poverty alleviation strategies, however. These involve eliminating subsistence poverty by setting up and improving the social security system for rural and urban areas, and emphasizing the need to embrace development, including by enhancement of the capabilities of the poor and acceleration of socio-economic development in impoverished regions. In today's China, where each and every resident contributes to building a well-off society, effective poverty alleviation policies are of gigantic significance for the sake of realizing common prosperity.

The *China Development Report* is a comprehensive research report compiled and released regularly by the China Development Research Foundation, based on its research efforts. The report touches upon themes of importance to China's economic and social development. This report, based on the 2007 report, is entitled *Eliminating Poverty through Development in China*, which not only shows the need to regard the elimination of poverty as an important goal of economic development, but also indicates that the ultimate solution for poverty elimination is the pursuit of development. China's development in the current phase has met those requirements.

The Report is based on the findings of in-depth research. It describes China's accomplishments in poverty reduction and the poverty situation today. Many of the report's conclusions touch upon the root causes of poverty and the means for reducing it. Overall, the contents are thought-provoking and worth much reference. I believe this Report is helpful for China's further implementation of her poverty alleviation programme, and also for the international community's understanding of China's progress and experience in poverty alleviation.

I would like to thank all the experts who have participated in the research efforts on which this report is based for their diligent input and sharp wisdom. I would also like to thank the China Development Bank and the Ford Foundation for their generous support.

Wang Mengkui

Former President of the Development Research Center of the State Council and Chairman of the China Development Research Foundation

Authors' Foreword

Eliminating Poverty through Development in China addresses the theme of poverty, briefly describes the history and status quo of the poverty issue in China, introduces other countries' experiences in poverty alleviation, analyses the characteristics of poverty in China today and the various reasons behind it, reviews and assesses various poverty alleviation policies in China and their effects, studies governmental practices in anti-poverty work, and puts forward multiple suggestions for policy makers based on data and analysis.

The Chinese nation is now undergoing a historically unprecedented renaissance of immense significance. On its path leading to prosperity and modernism, China needs to mobilize all its citizens to make concerted efforts to stride forward. Development is not the only objective; the goal of a harmonious society is equally significant. Both poverty elimination and economic growth are essential to this process.

In the past 30 years, China's anti-poverty efforts have achieved stunning results. Almost a quarter of a billion people have been lifted out of poverty; the provision of education, health care and other services has vastly improved across the country. China's amazing achievements have been widely acknowledged in the international community, while some other developing countries now see China as a role model. In the final analysis, China's anti-poverty accomplishments are credited to its fast economic growth and active poverty alleviation policies.

China today, however, still shoulders a heavy task in continuing its progress in reducing poverty, which has a number of causes. Economic growth, *per se*, will not make poverty vanish automatically. It is necessary to conduct further research on effective strategies, and mobilize people from all walks of life to make joint efforts to eliminate poverty entirely.

This report has made some new contributions towards this end.

First, in view of the latest developments in China and in line with the evolution of global thinking on poverty reduction, we calculate that the original rural poverty line used to assess whether or not subsistence needs are met does not adequately reflect the needs of rural residents to develop their own capabilities (principally with respect to health care, education, etc.).

Hence, this report puts forward a concept of a developmental poverty line that covers basic needs for health care and education. This concept covers more ground than the original poverty line and fits better into China's future poverty alleviation goals.

Second, as indicated by the findings of this report, poverty in rural areas increasingly stems from the lack of human capital in terms of health care and education, and the lack of related public services. In urban areas, the most obvious reason for poverty is underemployment, but limited health care, education and public services are important contributing factors.

Third, the report comprehensively analyses and assesses, for the first time, the poverty alleviation policies and measures adopted by the Chinese Government. It acknowledges that the previous development-oriented policies for poverty alleviation for some rural areas (inclusive of production and infrastructure development) have achieved marked results. The cancellation of agricultural taxes and other policies beneficial to peasants have assisted many low-income rural families. In the future, however, development-oriented poverty alleviation policies should pay more attention to human capital development, instead of just production development, and adopt such measures as support for education, job skills training and health care security to enhance the level of human capital. This will be an even more effective means of eliminating poverty, particularly if accompanied by a fully implemented social security system.

Fourth, it finds that China's constant efforts to alleviate poverty through government leadership have produced important results, but also given rise to a series of problems that have reduced efficiency in the use of poverty alleviation funds. Improving public administration will help bolster effectiveness.

Finally, suggestions are put forward in nine areas, targeting policy makers. These include issues related to poverty alleviation strategies, poverty line determination and concrete poverty alleviation measures.

Preparations for the report on which the report is based began in early 2006. The China Development Research Foundation undertook the organization of the project. Lu Mai, Secretary General for the Foundation, participated, from beginning to end, in the design of the framework for, discussions upon and amendments to the original report, making essential contributions. Wang Mengkui, former President of the China Development Research Center of the State Council and Chairman of the China Development Research Foundation, has put forward a host of important, concrete, constructive opinions regarding amendments to the draft report. Tang Min, Vice Board Chairman for the China Development Research Foundation, has taken part in amendments on the section 'Suggestions to Policy Makers'. In the course of research and compilation, many experts were involved and put forward an array of constructive suggestions. The National Bureau of Statistics of China and The Rural Economy Research Center, under the State Ministry of Agriculture, offered generous assistance in terms of data sourcing and field surveys.

Supported by the China Development Research Foundation, Chinese experts and some relevant organs offered 23 background papers for this project. Many data, analyses and opinions were integrated in the report. The papers are: 'International Theories and Practical Policies of Poverty Alleviation' (Liu Minquan and Yu Jiantuo), 'Influence of Rural Policies on the Poverty-Stricken Population' (Zuo Ting), 'Assessment of the Influence Wielded by Rural Compulsory Education Policies on Rural Poverty' (Jin Lian), 'Assessment of the Influence Wielded by Medicare Policies on Rural Poverty' (Han Jun), 'Research on Interest-Subsidized Loans for Poverty Alleviation Purposes' (Zhang Tao, Yi Cheng and Wang Tian), 'Assessment of Social Poverty Alleviation Endeavours and their Influence' (Li Zhou and Cao Jianhua), 'Report upon the Assessment of the Evolution of Industrialization Endeavours for Poverty Alleviation Purposes' (Li Zhou and Cao Jianhua), 'Immigration and Poverty Alleviation' (Li Xiaoyun and Tang Lixia), 'Assessment of the Poverty Alleviation Effect Generated by Training with Regard to the Transfer of the Labour Force' (Li Wen), 'Poverty Issues in Rural Areas of China – An Analysis into the Findings of a Survey of Rural Families' (Ma Yongliang, Zhao Changbao and Wu Zhigang), 'Report upon a Survey of Poverty in Rural Areas of East China' (Shanghai DataSea Marketing Research Co., Ltd), 'Research upon Parties Participating in the Formulation of Budgets of County and Township-Level Governments' (Beijing De Sai Si Chuang Consultation Centre), 'Influence Wielded by Minimum Livelihood Security Policies in Rural and Urban Areas upon the Poverty Scene' (He Ping), 'Institutionalization of China's Social Succor System' (Gu Xin), 'China's Urban Poverty Scene: Trends, Policies and New Problems' (Du Yang), 'Laying-off, Unemployment, Re-employment and Urban Poverty' (Cai Fang and Wang Meiyan), 'Descriptions of the Urban Poverty Scene and the Population Covered by the Minimum Livelihood Security System' (Wang Zhenyao), 'A Generation Living in a Crevice in the City' (Topical Research Group dedicated to studying the newly emerging unemployed population), 'Child Poverty in Rural Areas' (Yue Ximing), 'Nutrition, the Health of Underprivileged Children and Related Governmental Policies' (Ma Guansheng), 'Analysis of China's Urban Poverty Scene and Conditions of the Low-income Population since 1995' (Zheng Feihu and Li Shi), 'Appraisal Report upon Village-Wide Implementation Work' (Wang Sangui) and 'Structure of China's Poverty Alleviation Work' (Wang Sangui). In addition, Wang Chunhua has offered certain findings of his study in relevant documents.

To compile the original report for *Eliminating Poverty through Development in China*, the China Development Research Foundation organized a field survey of poverty in Chuxiong Prefecture, Wuding County within Yunnan Province, Hefei City, Shitai County within Anhui Province, Pingshun County, and Taigu County within Shanxi Province. The survey was conducted by the authors of this report, Lu Mai and Zhao Shukai with the China Development Research Foundation, assisted by Du Zhixin, Huang

Haili, Zhang Changdong and Chou Ting. Governmental departments in the prefectures, counties, townships, cities and provinces, and local villagers and cadres assisted the survey.

In addition, Zhao Shukai, Vice Secretary General of the China Development Research Foundation, Du Zhixin, Zhao Junchao, Huang Haili, Feng Mingliang and Zhang Changdong – all personnel with the Foundation – have undertaken many project-organizing tasks. We express our heartfelt thanks to all the organizations and individuals that have contributed to this report.

Wang Xiaolu, Li Shi and Wang Sangui

Contributors

ADVISERS

Wang Mengkui, Former President, Development Research Center of the State Council, and Chairman, China Development Research Foundation

Chen Xiwen, Deputy Director, The Office of the Central Leading Group for Finance and Economics, and Director, The Office of the Central Leading Group for Rural Affairs

Xie Fuzhan, Director General, National Bureau of Statistics of China

PROJECT COORDINATOR

Lu Mai, Secretary General and Research Follow, China Development Research Foundation

CHIEF AUTHORS

Wang Sangui, Professor, School of Agricultural Economics and Rural Development, Renmin University of China

Li Shi, Professor, School of Economics and Business, Beijing Normal University

Wang Xiaolu, Deputy Head and Research Fellow, National Economy Research Institute, China Reform Foundation

AUTHORS OF BACKGROUND REPORTS

Zhao Changbao, Deputy Head and Associate Research Fellow, Rural Studies Center, Ministry of Agriculture

Cai Fang, Director and Research Fellow, Institute of Population and Labor Economics, Chinese Academy of Social Sciences

Zheng Feihu, Lecturer and Doctor, School of Economics and Business, Beijing Normal University

Ma Guansheng, Deputy Director and Research Fellow, Nutrition and Food Safety, Chinese Center for Disease Control and Prevention

Han Jun, Head and Research Fellow, Department of Rural Economy Studies, Development Research Center, State Council

Sheng Laiyun, Deputy Head, Rural Survey Team, National Bureau of Statistics of China

Jin Lian, Lecturer and Doctor, School of Resources and Environmental Management, Guizhou Institute of Finance and Economics

Lv Liangming, Manager, DataSea (Shanghai) Market Research Company

Sun Liping, Professor, School of Humanities, Tsinghua University

Wang Liqun, Professor, Beijing Forestry University

Dong Mei, Lecturer, Nanjing Agricultural University

Liu Minquan, Professor, School of Economics, Peking University

He Ping, Director and Research Fellow, Research Institute of Social Insurance, Ministry of Labor and Social Security

Wang Pingping, Head, Rural Poverty Surveillance Division, Rural Survey Team, National Bureau of Statistics of China

Wang Sangui, Professor, School of Agricultural Economics and Rural Development, Renmin University of China

Zhang Tao, Deputy Director General, Research Bureau, People's Bank of China

Zuo Ting, Deputy Dean and Professor, School of Humanities and Development, China Agricultural University

Li Wen, Associate Research Fellow, Institute of Agricultural Economics and Rural Development, Chinese Academy of Agricultural Sciences

Zheng Xiaoxian, Professor, Beijing Forestry University

Li Xiaoyun, Dean and Professor, School of Humanities and Development, China Agricultural University

Gu Xin, Professor, Research Institute of Social Development and Public Policies, Beijing Normal University

Yue Ximing, Professor, School of Finance, Renmin University of China

Du Yang, Associate Research Fellow, Institute of Population Studies, Chinese Academy of Social Sciences

Li Yingxing, Associate Research Fellow, Institute of Agricultural Economics and Rural Development, Chinese Academy of Agricultural Sciences

Wang Zhenyao, Head, Department of Disaster Relief and Succor, Ministry of Civil Affairs

Li Zhou, Deputy Director and Research Fellow, Research Institute of Rural Development, Chinese Academy of Social Sciences

HEAD OF THE PROJECT IMPLEMENTATION OFFICE

Zhao Shukai, Vice Secretary General and Research Fellow, China Development Research Foundation

STAFF MEMBERS OF THE PROJECT IMPLEMENTATION OFFICE

Du Zhixin, Huang Haili and Feng Mingliang, China Development Research Foundation

1 Introduction

Since China began its reform and opening to the outside world, rapid economic growth has not only elevated the living standards of people in both urban and rural areas, but also sharply decreased the number of people in poverty. In the course of three decades of economic development, the numbers of the rural poor population have shrunk dramatically, according to various measurements. Based on China's official poverty line, there were 250 million rural poor people in 1978. By the end of 2005, there were only 23.65 million rural poor people. The rate of poverty fell from 31 percent to 2.5 percent in that period.[1] Even if the measurement is done according to a relatively high poverty line, such as that of the World Bank (US $1 dollar per day per person), the size of the poor population in rural areas and the incidence rate of poverty in China have declined in a largely identical way.[2]

Prior to reform, the restrictions on China's economic development and system meant the rate of poverty was far beyond the average in other countries. Today, China's rate is markedly below the world's average (Chen and Ravallion 2004). Propelled by the Government's developmental poverty alleviation strategy, poor regions in the country have embraced development in terms of culture, education, health care and other social undertakings, to different extents. China has become a role model for some other developing countries due to its stunning accomplishments in poverty alleviation and the commendation it has earned from the global community.

Nevertheless, China is still faced with a rather formidable poverty alleviation task. On the one hand, the remaining poor mainly comprise people who cannot be helped out of poverty that easily. On the other hand, with social advancement and people's increasing awareness of poverty, the term 'poverty' today is not meant for inadequate income alone. It also manifests through poor capabilities. A better awareness of poverty has raised standards for poverty alleviation, while the yardstick for poverty measurement has also moved as a consequence of economic development, becoming more prone to the influence of concepts of social development. The elimination of poverty no longer means merely meeting the minimum subsistence needs of the poor population. Instead, it is necessary to provide a basic capability for embracing development. Chinese society is undergoing a significant transformation as far as poverty alleviation strategies are concerned.

China's victory over poverty is accredited to two factors: rapid economic growth and ambitious poverty alleviation policies. Economic growth is, in large part, due to China's economic reform and opening-up policy. Poverty alleviation policies have been fuelled by the Chinese Government's determination and committed efforts.

It is essential to sum up China's successful experiences in poverty alleviation and also to analyse influential factors. Among them, swift economic growth is the most notable but that alone is not enough. In an economic scenario featuring a widening income gap, for the sake of poverty alleviation it is of paramount importance to make the mode of economic growth more beneficial to the poor and more conducive to the income growth of low-income earners. A mode beneficial to the poor will enable those people participating in economic activities to escape poverty in the shortest time. It will, however, be less helpful to those poor families with no labour capability. The roots of subsistence poverty cannot be eliminated unless a basic social security system, comprising social relief, is established. It is even more necessary to become aware that solving subsistence poverty is simply the first goal. Alleviating and eventually eliminating capability and developmental poverty is the ultimate goal, involving elevating the quality of the labour force and the potential capabilities of humans.

In today's China, where citizens are making concerted efforts to contribute to a harmonious society, the formulation of ambitious and effective anti-poverty policies is of extraordinary significance.

A REVIEW OF CHINA'S POVERTY AND ANTI-POVERTY EFFORTS

Prior to 1949, China was an economically backward country, with an enormous population of people in poverty. At that time, China was among those countries registering the highest rates of poverty. The founding of the People's Republic of China provided an important political foundation for poverty alleviation. Over the past half century, China has achieved historic results in its anti-poverty efforts, although the story includes numerous twists and turns.

China's poverty before its reform and opening up

Before the People's Republic of China was founded in 1949, China had carried out rural land reform in some Liberation Zones. After the founding of the People's Republic of China, the country launched a nationwide land reform that ended the 2000+ years old feudal land system, thus boosting productivity in rural areas. On the basis of national economic recovery,

China started to implement the first 'Five-Year-Long National Development Programme' in 1953. In 1957, China's economy experienced a historic boom, while the size of the poor population in both rural and urban areas reached a record low.[3] Nevertheless, the public ownership system, formed in the wake of the socialist transformation of ownership of the means of production in the mid 1950s, and the planned economic system established on its basis featuring a high degree of centralization, were not adapted to China's productivity level at that time. The country adopted a development mode that prioritized heavy industry, which, along with the burgeoning of people's communes and the 'Great Leap Forward' campaign, heavily jeopardized China's economic development. In the late 1950s and early 1960s, the country saw the yield of agricultural products drop sharply, peasants' incomes fell dramatically, the living standards of rural and urban residents declined markedly, and the rate of poverty rose steeply. Later, China made some adjustments to its economic system that enabled the national economy to regain steam. The rate of poverty began to fall to a level consistent with the stage of economic development at that time.

During the 10-year-long Cultural Revolution, the nominal growth of China's economy did not alleviate the roots of its poverty levels. Political movements exerted a negative impact on economic development, the population grew excessively fast, and hidebound economic and management systems gave rise to appalling wastage and low efficiency. Fast economic growth that was the result of immoderate accumulation did not benefit the multitudes in pragmatic terms. As some pertinent data indicate, the per capita income of rural residents from 1966 to 1977 was up by only RMB 18 yuan (Zhou Binbin 1991), which is less than half of the per capita income growth recorded by rural residents in 1979 alone. In that period of time, the annual growth rate of peasants' income on average was less than 1.5 percent, while the per capita food intake of rural residents did not reach 2100 calories per day (ibid.). When measured by the nutrition yardstick, 40 percent to 50 percent of rural residents were in a state of subsistence poverty.

China's development and the evolution of anti-poverty efforts since reform and opening up

According to the National Bureau of Statistics of China, in 1978, shortly after China adopted a policy of reform and opening up, the size of the poor population in rural areas was 250 million, and the rate of poverty was up to 31 percent (using China's officially announced poverty line, which is on the low side).[4] Measured by the rural poverty line, the size of the poor population in urban areas could have been deemed negligible.[5] At that time, the Chinese Government focused its efforts on rural poverty, an inevitable task.

Since then, the country's anti-poverty campaign has evolved in three stages. The first stage featured a mode of poverty alleviation principally based on the pursuit of economic growth; the second stage emphasized developmental poverty alleviation policies; and the third stage has been characterized by multiple public policies beneficial to peasants.

In the late 1970s and early 1980s, propelled by the reform of the land rights use system in rural areas, Chinese peasants demonstrated unprecedented initiative that resulted in a historic boom in agricultural production. Grain output reached record highs for many consecutive years. The Government kept increasing grain prices, so peasants' incomes continued to grow from one year to another. From 1978 to 1985, China's total grain output was up by 24 percent, while the per capita grain output of rural residents was up by 84 kilos. China's total cotton output rose by 91 percent. Its oil output increased 202 percent. In the same period, the grain price was up by 102 percent, and the prices of agricultural products rose by 67 percent; both price increases exceeded the growth rate of the price of industrial products from rural areas.[6] As a consequence, the real per capita net income of rural residents was up by 169 percent in that period, yielding an annual growth rate of up to 15.1 percent. Since the economic reform, as such, emancipated production potentials in underdeveloped regions of China to a great extent, the income gap among rural areas started to shrink.[7] The income growth had an immense impact, combining with an income distribution effect to mitigate poverty, in sharp contrast to the scenario emerging after 1990.[8]

Figure 1.1 shows the trend in the size of the poor population in rural areas since China's reform and opening up. It is not hard to see that within seven

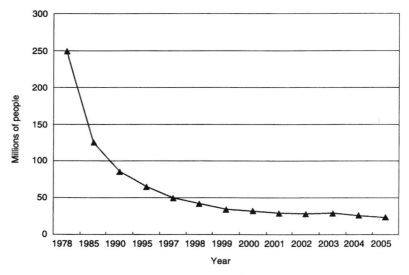

Figure 1.1 Changes in the poor population in rural areas of China from 1978 to 2005.

Source: China Statistical Summary 2006.

years (from 1978 to 1985), the population was halved, falling to 125 million persons from 250 million persons. In the same period, the rate of poverty in rural areas dropped from 31 percent to 15 percent. From the research documentation available now, Chinese and foreign scholars have mostly shared a common understanding of the reasons for such significant progress. These include the income growth of peasants due to the reform of the land use rights system and the increased prices of agricultural products as the most important driving forces.[9] Under the policy of equal distribution of land use rights, the growth of income from agriculture became, in quite a large part, a pro-poor growth strategy. Behind the growth was peasants' enhanced productivity, which came from the fact that peasants were provided with greater economic freedom and enabled to dispose of their means of production freely, due to the general adoption of market principles in the selling of agricultural products and the rationalization of their prices. To sum up, economic liberalization and the market-based allocation of resources have offered an effective institutional guarantee and an incentive to speed the growth of the rural economy, even as market-driven growth has been manifested, to a certain degree, in a pro-poor manner.

In the late 1980s, the rate of poverty in rural areas of China started to fall at a decreasing pace, especially from the middle of the 1980s to the middle of the 1990s. From 1978 to 1985, the annual average size of the Chinese population helped out of poverty was 17.86 million persons; from 1986 to 1990, the annual average was 8 million persons; from 1991 to 1995, the annual average was 3.92 million persons; from 1996 to 2000, the annual average rose to 6.66 million persons; from 2001 to 2005, the annual average dropped to 1.69 million persons.[10] Such changes correlate, in part, to the slow growth of peasants' income, and in part to constantly widening income gaps in rural areas in this period. Compared to the early 1980s, the annual average growth rate of real per capita income of peasants from 1986 to 1995 fell sharply, reaching as low as 3.6 percent. Except for 1996, when the growth rate of the real per capita income of peasants reached 9 percent, most other years since the late 1990s have seen the growth rate at below 5 percent. Income inequality in rural areas has been rising, and the income gap among rural residents, measured by various indexes, has been widening. For instance, the Gini coefficient of the income gap in rural areas, roughly estimated according to the rural household survey conducted by the National Bureau of Statistics of China, was 0.31 in 1990. It rose to 0.35 in 2000 and 0.38 in 2005 (see Figure 1.2). Today, the composition of the poor population is totally different from 20 years ago, and the causes of poverty have become increasingly varied. Realistically speaking, those people who can be easily helped out of poverty have already benefited from poverty alleviation. The remaining poor people will find it more difficult to leave poverty, and this has already been seen as having an inevitable influence on the average number of people emerging from poverty in the ensuing years. This situation is more complex, however, than the simple conclusion that the slower pace is an

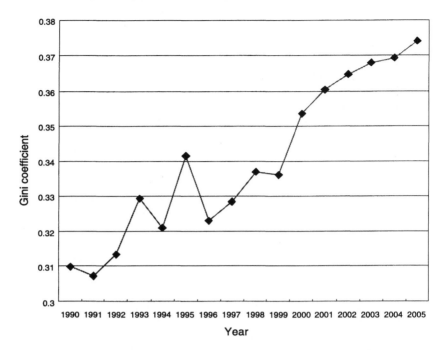

Figure 1.2 Changes in the income gap among rural areas of China from 1990 to 2005: Gini coefficient.

Source: China Yearbook of rural household survey 2006, p. 34.

indication that the Chinese Government's poverty alleviation policies have become ineffective.

Starting in the 1990s, the Chinese Government embarked on myriad poverty alleviation strategies. Throughout that decade, developmental poverty alleviation policies played an important role. In general, this mode of poverty alleviation means governmental departments at all levels confer financial subsidies on some selected regions with a high density of poor people. The aim is to enhance development capabilities, job opportunities and market competition capabilities in these regions. This helps to boost economic growth in a manner that eliminates poverty. From the size of the population helped out of poverty at that time, compared to the 1980s, people could easily conclude that poverty alleviation results in the 1990s seemed less remarkable. But the composition of the poor population and the reasons for poverty in the 1990s varied from those in the 1980s. The environment for applying poverty alleviation policies was also different, giving rise to greater difficulties. Nonetheless, the absolute size of the rural population suffering subsistence poverty dropped from 85 million in 1990 to 32 million in 2000.[11]

Since the start of the new millennium, the Chinese Government has, considering the latest characteristics of the location and composition of poor populations, made timely adjustments to its poverty alleviation policies. Developmental poverty alleviation policies have undergone significant changes in two respects: (1) when it comes to offering support to poor regions, the Government no longer targets certain counties, but focuses on particular villages through the 'Entire Village Coverage' project; such a close-up emphasis on concrete targets enables poverty alleviation projects and funds to reach the poor more effectively; (2) developmental poverty alleviation projects were adjusted structurally, and an increasing number of projects to enhance capabilities in poor regions and populations were added, mostly taking the form of investments in education and the training of migrant labourers from poor regions. In addition, other pro-peasant policies have been launched in recent years. For example, an agricultural tax exemption has mitigated peasants' financial burden, especially for the poor. The ration allowance policy has benefited peasants engaged in farming, who are most prone to poverty. The policy of reducing and exempting the tuition fees and incidental charges of rural students has not only mitigated peasants' financial burdens from education, but also exposed children in rural poor families to more educational opportunities. The rural cooperative medical system has improved, to a certain degree, both living conditions and medical services. The comprehensive implementation of the rural minimum livelihood security system has made it possible to eliminate subsistence poverty in some rural areas. Due to the combined effects of these policies, in 2005 the size of the rural population suffering subsistence poverty fell just below 24 million people, and the rate of poverty dropped to 2.5 percent.[12] Pro-peasant policies also assisted low-income groups. According to the latest statistical data, from 2000 to 2005, the number of low-income people in rural areas fell from 62 million to 41 million, a decrease of one third.[13]

In China, urban poverty, when compared with rural poverty, has its own traits in terms of both size and causes. Starting from the mid 1990s, as Chinese cities underwent an economic restructuring and the Chinese Government carried out enterprise reform, urban poverty worsened. Some urban households were affected when wage-earners were laid off. Poverty grew especially in industrial regions and areas lagging behind in the pace of economic restructuring.[14] The Chinese Government adopted timely measures to expand the minimum livelihood security system for urban residents, and succeeded in establishing an urban anti-poverty system.[15] Urban poverty was quickly mitigated, and in recent years has been alleviated markedly in comparison to the 1990s, when measured by whatever kind of poverty yardstick.[16] Today, poverty in urban areas is also undergoing structural changes. An increasing number of rural residents have arrived in urban areas, where they earn unstable wages due to unsteady job opportunities. They are unable to access social security assistance for urban residents and now constitute a major component of the poor population in urban areas.[17]

China's contribution to the world's anti-poverty campaign

China's anti-poverty accomplishments have redefined the world's history of poverty alleviation efforts. In three decades, the absolute size of the world's poor population has significantly shrunk, but huge discrepancies in progress exist among the five continents and their countries (Sachs 2006). From 1981 to 2001, according to the poverty line of US $1 dollar per day per person, the world's rate of poverty fell from 40.4 percent to 21.1 percent. In the same period, China's rate of poverty dropped from 63.8 percent to less than 17 percent (Chen and Ravallion 2004). According to the same poverty line, in 1981, China's rate of poverty was higher than the world's average by 23.4 percent. In 2001, China's rate of poverty was lower than the world's average by 4.5 percent (see Figure 1.3). In 1981, the Chinese poor comprised 43 percent of the global population in poverty; by 2001, the figure was less than 20 percent.

During these two decades, the Chinese population comprised 108 percent of the total world population that emerged from poverty. It constituted 81 percent of the total population that left poverty in all the countries of East Asia.[18]

One of the eight Millennium Development Goals (MDGs) endorsed by the United Nations is to halve the world's (extreme) subsistence poverty from 1990 to 2015. But progress has been slow. According to the *MDG*

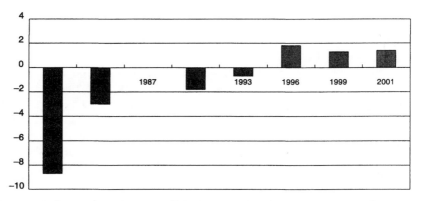

Figure 1.3 Comparison between China's rate of poverty and the world's rate of poverty (%).

Source: Chen and Ravallion 2004.

Note: The horizontal axis in the figure stands for years, and the vertical axis represents the discrepancy between the world's rate of poverty and China's rate of poverty. A positive discrepancy means the world's rate of poverty is higher than China's. A negative discrepancy means the world's rate is lower than China's.

Report released by the UN (2005), as of 2001, the rate of subsistence poverty in all developing countries has been cut by nearly 24 percent. The rate of subsistence poverty in East Asian countries (including China) has declined by 49.7 percent, which comes close to the MDG poverty alleviation goal (United Nations 2005). The sharp decrease is chiefly accredited to China's poverty alleviation accomplishments because, during this period, the rate of subsistence poverty in rural China was reduced by nearly two-thirds.[19]

Poverty alleviation and the establishment of a harmonious society

Poverty is an important factor behind social disharmony. As shown by the findings of one international study, the rate of poverty is negatively correlated, to a marked degree, with the political stability of a country; namely, the higher the rate of poverty in a country, the lower its political stability will be. In a society where most people remain in poverty, it is hardly possible to achieve political stability and social harmony. In today's world, certain countries whose economies have been appallingly backward and where most citizens remain in a stage of extreme poverty have adopted two primary means to maintain their social stability: either strong-arm governments or seclusion and the blockage of information from the outside world. Such means of maintaining social stability are not Chinese government policy. Besides, social stability does not automatically stand for social harmony. Social stability can be an exogenous outcome that is realized through external coercion, while social harmony is an endogenous outcome that stems from the free choices made by members of a society.

The existence of a large population that suffers extreme poverty is not conducive to long-term economic development, which is a basic precondition for social harmony. As indicated by the findings of one study, poor people are unable to make human capital investments in their children, such as education. In modern times, economic development is increasingly dependent on the growth of human capital. In those poor families, as parents are unable to pay tuition fees, their children will lose the rights and chances to receive an education, more often than not.[20] If the children of poor families cannot receive necessary education, poverty is bound to pass from one generation to another. It becomes like an inherited disease that cannot be eliminated at the root.

The experience in China and other countries has indicated that, besides extreme poverty, relative poverty is also a key factor resulting in social instability and disharmony. In large part, relative poverty manifests in the form of a relatively big income gap; growing relative poverty occurs through a constantly widening income gap. A widening income gap combined with an expanding population suffering relative poverty will exert a negative influence upon economic growth in the long run.[21] In developing countries, the slowdown of economic growth will be more harmful for people in extreme poverty, as their job opportunities will shrink accordingly. With an incessantly widening income gap, a large population stricken by relative poverty will emerge. In a society where social wealth is distributed in an excessively unbalanced way and human beings are categorized strictly by economic standing, those people at the bottom will not be able to maintain their human dignity and integrity, which reduces the prospects for social harmony.

As indicated by experiences in other countries, a high crime rate and a high incidence of violence are closely correlated with excessive inequality in income distribution or excessively high rates of poverty. A study conducted by Fajnzylber *et al.* (1998; 2000), did a regression analysis on the crime and murder rates in over 40 countries. It found that the estimated coefficient of the income gap variable turned out to be a significantly positive value. The income gap variable is always highly significant, no matter when the Gini coefficient was adopted or the income share of the lowest quintile group was employed. This means an excessive income gap has become a variable that explains the discrepancies among different countries in terms of the murder rate. When doing a regression analysis of the discrepancies in terms of the rates of robbery cases, Fajnzylber *et al.* (1998) discovered likewise that inequality in income distribution was a stable but remarkable explanatory variable.

In general, a harmonious society depends on effective anti-poverty efforts. As long as the extremely poor part of the population is unable to benefit from economic growth, and the segment of the population in relative poverty keeps growing, it will not be possible to achieve a harmonious society.

SOCIOECONOMIC DEVELOPMENT AND POVERTY REDUCTION

Economic development is one of the most important conditions to reduce poverty. Without constant economic growth, anti-poverty strategies cannot produce steady and consistent progress. Experiences in some developing countries, including China, have indicated, however, that economic growth will not automatically result in poverty reduction. Only pro-poor growth will generate direct effects. When poverty reduction is viewed more broadly than merely as income and consumption poverty, and regarded as involving individuals' lack of potential capabilities, only social development can ensure the long-term effectiveness of poverty reduction measures.

Economic development and anti-poverty strategies

Historically, poverty has been deemed a result of backward economies. In the last 100 years, the world's rate of poverty has continually decreased due to economic development. As Bourguignon and Morrisson (2002) have indicated, pursuant to the globally acknowledged poverty line announced in 1985 (i.e., US $1 dollar per day per person), the world's rate of poverty reached 75 percent in 1879, but dropped to 24 percent by 1992. In that period, the world's per capita income, measured by the 1985 purchasing power parity of the US dollar, increased 4.5 times. From the early 1980s to 2001, the world economy kept growing at a fast pace. Subsequently, the size of the global poor population continued to shrink, falling to 400 million people as measured by the global poverty line (Banerjee, Benabou and Mookherjee 2006).

Ninety percent of the poor live in developing countries, whose total population constitutes 70 percent of the world's aggregate. Seventy percent are in low-income countries, whose total population comprises only 40 percent of the world's aggregate. Eighty percent live in African and Asian countries where per capita incomes have all remained below the world's average (ibid.).

One international study indicated that continued economic growth has played a rather marked role in poverty alleviation. When the changes in poverty are ascribed to two factors (namely, economic growth and income distribution), then the economic growth factor produces 75 percent of short-term progress in poverty reduction and 95 percent of long-term changes (Kraay 2005). For an overwhelming majority of developing countries, the first and foremost task for poverty alleviation is to pursue economic development.

Economic development's usefulness in poverty alleviation has two aspects: (1) economic development provides more and better job opportunities for the poor; and (2) economic development enables governmental finance organs to earn more, thus making the Government more capable of helping the poor. The first aspect shows the direct effect generated by economic development on poverty alleviation; the second aspect has an indirect effect on poverty alleviation.

China's development experience has indicated that economic development is the primary driving force behind poverty alleviation. The years from the late 1970s to early 1980s were a prime period in which peasants' incomes kept growing robustly, and the size of the rural poor population significantly declined. From 1978 to 1985, the real net income of peasants was up by 1.69 times, with an annual average growth rate of up to 15.2 percent. During the same period, the size of the rural poor population fell by 125 million people, and the rate of poverty dropped from 31 percent to less than 15.5 percent (see National Bureau of Statistics of China 2005). Statistical data from different provinces have also shown a positive correlation between the rate of poverty and economic development in rural areas. Figure 1.4 shows the rates of extreme poverty in rural areas of different provinces in 2004.[22] In the horizontal axis, all the provinces are ranked by per capita net income. It is not hard to see that the rate of rural poverty has a strongly negative correlation with the degree of economic development. Within those provinces where the per capita net income exceeds RMB 4000 yuan, the rates of extreme rural poverty are low and even negligible in some cases. In those provinces where the per capita net income is between RMB 2300 yuan and RMB 4000 yuan, the rates of poverty (except for certain provinces) are

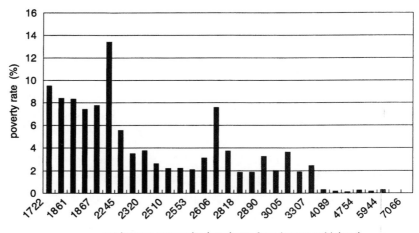

Figure 1.4 Income level and poverty rate at provincial level in rural China, 2004.

Source: Based on the data in *China Statistical Yearbook*.

mostly between 2 percent and 4 percent. In those provinces where the per capita net income is below RMB 2300 yuan, the rates are all above 6 percent and even above 10 percent in some provinces.

In the past three decades, the sharp decrease in the size of the rural poor population stems from rapid economic growth. From 1978 to 2005, the per capita net income of rural residents in China increased by 5.25 times and recorded an annual average growth rate of 6.6 percent. Meanwhile, according to the official poverty line, the size of the rural poor population fell to 23.65 million people from 250 million people, representing a decrease of nearly 9 million people a year, on average. From the late 1970s to the mid 1980s, peasants' incomes grew rapidly, while the size of the rural poor population fell by 125 million people, and the rate of poverty was halved. Yet in the same period, an overwhelming majority of rural areas in China were still adopting out-dated poverty alleviation measures originally worked out under the traditional economic system. These featured the provision by local governments of rather limited social support and relief to a small portion of extremely poor families. The sharp decrease in the size of the rural poor population was primarily due to the development of the rural economy and the fast growth of incomes.

Figure 1.5 portrays the relationship between the growth rate of per capita incomes of rural residents and the decrease in the rural poverty rate. It is not hard to see that from 1978 to 2005 the correlation was quite remarkable. Prior to 1985, the high growth rate of per capita net income coexisted with the sharp decrease of the rural poverty rate each year. In those years when the growth of per capita net income was above 10 percent, the rate of rural

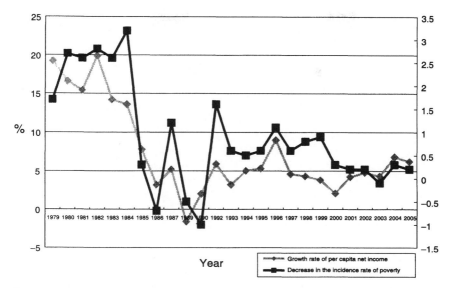

Figure 1.5 Relevancy between the growth of per capita net income and the decrease in the incidence rate of poverty in rural areas of China from 1979 to 2005.

Source: From calculations based on the data in *China Statistical Summary 2006*.

poverty reduction was about 2 percentage points annually. From the late 1980s to the mid 1990s, peasants' incomes fluctuated largely, as did the decrease of rural poverty rates. The growth rates of per capita net incomes of rural residents in some years were less than 3 percent and were even negative at times. Accordingly, the decrease in poverty rates in rural areas seemed negligible and even reversed in some years.

After the mid 1990s, the slow growth in incomes coexisted with the slow decrease in the rate of poverty. In most subsequent years, the income growth rates were less than 5 percent. The rate of poverty decreased by about 0.5 percent.

It follows that high economic growth in rural areas that propelled quick rises in peasants' incomes has been critical to the alleviation of rural poverty.

Economic development alone is inadequate

Economic development is not the exclusive factor behind poverty alleviation. Another factor is equality in income distribution. It is only when the poor can share in the outcomes of economic growth that it contributes fully to poverty alleviation. In China, most income earned by poor populations comes from agriculture, so increases in incomes from agriculture will, more or less, directly influence the size of the rural poor population. Increased income from agriculture depends on two factors: (1) the increase of per capita yield of agricultural products; and (2) the increase of relative prices of agricultural products. Prior to the mid 1980s, peasants' increased incomes derived from the rising yield of agricultural products and their relative prices. Economic growth in rural areas in that period was pro-poor.

In the late 1990s, even if governments at all levels stepped up their efforts in poverty alleviation, the results were not sufficient, primarily because peasants' incomes from agriculture in this period started to fall and remained on a low level. Starting in 1997, the per capita income of rural residents from agriculture declined and did not rise until 2000. According to a constant price index, the decrease was as high as 17 percent. From 2000 to 2003, peasants' incomes from agriculture recorded a growth rate of only 6 percent. The per capita income of peasants from agriculture in 2003 was still 10 percent lower than in 1997. Although from 1997 to 2003 the per capita net income of peasants was up by 5 percent, the per capita income of peasants from agriculture was down by 10 percent. The increase in peasants' incomes at this time was fully dependent on non-agricultural income, while the growth of agriculture did not benefit the poor and low-income populations.

In each society, there are always people either unable to participate in economic activities due to a lack of labour, or hardly able to make a living due to natural disasters or emergency events. In their eyes, the first and foremost thing is not an employment opportunity or a high-paying job, but a secure income sufficient to keep them alive. In this situation, providing necessary public services and social security is one of the requisite conditions for eliminating poverty at the root.

Social development and anti-poverty strategies

In order to enable the low-income population to earn more from economic growth and allow the poor to escape poverty in a more effective way, it is essential to encourage the common development of members of society, including that the results of social development benefit the poor. From China's experience, excessive emphasis on the pursuit of economic development and ignorance of the importance of social development have blocked the full effectiveness of poverty reduction strategies.

Figure 1.6 illustrates the correlation between the rates of rural poverty and degrees of human development in different provinces of China in 2004. On the horizontal axis, provinces are ranked by the human development indexes of their respective rural areas; on the vertical axis, the rates of rural poverty are listed. In those provinces with higher human development indexes, the rates of rural poverty are relatively low. In those provinces with low human development indexes, poverty rates tend to be high. Among the 30 provinces, the average poverty rate in the eight provinces with the lowest human development indexes was 8.3 percent. The average poverty rate in the eight provinces with the highest human development indexes was less than 0.7 percent, or more than 10 times lower.

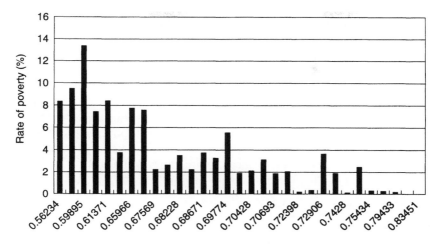

Ranking of provinces by human development index

Figure 1.6 Human development index and rate of poverty in rural areas by province in 2004.

Source: The human development indexes of different provinces were abstracted from the *China Human Development Report 2005*, while the National Bureau of Statistics of China provided data on rates of poverty in different provinces.

Public services and anti-poverty strategies

An effective method for poverty alleviation in the short term is to raise the income level of the poor. From a long-term perspective, focusing efforts merely on income growth for the sake of poverty alleviation is not enough; it is necessary to enable the poor population to develop capabilities to escape poverty on their own. Basic capabilities include the capability to create income (i.e., possessing physical health and human capital desired by society) and the capability to take part in social activities (i.e., being endowed with basic social and political rights). Public services provide opportunities for all citizens to realize their potential capabilities. For the poor in particular, public services are indispensable, as they are unable to utilize their own resources to better their latent capabilities.

As shown by experiences in most developing countries, the labour flow from backward regions to developed regions (or from low-income occupations to high-income ones) often acts as an important means for helping the poor out of poverty. As the labour market becomes segmented due to institutional barriers, however, labour mobility and employment suffer restrictions to different degrees. These have a greater impact upon the poor. Migrant labourers need more assistance and support, employment information, pre-job training and necessary legal aid.

In both developing and developed countries, poor people who want to advance in their lives will encounter a variety of difficulties. One of the biggest is obtaining financing from financial institutions. The poor normally do not receive loans to start their own businesses or cannot secure enough funds to invest in human capital. Generally, small and medium-sized financial institutions, instead of giant banks, provide the poor with financial aid, often in the form of microcredit.

Poorer people are frequently unable to afford medical charges to maintain their physical health at the society's average level. Ensuring access to medical services should be a primary component of any anti-poverty strategy. The establishment of a government-guided public medical system and the provision of basic medical security to the poor are two crucial tasks.

Social security and anti-poverty strategies

Reducing poverty is an inclusive, multilevel task. Inclusiveness means it is essential to assist both the rural and urban poor. The multilevel aspect implies treating different types of poor people in different ways and taking poverty alleviation measures that correlate with the concrete reasons for their poverty. The developmental approach to poverty alleviation that has been implemented by China for many years has played a big role in addressing rural poverty. Within the past few years, when new poverty issues arose in urban areas, the Chinese Government did not simply reapply this experience. It adopted a social welfare approach to poverty alleviation, in tune with the characteristics of urban poverty. This is appropriate, because the developmental approach to poverty alleviation can hardly bear fruit in the short term when supply exceeds demand in the labour market.

The selection of a poverty alleviation approach depends not only on local circumstances, but also on timing and the target population. In rural areas, regardless of which poverty line is employed, the composition of the poor population differs today from 10 or 20 years ago. With the shrinking of the size of the extremely poor population, an increasing portion of the poor population is known to be those people who are stuck in poverty due to lack of labour capabilities, sickness, or accidents or disasters. One group of rural residents has an income level inadequate for them to get out of developmental poverty, even though their income is above the subsistence poverty line. They are unable to give their children access to compulsory education or afford basic medical expenses. They constitute the rural developmentally poor population mostly targeted by this report. Faced with such changes in the mixture of the poor in rural areas, is it necessary to change the poverty alleviation approach accordingly? The answer is yes.

Making corresponding adjustments to poverty alleviation strategies means addressing three aspects simultaneously. These involve: (1) continually carrying out a developmental approach to poverty alleviation, and making poverty alleviation policies focus mainly on those families that have certain labour capabilities, but lack job opportunities or earn an inadequate income; (2)

adopting the social welfare approach to poverty alleviation, and mainly targeting those families in rural areas that lack labourers and those poor people who have been impacted by natural disasters or disease; and (3) improving public services, and providing poor and low-income populations with gratuitous compulsory educational opportunities and basic public medical services.

In a modern society, poverty alleviation is inseparable from public services and a social security system, for two reasons: first, a social security system is the optimal arrangement for responding to several factors that can cause or sustain poverty (such as employment risks, disease, natural disasters and misfortune, etc.). In the late 1990s, a great number of workers were laid off after reforms in corporate management systems and economic restructuring, thus causing the urban poverty rate to rise. To solve this problem, the Chinese Government later expanded the coverage of its minimum livelihood security system for low-income populations in urban areas, thus enabling those urban residents whose income level remains below the minimum subsistence line to maintain a minimum standard of living. This has proven to be a timely, effective method for urban poverty alleviation, and has provided good experience for the establishment of a similar system for rural areas.

Second, in a broader sense, 'poverty' does not only mean 'income poverty'; there are many reasons for poverty besides inadequate income. Even income poverty is caused by multiple factors. Physical health and a sound education are two basic preconditions for participation in a competitive labour market, and achievement of a relatively high and stable income. These require solid medical and educational services.

In the past few years, some provinces have tried minimum livelihood security programmes on a trial basis in selected rural areas. By the end of 2006, up to 18 provinces (autonomous regions and municipalities) had established these, as had some counties (prefectures) within other provinces (autonomous regions and municipalities). At that point, 15 million rural people were accessing the minimum livelihood security system, about 12 million of them categorized as extremely poor.[23] At the National Conference on Rural Work held in December 2006, the leaders of the State Council officially announced the implementation of the minimum livelihood security system across the country, starting from 2007. This means an increasing number of people in subsistence poverty will receive income support from governments at all levels and have a chance to eliminate their poverty.

EVOLUTION OF POVERTY CONCEPTS AND OTHER COUNTRIES' EXPERIENCES

Over the past half century, Chinese and foreign scholars have discussed poverty in depth and gained a more profound understanding of the phenomenon from different perspectives. Their endeavours have included formulating the relative poverty concept, which is different from the absolute poverty concept; developing the subjective poverty concept, which is the opposite of the object- ive poverty concept; and creating the lack of capability poverty concept, which is distinct from the income poverty or consumption poverty concepts.

Since World War II, most countries have made varying progress in poverty alleviation. Some have achieved outstanding results; others have seen their poverty rates linger at certain levels until now. The following section sums up different experiences and analyses the lessons learned.

The evolution of poverty concepts

Absolute poverty, relative poverty and subjective poverty

The absolute poverty concept can be traced back to the innovative study conducted by the British scholar S. Rowntree on Britain's poverty at the end of the nineteenth century. He unambiguously put forward the concept of absolute poverty in his book *Poverty: A Study of Town Life*, which was pub- lished in 1901. According to his definition of poverty, a family is stuck in poverty because its earned income is not enough to satisfy its minimum phys- ical needs. Based on such a definition, people will naturally come up with two questions: What are the minimum physical needs? How should societies ascertain if a family's income is enough to satisfy the minimum physical needs of its members? When these two questions are answered, it becomes possible to identify poor families and poor populations, and to estimate the extent of poverty. This opened up the empirical study of poverty. Rowntree estimated the minimum physical needs of ordinary British families at that time in the earliest study of the absolute poverty line.

Rowntree's definition of absolute poverty and subsequent thinking influ- enced the study of poverty in the twentieth century, with some adjustments and expansion of the notion of minimum physical needs. Rowntree came to realize that his definition of needs was too narrow. From a long-term view, satisfying physical needs alone is inadequate. Consideration must be given to other needs as well. This idea was accepted over time. For example, the UN Development Programme (UNDP) and the International Labour Organization (ILO) have linked poverty with basic human needs defined as physical needs (such as food, clothing, housing and medical care) and basic cultural needs (such as education and entertainment). Khan (1977) elabor- ated basic needs as comprising food, clothing, housing, medical care, educa- tion and drinkable water. In sum, the scope of and standards for basic needs have increased. As some poverty researchers have pointed out, basic needs change over time and by location. This implies changes in the income necessary for maintaining and satisfying basic needs, and an increase in the absolute poverty line.

Since the absolute poverty concept is connected with a certain social back- ground and degree of economic development, it is relative to some extent. In the 1960s and 1970s, some scholars put forward the relative poverty concept (see Box 1.1). Victor Fuchs, an economics professor at Stanford University in the United States, defined this and became the first scholar to use it. When estimating poverty in the United States, he set the poverty line at a level tantamount to 50 percent of the median income for the US population. Subsequent scholars used the average income or 40 percent of the median (average) income. In spite of such differences, these approaches were all based on the same concept of treating poverty as a relative phenomenon. The detailed description given by the British scholar P. Townsend (1962) is worth mentioning, since it heavily influenced most West European countries' adoption of the concept. Townsend insisted that poverty could only mean relative poverty, referring to the state of living of the portion of people whose income falls far below the average in a society. Strictly speaking, as long as any income gap and low-income group exist, it is impossible to get rid of poverty. Poverty has nothing to do with the degree of socioeconomic development and only correlates with the income gap.

Box 1.1 The relationship between absolute poverty and relative poverty

In a given society, what conclusion will be reached when the definition of absolute poverty and the definition of relative poverty are employed simultaneously to evaluate poverty? What difference will occur between the rate of poverty determined by use of the absolute poverty line and the relative poverty line? The answers to these questions will depend on the degree of economic development. With a given income gap, the rate of relative poverty may remain unchanged. The rate of absolute poverty may change with income: the lower the income level, the higher the rate of absolute poverty, and conversely.

The following figure illustrates such a relationship. The horizontal axis stands for the income level, while the vertical axis stands for the size of poor population or the rate of poverty. The line RP1 parallel to the horizontal axis shows the rate of relative poverty corresponding to the income gap I1. As it has nothing to do with the income level, in the case of a fixed income gap it will remain unchanged. In the case of changes in the income gap, it will move up and down. For example, when the income gap climbs to I2, the line of the rate of relative poverty will climb to RP2. The oblique line AP shows the rate of absolute poverty, and corresponds to the income gap I1. Different from the rate of relative poverty, the rate of absolute poverty keeps falling with the rise of income level.

The vertical line D is used to measure the levels of economic development, with low-income levels on the left-hand side and high-income levels on the right-hand side. In a preliminary stage of economic development, when the income level is on the relatively low side, the rate of

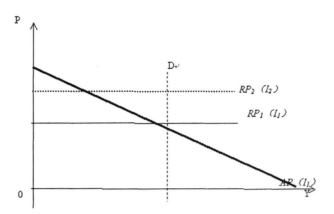

Box 1.1 The relationship between absolute poverty and relative poverty.

absolute poverty is higher than that of relative poverty: the lower the income level, the bigger the discrepancy between these two rates. In a high stage of economic development, however, when the income level is on the relatively high side, the relationship between these two rates is exactly opposite. The rate of absolute poverty is lower than that of relative poverty, and the higher the income level, the bigger the discrepancy between these two rates.

Perhaps because of different definitions of the term 'poverty', and adoption of different poverty lines, varying conclusions about the size of poor populations have been reached. Most experts engaged in studying poverty have tended to endorse adoption of the absolute poverty definition for developing countries, and the relative poverty definition for developed countries (Ravallion 1994, p. 37).

So-called subjective poverty means poverty determined by a family or an individual, based on personal (and subjective) perceptions. This raises a series of questions, such as: Is it necessary to take into account the personal opinions of the general public when determining the poverty line and identifying the poor population? Can the general public accurately judge the quality and state of their living conditions? Since different types of families have dissimilar basic needs, do such discrepancies need to be considered when defining poverty? To all these questions, the answers offered on the basis of the study of both absolute and relative poverty are mostly no. Researchers of subjective poverty, however, advocate taking full account of the subjective judgement of individuals and contend that people best understand their own living conditions. They maintain that discrepancies among individuals in terms of their judgement of poverty have arisen from their actual lives, so these should be acknowledged and contribute to defining poverty.

Capability poverty and developmental poverty

The concept of capability poverty is inseparable from the renowned economist Amartya Sen. In Sen's view, an individual's well-being is guaranteed by his or her capabilities. Poverty is derived from the lack of capabilities, defined as a series of functionings such as being free from starving, being free from disease, receiving education, obtaining adequate nutrition, securing basic housing, etc. The loss of any or all of these functionings is not only a manifestation of poverty, but a cause of it (Sen 1983). This approach does not require setting a uniform income or expenditure poverty line. Instead, to judge if a family or an individual is in poverty, the presence of functionings must be assessed, along with the extent of any gaps.

THIS REPORT'S APPROACH

This report has briefly introduced a few common poverty concepts for two purposes:

1 The question 'what is poverty?' seems easy to answer, but is tricky in reality. There have been many controversies over this question.
2 With the rural poverty line that the Chinese Government has adopted, poverty has been simply deemed a sort of living condition featuring an inability to satisfy one's minimum physical needs. In other words, a person who is merely able to satisfy his or her minimum physical needs will be excluded from the poor population, even if other needs are seldom taken into account.[24] This report maintains that the rural poverty line set by the Government is the subsistence poverty line. It then puts forward the developmental poverty concept and expounds on the method for defining the developmental poverty line.

How can poverty be fought effectively?

In gaining an increasingly profound understanding of poverty, people have also pondered how to help the poor escape poverty as quickly and effectively as possible. According to the traditional viewpoint of poverty alleviation, since poverty takes the form of an inadequate income, providing the poor with income allowances appears to be an obvious policy option. This is termed a 'blood transfusion' strategy. But for China in the 1980s, this strategy was obviously unfeasible because the size of the rural poor population was so large that the Ministry of Finance could not have afforded such income allowances. In view of these circumstances, some scholars put forward the 'blood producing' mode of poverty alleviation (Wang Xiaoqiang and Bai Nanfeng 1986). Later, the Chinese Government set up the developmental approach to poverty alleviation, which played a significant role in solving the rural poverty issue in the 1980s and 1990s. In fact, this is an effective solution for reducing subsistence poverty in most parts of the country, involving better infrastructure, new job opportunities through local economic development, and more efficient market mechanisms. The usefulness of the developmental approach is ultimately dependent on the degree to which concrete development measures benefit the poor.

By the late 1990s, the composition of the rural poor population had changed, as had the causes of poverty. These included not only the lack of job opportunities, but also sickness, the absence of necessary human capital and the lack of a necessary environment for subsistence. Certain scholars suggested carrying out developmental poverty alleviation and social welfare-based poverty alleviation simultaneously. The minimum livelihood security system for rural areas that the Chinese Government is preparing to implement nationwide is a positive response to such a suggestion.

The shift from subsistence poverty to developmental poverty will undoubtedly have a further bearing on the selection of poverty alleviation policies. Easing subsistence poverty offers only a temporary salve that does not resolve root development problems. When poverty stems from the lack of opportunities for embracing development and improving capabilities, then the most effective policy option is to provide the poor population with educational and medical services that enable them to accumulate necessary human capital. This is a key viewpoint in this report and an important suggestion for policy makers.

The evolution of poverty: global trends

Globally, the last century has seen poverty decrease through social advancement and economic development. The size of the poor population, measured by the poverty line of US $1 dollar per day per person, has been reduced by nearly 400 million people (Banerjee, Benabou and Mookherjee 2006). But poverty in today's world remains very serious. About 1.2 billion extremely poor people, or one fifth of the world population, still earn less than US $1 dollar a day. About 2.8 billion people, or nearly half the world's population, earn less than US $2 dollars a day (World Bank 2001). Most of the poor are in developing countries, particularly in Asia and Africa. As estimated by UNDP, in 2001 nearly 17 percent of the total population in East Asian countries was still in the state of subsistence poverty, earning less than US $1 dollar a day on average. Close to 30 percent of people in South Asian countries remained in subsistence poverty. In Africa, the rate of poverty was 46 percent, up 2 percent from the rate in 1990 (UN 2005). From 2000 to 2002, the percentage of people falling short of minimum required nutrition was 22 percent in South Asian countries and 33 percent in African countries (ibid.).

The most vulnerable group in terms of poverty, hunger and sickness is children from poor families. As estimated by UNDP, in developing countries, the rate of poverty among children is usually higher than among adults, because families with multiple children are more likely to be stuck in poverty.

In 2003, 28 percent of children below five years old in developing countries were suffering malnutrition. This figure was 29 percent in Southeast Asia, 31 percent in Africa and 47 percent in South Asian countries (ibid.).

Other countries' experiences with poverty reduction

The need for concerted action on poverty has become a common understanding in the international community, and especially among developing countries. Various countries have adopted different approaches in recent decades, seeking effective anti-poverty measures and policies that suit the social, economic and cultural characteristics of their respective communities. Many lessons have been learned. The main measures and policies can be categorized roughly as:

1   Policies that aim to directly strengthen the elements of production input, including human capital policies, those encouraging technological advancement (such as in the Green Revolution), population and migration policies, etc.;
2   Policies that aim to bolster the market climate, such as open trade policies (including domestic and foreign trade), financial development policies, etc.;
3   Policies that aim to improve production and living conditions, such as policies for investment in public infrastructure facilities and the protection of the environment;
4   Policies that aim to reduce the uncertainties in economic life, such as social security network policies;
5   Redistribution policies, such as finance and public expenditure policies, and land reform policies;
6   Public administration policies, such as those to boost participation and empowerment, reform the political system and basic social system, etc.; and
7   Agricultural modernization policies, industrialization and urbanization policies, etc.

All the policies in the above seven categories are often implemented in conjunction. Instead of reviewing each of them, this report will discuss only those that are important for China's anti-poverty strategies. These include policies for the construction of public infrastructure, investment in human capital, financial development for poverty alleviation and public administration.

Construction of public infrastructure

The construction of public infrastructure is of considerable importance for agricultural production, economic growth and poverty alleviation.[25] Some impacts are particularly important:

1   The construction of such infrastructure as roads, water and power systems, and communication facilities exposes the poor population to more chances for entering the market, conducting trade and saving trading costs;
2   The improvement of infrastructure helps enhance productivity, lower production risks, boost the development of non-agricultural industries and create job opportunities;
3   The construction of public infrastructure supplies the poor directly with employment opportunities and increases their economic gains (through jobs instead of financial aid); and
4   The improvement of infrastructure exposes the poor to more opportunities to get educational and medical services, thus increasing their human capital.

One study has directly estimated the influence of improved infrastructure on poverty alleviation. As indicated by Kwon (2001), who analysed factors determining poverty alleviation effects in 21 provinces of Indonesia from 1976 to 1996, those provinces furnished with more roads were more likely to receive better services and produce agricultural products of better quality. Residents were able to find more job opportunities beyond the agricultural industry. Dercon and Krishnan (1998) used data from a family survey in Ethiopia in 1989, 1994 and 1995 to demonstrate that groups of people with access to better road services have a lower degree of poverty. Fan and Chan-Kang (2005) evaluated the influence of China's road construction work on poverty alleviation, and discovered that it has played the most evident role in alleviating urban poverty in north-western and north-eastern China, and rural poverty in north-western and south-western China. This offers an important reference for determining the direction of investment in future transportation infrastructure.

Infrastructure can also have a negative influence on the poor, as experience reveals.[26] Some giant construction projects will cause some peasants to lose their lands and houses, along with incomes and employment opportunities. In the same community, different people will have different capabilities in using public infrastructure facilities. Agricultural modernization and the development of non-agricultural industries spurred by improved infrastructure might worsen economic inequalities, offsetting gains in income growth. Benefits for the poor from infrastructure also rely upon auxiliary conditions. For example, the usefulness of transportation infrastructure depends on investment in other kinds of infrastructure, such as that for education, power, etc.

Human capital investment

Human capital plays an obvious role in propelling the growth of personal income and macroeconomic growth. Many anti-poverty policies in many countries have emphasized increased investments in education and health care, particularly for the poor.

Basic education policies

Investment in basic education enjoys top priority. Many studies and experiences have confirmed that investments in basic education, especially in backward areas and for girls, accomplish a higher rate of return (World Bank 1995, 1999a and 2001; Sen 1999). Therefore, stepping up investment in basic education has become a mainstream poverty alleviation policy. Since the direct educational costs of families, namely tuition fees, are a key factor influencing the schooling rate, policies tend to emphasize basic education allowances, low tuition fees and even free basic education.[27] Avenstrup *et al.* (2004) reviewed free basic education in Kenya, Malawi, Lesotho and Uganda, which have each recorded a dramatically enhanced schooling rate and a greatly increased number of students in schools. In Uganda, the schooling rate of those children from the poorest classes has come close to that of the wealthiest children.

Medical services and health care

Disease is an important dimension and cause of poverty. In developing countries, increasing the supply of basic medical services is essential to enhancing health in ways that helps people build human capital and reduce their level of poverty. Compared with urban residents, rural residents are disadvantaged in terms of economic standing and access to social welfare services. An important issue has become how to expand primary health care services for peasants through innovation and the mobilization of limited resources. In many developing countries, this is increasingly considered a key strategy in closing gaps in services between rural and urban areas. For example, Iran's primary health care system, which has put health centres in remote and scarcely populated regions staffed by medical specialists, is now regarded as a successful example of a simple but integrated health care information system.[28] Iran's experience has indicated that, even in a relatively poor country with rather limited natural resources, so long as the Government is able to make a reliable commitment, and develop an effective and innovative system (including the division of powers and coordination in the allocation of resources, a focus on targets, personnel training and supervision, etc.), it is possible to provide everyone with primary health care.

Microcredit

In many developing countries, factors such as the lack of information, trading costs, monopolies and governmental interference have prevented financial markets from realizing their full capacity to support development. Small and medium-sized enterprises and households (especially those in rural areas) have been unable to garner a whole gamut of regular financial services, due to a lack of collateral and other guarantees, and also on account of the uncertainties in their economic life.[29] They accumulate capital, both physical and human, at a slow pace (McKinnon 1983, Shaw 1973, Besley 1995 and Morduch 1999). In order to expand the supply of regular financial services, since the 1950s and 1960s, some national governments have attempted to enlarge financial capacities through compulsive loan arrangements, interest rate restrictions, and so on. After two to three decades, these forms of interference have been useful to a certain extent, but there have been problems as well, such as bad loans, multi-tiered moral hazards between governments and financial organs, and inabilities to target prospective borrowers. In the 1980s, when most theoreticians felt pessimistic pursuing development and alleviating poverty through interference in financial markets, the emergence of microcredit seemed hopeful.

Microcredit organizations – such as Bangladesh's Grameen Bank, Indonesia's Bank Rakyat Indonesia Unit Desa and Badan Kredit Desa, Bolivia's BancoSol and Latin America's FINCA Village Bank – have from their inception distinguished themselves from traditional financial organs in the following respects: (1) many made it clear that they were providing not only financial services, but also pursuing diverse social objectives (such as broadening participation, empowering women, alleviating poverty, offering legal aid, etc.; (2) most target those people excluded by traditional banks; (3) most operate on a small scale, and their loan terms are relatively short; and (4) as far as loan risk control techniques are concerned, microcredit organizations have applied a number of creative mechanisms such as companion selection, companion supervision,[30] dynamic incentives and mortgage substitution based on social capital. Microcredit has also made a difference in terms of issues such as creative arrangements for deposits, advocacy for sustainable commercial operations, etc., which are all significant breakthroughs for finance and poverty alleviation. In two decades, microcredit organizations have spread quickly. The Grameen Bank has had more than 3.2 million borrowers (95 percent of whom are women), established 1178 branches for service to over 41,000 villages and possessed assets of more than US $3 billion (Mainsah *et al.* 2004). Bank Rakyat Indonesia has provided deposit services for nearly 30 million customers and offered loan services for 3.1 million customers (Maurer 2004). Such operating modes have spread and been copied not only in developing countries, but also developed countries (Colin 1999). Even traditional financial organs have started to use microcredit operating modes (Morduch 1999).

Social security network

The social security network refers to transfer payment programmes and policy arrangements specifically for poor and vulnerable populations; it can also be known as social relief or social welfare. An ordinary social security network comprises such modules as cash transfer payments, food-related plans, price and other allowances, public work services, etc. It also covers the intention to provide access to basic public services (such as health care, education and power supplies).

Conditional cash transfer is one creative institutional arrangement that has attracted attention from academia and policy makers internationally. This is a policy arrangement that reduces poverty by use of monetary and material allowances. It requires the adults in a poor family to participate in public projects and make human capital investments in the next generation, so as to reduce the probability of their family remaining in poverty. The amount of such allowances does not vary with the income level of family members. In traditional allowance policies, the amount often slides down with the enhancement of income, thus giving a reverse incentive to receive a higher allowance by reducing labour input (Skoufias and di Maro 2006). Mexico's PROGRESA, Brazil's Bolsa Escola and Ecuador's Bono de Desarrollo Humano are relatively representative conditional cash transfer projects.[31]

Financial decentralization and broader participation

Globally, thinking and practice in poverty alleviation have made decentralization and the broadening of participation not only objectives, but also normative requirements, among others. These elements govern policy formulation, especially in arrangements made by international development institutions such as the World Bank, UNDP and International Monetary Fund.

Financial decentralization means the delegation of decisions on financial matters to lower-level governments (UNESCO 2005). The role of financial decentralization in boosting poverty alleviation includes: (1) as local governments undertake more decisions, they can be more likely to provide public services according to the needs of the poor, and in a more effective way; (2) local governments have better mastery of local information about the needs of the poor, so decentralization can ensure more public financial expenditures reach the poor and poor regions; and (3) financial decentralization can enhance local government abilities in implementing pro-poor public policies (Rao 2005, UNESCO 2005 and Boex 2005).

Financial decentralization has been a trend in many developing countries. As indicated by research in Indonesia, Pakistan and the Philippines, after decentralization, local governments have proffered public services of markedly better quality (UNESCO 2005).[32] There have also been opposite experiences. According to Faguet (2000), decentralization in Bolivia produced better quality public services for health care, hygiene, education and so on, but local governments remained unresponsive to appeals for some types of public services (such as water management). The central Government has a better record on some issues. Gu Xin and Fang Liming (2004) analysed China's public health care policies for rural areas, and determined that financial decentralization might be one of the reasons giving rise to the ongoing shortages in services. A similar conclusion was reached in the *China Human Development Report 2005*. A study by Ellis, Kutengule and Nyasulu (2003) on Malawi's poverty reduction strategy paper found that financial decentralization was impeding poverty alleviation in rural areas when local governments were aiming primarily to increase the income level.

The emphasis on broadening participation in poverty alleviation policies in different countries manifests on multiple fronts, from the formulation of strategies, to planning for the public development of communities, to participatory poverty assessments. The rationale for this approach has several aspects. First, through participatory development, the poor have more chances to express their interests, which makes it easier to locate target populations, make customized policy arrangements, and allow the poor to share in a wider range of development outcomes (Karl 2000; UNESCO 2005). Second, participatory development is not only a process of finding out about the needs of the poor, but also a course in which poor people demonstrate their creative power to facilitate policy innovation. This can enhance the effectiveness, efficiency and sustainability of poverty alleviation projects, as well as the sense of government responsibility (Pretty *et al.* 1995; Karl 2000, Beresford and Hoban 2005; Hjorth 2003). Third, via participatory development, poor people can foster their own capabilities and independence, which supports sustainable poverty alleviation (Beresford and Hoban 2005). Finally, since they play the principal part, the poor should not only act as passive beneficiaries of development, but also participate in the development course (Sen 1997; Sen 1999).

Pursuant to the review by Turk (2001) of practices in Vietnam, participatory poverty evaluation has generated a positive influence in changing the course and direction of central and local government policy formulation, and improving the design, supervision and evaluation of poverty alleviation projects. Due to the implementation of such policies, the economic life and well-being of poor populations have also improved. A participatory project in Nayong County of Guizhou Province of China, which was sponsored by the Asian Development Bank, found that community residents' opinions on the estimation of poverty, its causes and necessary policy responses were immensely different from local government beliefs. In this sense, participatory poverty evaluation is helpful in closing gaps between policies and actual needs.[33] Public community resources have had a greater bearing on the poor's welfare than on that of the rich, and the management of resources has improved (Sunderlin 2006; S. Kumar 2002; N. Kumar *et al.* 2000; World Bank 2001). A joint forestry management project in Madhya Pradesh in India enabled the forestry administration and forest users to share decision-making rights for woodlands, which encouraged controlled development and other positive outcomes.

Notes

1 See Rural Survey Group of the National Bureau of Statistics of China (2006, p. 98).
2 When the World Bank's advocated poverty line of US $1 dollar per day per person is employed, the incidence rate of poverty in rural areas of China is estimated at 64 percent in 1981, dropping to 16.6 percent in 2001 (see Chen and Ravallion 2004).
3 According to data provided by Zhou Binbin (1991), the consumption level of peasants in 1957 was 17 percent above that in 1952; however, during the 'Great Leap Forward' period, this level fell markedly, before rebounding to the 1957 level in 1965.
4 See Rural Department of the National Bureau of Statistics of China (2006a, p.45).
5 Although using the poverty line for rural areas will result in an underestimation of poverty among urban residents, in comparative terms, both the size of the poor population in rural areas and the degree of their poverty have exceeded those of the poor population in urban areas.
6 See National Bureau of Statistics of China (1999).
7 According to the rural household survey data offered by the National Bureau of Statistics of China, the estimated Gini coefficient of net income distribution of rural residents in 1980 was 0.241. It dropped to 0.227 in 1985 (see Rural Department of the National Bureau of Statistics of China 2005).
8 From a macro point of view, the two main factors influencing the changes in the rate of poverty are income growth and income distribution. The former is negatively correlated with the rate of poverty (i.e., income growth will help reduce poverty), but the latter is positively correlated with the rate of poverty (namely, a widening income gap will cause worsening poverty). After 1990, Chinese peasants saw their income grow slowly, and the income gap among rural people kept widening. Therefore, the effect on poverty alleviation generated by income growth was offset, in quite a large part, by the widening income gap.
9 From 1979 to 1984, the growth rate of the per capita actual income of peasants exceeded 10 percent for six consecutive years; in some specific years such as 1982, this growth rate was up to 20 percent (see National Bureau of Statistics of China 2006, p.108).
10 The data on the population helped out of poverty annually in different periods are calculated from the data in National Bureau of Statistics of China (2006, p.110).
11 See National Bureau of Statistics of China (2006, p.110).
12 Ibid.
13 See Rural Survey Group of the National Bureau of Statistics of China (2006, p.98).
14 As indicated by the estimate of Hussain (2003), when income was adopted as the measurement, the rate of poverty in urban areas of China in 1998 was 4.7 percent. When consumption expenditure was employed as the measurement, the rate of poverty in the same year was 11.9 percent. As indicated by the findings of a study on urban poverty in the late 1990s, the rate of poverty rose a certain degree in that period (see background paper, Zheng Feihu and Li Shi, 'Analysis of China's Urban Poverty-Stricken Population and Low-Income Population since 1995').
15 The minimum living security system for urban areas has been widely implemented since 2002. The population covered by this system grew quickly to 20.64 million people in 2002, up from only 4.02 million in 2001. In the ensuing few years, the population this section covers has basically remained at this level. According to the Chinese Ministry of Civil Affairs, the minimum living security system for urban areas has, by and large, covered the poorest population in urban areas, and

has honoured its objective of covering every urban resident entitled to benefit from the system (see background report, Wang Zhenyao 2006).

16 According to the estimates of Khan (2007) and as indicated in the background paper offered by Zheng Feihu and Li Shi (2006), the rates of poverty in urban areas from 1995 to 2002 have been dropping dramatically, regardless of which income concept is adopted for measurement (either the income concept of the National Bureau of Statistics of China or the amended income concept) and which poverty line is used (either a higher or lower poverty line).

17 According to Khan (2007), the rate of extreme poverty among urban residents in 2002 was 2.1 percent, while the rate of extreme poverty among rural migrants to urban areas was 5.5 percent. There has been a sharp increase in the size of migrant populations in urban areas. Since they are excluded from the minimum living security system, they constitute a major component of the urban poor.

18 From 1981 to 2001, except for some East Asian countries (including China) that saw the sizes of their poor populations drop markedly, other countries did not make substantial progress. Poor populations grew in some Latin American countries and most African countries, as well as in the Central Asian and Eastern European countries. In India, the rate of poverty fell, but the size of India's poor population was not much reduced, mainly due to excessive population growth rates (see Chen and Ravallion 2004).

19 From 1990 to 2001, the rate of subsistence poverty in rural areas of China fell from 9.4 percent to 3.2 percent, down by 66 percent (see National Bureau of Statistics of China 2006, p.110).

20 The retention rate of compulsory education in western China is relatively low, but the dropout rate has remained high for years. For instance, the retention rates of students in grade five in elementary schools in a few provinces in western China are below 80 percent, including Tibet (75.88 percent), Gansu (77.67 percent), Qinghai (79.11 percent) and Ningxia (73.96 percent). This means that in these regions, more than 20 percent of the students in elementary schools are unable to finish their studies and have to leave their schools ahead of schedule. According to the Rural Survey Group of the National Bureau of Statistics of China (2003, p.33), in 2002, 9.1 percent of children aged 7 to 15 years in poor counties of China discontinued their studying (the rate for boys was 7.2 percent and for girls 10.8 percent). According to an analysis of the reasons, nearly 50 percent of these children stopped going to school due to financial difficulties. According to research conducted by Emily Hannum (2003), who carried out a regression analysis on the schooling rate of 83,379 rural children aged 12 to 14 years in 1992, the schooling rate of male children from families in the lowest income quintile was 6 percent less than that of children from the top income quantile. As far as female children are concerned, the discrepancy is nearly 15 percent. News reports on high school graduates who cannot afford the tuition fees in colleges and universities, even though they have successfully passed the matriculation examination, have drawn attention to the financial difficulties suffered by children from poor families in seeking higher studies.

21 Some empirical studies have utilized data from different countries to estimate the effect of income gap on economic growth. According to the results of estimations such as these, the original income gap in countries is apparently negatively correlated with their economic growth rate (see de Ferranti *et al.* 2004). That is also to say, a country with a smaller income gap is more likely to achieve higher economic growth; an excessive income gap will impede economic growth.

22 The extremely poor population in each province has been defined per the Government's announced poverty line. In 2004, the official extreme poverty line in rural areas was RMB 668 yuan (see National Bureau of Statistics of China 2005).

23 See the data from the *Quick Statistical Report on Civil Administration in 2006* (Ministry of Civil Affairs of the People's Republic of China 2006b).

24 The rural poverty line adopted in 1998 was RMB 635 yuan, which is actually a subsistence poverty line, because the Engel's coefficient in use when setting this poverty line was 85 percent (Sheng Laiyun 2001).

25 Research documentation includes Binswanger *et al.* 1993, Fan *et al.* 1999, Jacoby 2000, Jalan and Ravallion 2002, Limao and Venables 1999, Kandker 1989, Fan *et al.* 1999, Fan and Rao 2002, Escobal 2001, Zhu Ling *et al.* 1994, Zhang Weixin 2000, and Fan and Chan-Kang 2005.

26 For research on the negative influence of infrastructure upon the poor, please see Songco 2002, Benjamin and Brandt 1999, Rozelle 1994, Khan and Riskin 2001, Fan and Chan-Kang 2005, Escobal 2001, Chatterjee 2005 and Escobal 2001.

27 See Avenstrup, Liang and Nellemann 2004, Ravallion and Wodron 2000, Behrman and Sengupta 2005, and Zhang 2004.

28 Since its implementation, the primary health care system played a rather significant role in improving the health conditions of rural residents in Iran. For instance, from 1974 to 2000, the mortality rate of newborns dropped from 39 percent to 20.6 percent, while the mortality rate of infants dropped from 12 percent to 3.02 percent, thus coming close to rates in urban areas. However, the mortality rate of children below five years of age fluctuated largely during these few years and did not decline markedly. The mortality rate of every 10,000 pregnant women and those in confinement who gave birth to babies alive fell from 370 persons to 35 persons. Many indicators related to immunity concerns and drug use have all come close to, or even outstripped, those in urban areas (Mehryar 2004).

29 New methods of finance have, to a certain degree, complemented the regular financial sector. For discussions upon the strong and weak points and economic usefulness of these new methods, please refer to the descriptive article by Liu Minquan *et al.* (2003).

30 The team-based companion selection and supervision system is a critical institutional arrangement in the Bangladeshi model. As indicated by an analysis of the theories and proven experience with this system, an effective internal supervision mechanism helps reduce the moral hazards of borrowers (Stiglitz 1990; Varian 1990; Wydick 1999; Hermes *et al.* 2003, 2005).

31 Mexico's PROGRESA is a large conditional cash transfer payment project for education, health and nutrition in poor rural regions that has been relatively successful. See Skoufias *et al.* 2001, Skoufias and di Maro 2006, and Gertler 2004.

32 See the World Bank, 'Majority of Indonesians says public services improving after decentralization, says new survey' [http://web.worldbank.org/WBSITE/EXTERNAL/COUNTRIES/EASTASIAPACIFICEXT/INDONESIAEXTN/0], and the ILO (2004).

33 See Foreign Capital Project Management Center (Leading Group Office of Poverty Alleviation and Development, State Council of the People's Republic of China) and Center for Community Development Studies of Yunnan (2001).

2   New characteristics of poverty in China today

The last three decades have not only seen China's success in implementing reform and achieving greater openness and speedy economic growth, but have also witnessed concerted anti-poverty initiatives. Through the efforts of people in poor regions and governments at all levels, the size of China's poor population has dramatically declined. In the present stage of China's economic development and reform, considerable changes have happened in terms of the mixture of rural and urban poverty. This chapter discusses this shifting dynamic and the basic characteristics of rural and urban poverty, including geographical and demographic distribution. A basic condition for defining the poor population is first to elaborate what poverty means and select a poverty line.

THE ABSOLUTE POVERTY LINE IN CHINA

Official rural poverty line, one-dollar line, low-income line, urban line for minimum subsistence

Since the early 1980s, the Chinese Government has applied a rural poverty line set by the National Bureau of Statistics of China. This is used to determine the size of the population in poverty and the incidence of poverty in rural areas. The method for setting this poverty line has complied with international criteria. First, it was necessary to define a nutrition standard, so the National Bureau of Statistics of China decided on a standard of 2100 calories per day. The second requirement was to establish the volumes of different foodstuffs necessary for measuring up to this nutrition standard, in line with the consumption structure of the lowest quantile, before calculating the corresponding monetary value according to the prices of foodstuffs. Such a monetary value then becomes the food poverty line. Second, the non-food poverty line needed to be calculated by either a simple or a slightly more complex method. The simple approach is to either subjectively determine the percentage taken up by the food poverty line in the total poverty line, or to calculate this percentage by reference to the Engel's coefficient of the entire society or the Engel's coefficient of the low-income population. For detailed discussions upon a more complex method, see Rural Survey Group of the National Bureau of Statistics of China (2000, pp. 130–131).

Figure 2.1 illustrates the changes in the rural poverty line. At the top is the official poverty line in current prices; the bottom line denotes the poverty line in constant 1985 prices. Although the nominal poverty line kept increasing from year to year prior to 1997 with the increase of consumption prices in rural areas at large, in some of the following years, the increase of the latter has even exceeded that of the former. This can be corroborated by observation of the variation trend of the real poverty line. As shown in Figure 2.1, the poverty line in 1985 is determined at RMB 206 yuan; in the ensuing two decades, the poverty line measured by constant 1985 prices has remained around RMB 200 yuan on the whole. The real poverty line has remained generally stable.

During the last 20 years, the per capita income of rural residents has grown markedly. Real per capita income from 1985 to 2005 rose 1.38 times. As a result, the ratio between the rural poverty line and the per capita income of rural residents has continuously fallen. As shown in Figure 2.2, the ratio between the poverty line and per capita income was 52 percent in 1985, and dropped to 40 percent in 1992, 29 percent in 1998 and 21 percent in 2005. As indicated by some international research, compared with other countries, China has registered the lowest ratio between the rural poverty line and per capita income of rural residents. The comparison has triggered questioning of the rationality of the poverty line, with an increasing number of people suggesting that the official poverty line for rural areas has been underestimated.[1]

While China is still applying a poverty line that is relatively low, certain international organs have put forward poverty lines with higher standards. For example, the World Bank has offered a few optional poverty lines: US $1 dollar per person per day (shortened as the one-USD poverty line) and US $2

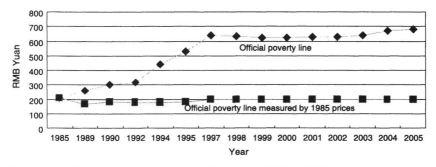

Figure 2.1 Official poverty line in rural China from 1985 to 2005.

Source: After an estimation based on rural poverty lines issued by the National Bureau of Statistics of China (*China Yearbook of rural household survey 2006*, p. 45) and rural consumption price indexes of the pertinent years.

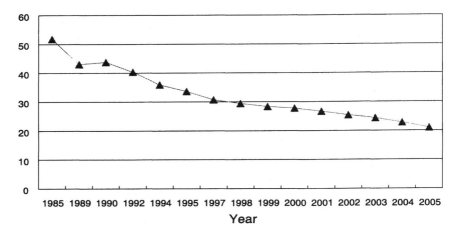

Figure 2.2 Ratio between the official poverty line for rural areas and per capita net
income of rural residents from 1985 to 2005 (%).

Source: Based on the data in *China Statistical Summary 2006*.

dollars per person per day (shortened as the two-USD poverty line). These
poverty lines accord with the factual consumption levels of most developing
countries.[2] The bank defined the one-USD poverty line as the lowest standard
poverty line, equivalent to the minimum subsistence line. Those below the line
are considered extremely poor.

So far in China, no uniform standards exist for assessing urban poverty
and the urban poor. To define impoverished populations in urban areas, a
widely acknowledged practice is to refer to a city's security line for minimum
subsistence. Those people whose per capita disposable income level is lower
than the city's security line for minimum subsistence are considered poor. At
the end of 2006, there were 22.41 million urban residents in China receiving
minimum subsistence security benefits, accounting for 3.9 percent of the total
population in urban China. The average security level is RMB 169.6 yuan per
person per month or an average of RMB 2035 yuan per year, which roughly
equals 17.3 percent of the annual per capita disposable income level for urban
residents (Ministry of Civil Affairs of the People's Republic of China 2007a
and 2007b, and National Bureau of Statistics of China 2007).

The urban security line for minimum subsistence in each city is set up by
the local government according to its own fiscal payment capability; there is
no nationwide standard. In 2006, Shenzhen had the highest level at RMB
4128 yuan, and Suihua had the lowest level at RMB 1248 yuan. Data analysis
reveals a strong correlation between local minimum security levels and the
per capita income of urban residents. Figure 2.3 demonstrates the relationship between the per capita disposable income and average minimum security
level in each province.

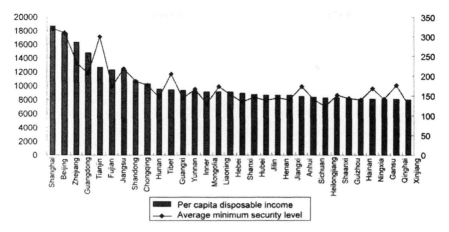

Figure 2.3 Correlation between the minimum security level and per capita disposable income of urban residents in each province (RMB yuan).

Source: Ministry of Civil Affairs 2007 and National Bureau of Statistics of China 2006.

Note: The left vertical axis sets forth the per capita disposable income of urban residents (2005 data) calculated on an annual basis. The right vertical axis sets forth the average minimum security line in each province (2006 data) calculated on a monthly basis.

Wang Youjuan (2005) adopted the Martin Ravallion (1994) method (i.e., the food poverty line is assumed to be 2100 calories per person per day, and the non-food poverty line is determined by regression analysis) to calculate the urban poverty lines for the nation as well as for provinces, autonomous regions and municipalities directly under the central Government in 2004. According to this calculation, the national urban poverty line was RMB 2985 yuan in 2004, and the urban poverty lines for different provinces ranged between RMB 2303 yuan and RMB 4397yuan. These urban poverty lines all positively correlated with local economic development or per capita income level. The relationship between the calculated urban poverty line for each province and the average security line for minimum subsistence remained stable.

Strictly speaking, the security line for minimum subsistence is not equivalent to the poverty line, but in some cities, the security line for minimum subsistence is close to the poverty line. Since it is necessary to take into account the feasibility of policy implementation while setting up security lines for minimum subsistence, the lines will turn out to be relatively high for cities with advanced economies and strong fiscal pictures, and relatively low for cities with backward economies and weak fiscal health. It can be inferred that the security line for minimum subsistence deviates from the actual poverty line for a majority of cities.

Table 2.1 reports a finding from an evaluation report on minimum livelihood policies for urban areas which utilized well-structured statistical data to

Table 2.1 Comparisons between poverty lines and security lines for minimum subsistence of urban residents in China in 2004

Region	Poverty line (RMB yuan)	Security line for minimum subsistence (RMB yuan)	Security line for minimum subsistence/ poverty line (%)
Eastern China	3,411	2,407	71
Central China	2,610	1,670	64
Western China	2,664	1,735	65
Nationwide	2,985	2,016	68

Source: Wang Youjuan 2006 ('Evaluations of the Implementation of Minimum Livelihood Security Policies for Urban Residents').

estimate urban poverty lines in different provinces, and to compare poverty lines and security lines for minimum subsistence in three regions in China. There is a marked difference between the security line for minimum subsistence and the estimated poverty line. An obvious finding from the table is that the differences between the two lines are more drastic for the relatively underdeveloped economic regions in the central and western parts of the country.

As determined by the security line for minimum subsistence, the urban population in poverty is underestimated. Even making the calculation based upon the existing lines, the number of people that have received security benefits is much smaller than the number entitled. According to a calculation by Wang Youjuan (2006), in 2004, 3.9 percent of residents in 35 large and medium cities received security benefits for minimum subsistence. According to calculations based upon the security lines for minimum subsistence in different cities, 8.1 percent of residents were entitled. Benefits therefore reached only about half of the target population.[3]

Nevertheless, the calculation based on the survey data of urban residents administered by the National Bureau of Statistics of China has illustrated that, to some extent, the definition of who is eligible for benefits is accurate. The incomes of 67.6 percent of the target population entitled to benefits are lower than the security lines, while only 32.4 percent of beneficiaries have higher incomes. In addition, 87.4 percent of the target population is distributed in low-income families, which account for 20 percent of the total number of families in urban areas. The data suggest that despite some acknowledged errors, the inaccuracy rate is in an acceptable range, and accords with international experiences (Wang Youjuan 2006).

Developmental poverty line

The above comparison of rural poverty and urban poverty lines suggests a huge difference exists. As estimated by Wang Youjuan (2005), the average value of the urban poverty line in 2004 was RMB 2985 yuan, while that of the official rural poverty line in the same year was RMB 668 yuan; the former is 4.47 times more than the latter. Such a difference has occurred due to the disparity in terms of living expenses between rural and urban areas, and more importantly the discrepancy between the poverty standards applied to rural and urban areas. The rural poverty line is established on the concept of subsistence. The urban poverty line has transcended this concept by covering not only expenditures on food to achieve minimum nutrition, but also expenditures on basic education and health care. In a sense, the urban poverty line is rooted in the developmental poverty concept, which includes the subsistence poor and the developmentally poor.

As far as rural poverty is concerned, it is not enough to consider subsistence poverty alone. From the angle of human development, the most important objective of poverty alleviation is to enhance people's capabilities to pursue development, instead of simply providing them with bare subsistence. To eliminate the root causes of poverty and help the poor achieve a better life requires education, training and health care.

It thus appears essential to appropriately amend the official poverty line for rural areas – namely, the subsistence poverty line indicating the income level that the rural poor need for bare subsistence. This report instead proposes the developmental poverty line, which is an income/consumption expenditure line above the subsistence poverty line. It includes not only the income necessary for bare subsistence, but also the payment capability required for securing average education and health care services. The following formula illustrates the developmental poverty line for rural areas:

$$DPL = SPL + \sum_{i=1} \left(E_{ni} - E_{pi} \right)$$

In this equation, DPL is the developmental poverty line, SPL is the subsistence poverty line, E_{ni} is the average of the expenditures in rural areas under item 'i' necessary for enhancement of development capabilities, and E_{pi} is the amount of expenditures under item 'i' of the poor population.[4] A detailed discussion needs to determine which expenditures are necessary for enhancing development capabilities. Whether an item should be included will depend on the extent to which it correlates with the development of individuals' potential capabilities. Without doubt, expenditures for children's compulsory education, the training of unskilled labourers and basic medical expenditures should be included. Since the developmental poverty line covers educational and medical fees, it is more likely to be influenced by the modes of provision and prices of these two services. If they are entirely paid for by the Government, then the developmental poverty line will slide down and may even be equal to the subsistence poverty line. On the other hand, if the two services are fully paid for by individuals, and their prices go up excessively, the developmental poverty line will naturally be elevated.

Therefore, in different periods, the developmental poverty line is more likely to fluctuate.

POOR POPULATIONS IN RURAL AREAS OF CHINA

Size, geographical distribution, demographic distribution and changes in populations

In this section, we will describe the size, geographical and demographic distribution, and evolution of rural populations living in subsistence and developmental poverty, respectively. As far as subsistence poverty is concerned, the size of the rural poor population has continued to shrink, along with the incidence of poverty. As shown in Figures 1.1 and 2.4, in the first half of the 1980s, the size of the poor population in rural areas dropped sharply. In the ensuing two decades, the decline slowed, but the decrease has been satisfactory overall. As estimated by the National Bureau of Statistics of China, by the end of 2005, the size of the rural population in subsistence poverty had fallen below 24 million persons.[5] Even according to a higher poverty standard (such as the one-USD poverty line or low-income line), the size of the poor population in rural areas has been decreasing at an almost identical pace.

Figure 2.4 shows the changing size of the population in developmental poverty since 1980. It comprised 253 million or so people at that time, dropping to 160 million people in 1985, 110 million people in 1995 and 85 million

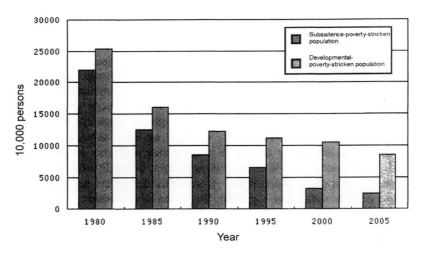

Figure 2.4 Changes in the population in subsistence and developmental poverty in rural China.

Source: Calculated after the estimation based on *China Statistical Yearbook.*

people in 2005. This is roughly equal to the size of the low-income population in rural areas announced by the Government. In nearly three decades, the size of the population that is developmentally poor has, by and large, fallen at the same pace as the size of rural populations in subsistence poverty. This is best demonstrated prior to 1990. An in-depth comparison shows that in the mid and late 1990s, quite a big difference occurred between the pace of decline for the two populations, with the decrease much slower for developmental poverty. Figure 2.4 shows that by 2000, the subsistence poverty population had declined by 33.3 million people since 1995. The size of the population in developmental poverty was reduced by less than 6 million. This means a considerable portion of people escaped subsistence poverty, but not developmental poverty. In other words, as far as the low-income population in rural areas is concerned, it is harder to reduce developmental poverty than subsistence poverty. This is partly because of the slow income growth of low-income populations, and also due to the fact that rural residents are paying an increasingly higher price to obtain development capabilities. The most typical instance is the fact that increasing tuition fees and incidental charges have been levied on rural students. Medical charges in rural areas have gone far beyond the growth rate of per capita income of rural residents as a whole, posing special burdens for low-income populations.

Geographical distribution

While the size of the population in subsistence poverty has fallen markedly, the composition of this group has also changed. An analysis conducted by the National Bureau of Statistics of China in 2005 found that most people in subsistence poverty live in central and western China. Among the 23.65 million rural poor, 3.24 million people are in eastern China, 8.39 million in central China and 12.03 million in western China, constituting 13.7 percent, 35.5 percent and 50.8 percent of the total respectively (see Table 2.2). The rates of subsistence poverty in central China and western China are 3.1 times and 6.5 times, respectively, that of eastern China. In 1993, the percentage of people in subsistence poverty, out of the total rural population in subsistence poverty, was 19.5 percent, 31.1 percent and 49.4 percent in eastern, central and western China, respectively (see Wang Sangui and Li Wen 2005). In 1998, these three percentages were 14.8 percent, 37 percent and 48.2 percent, respectively (see Table 2.2). From 1993 to 2005, changes in the geographical distribution of the rural population in subsistence poverty mostly manifested in the decrease of the percentage in eastern China, and the increase in central China. The percentage in western China did not vary largely. The decrease in eastern China exceeded the country's average. The decrease in western China has been equal to the country's average, while the decrease in central China has been less than the country's average.[6]

Table 2.2 indicates that by the end of 2005, the population in subsistence poverty in central and western China still constituted a major part of the country's total population in subsistence poverty in rural areas. The number of people who have left poverty in these two regions has also constituted an absolute majority of the total number of rural people helped out of poverty nationwide. From 1998 to 2005, the size of the population in subsistence poverty in rural areas fell by 18.45 million persons. The decrease in central China involved 7.2 million persons, and in western China 8.27 million persons, comprising 39 percent and 45 percent, respectively, of the total number of people in rural areas helped out of poverty. While central and western China have contributed to the decrease in the size of the rural poor population, they must shoulder an even greater responsibility for rural poverty alleviation in the future.

The discrepancy in terms of the rate of poverty in rural areas is likewise apparent among different provinces. Table 2.3 shows the rate in each province in each of the years from 1998 to 2005. Those provinces with a 2005 rate in excess of 5 percent (twice the country's average) are Inner Mongolia, Guizhou, Yunnan, Tibet, Shaanxi, Gansu, Qinghai and Xinjiang, most of which are in western China. In the same year, eight provinces registered a rate below 1 percent; they are mostly in eastern China. Some provinces, such as Beijing, Tianjin, Shanghai, Guangdong, Fujian, Zhejiang and Jiangsu, have mainly ended subsistence poverty in their territories.

Another dimension of geographical distribution is the difference between poor and more well-off regions in the rate of poverty. In the past, local governments at all levels concentrated their poverty alleviation efforts on poor regions. Under such a policy framework, changes in poverty arrested the attention of the general public and became factors for assessing policy effectiveness. Table 2.4 lists the sizes of the populations in subsistence poverty, and the rates of poverty in poor and better-off regions from 2001 to 2005. It is not hard to see that most of the subsistence poor have converged in nationally designated poor counties. Although the total population within nationally designated poor counties takes up about 21 percent of China's aggregate rural population, the percent of subsistence poor in these counties is over 60 percent of the total population in subsistence poverty. From the perspective of the rate of subsistence poverty, the difference between nationally designated poor counties and other poor counties has become more evident. The rate in the former is five to six times that of the latter. Prior to 2004, there was no evident difference between these two types of regions in terms of poverty alleviation results.

As shown in Table 2.4, from 2001 to 2004 the size of the population of subsistence poor in nationally designated poor counties declined by 12.3 percent. The size of the population in subsistence poverty in other poor counties fell by 11.8 percent. In 2005, the decrease in nationally designated poor counties went far beyond that in other poor counties. The decline in the former was up to 12.8 percent, but only 6.7 percent in the latter. From 2001 to 2005, the size of the population in subsistence poverty in rural areas dropped by 5.62 million persons, 3.82 million of whom were in nationally designated poor counties. They constituted 68 percent of the total number of people helped out of poverty.

Child poverty

It is of paramount importance to help children escape poverty. For everyone, childhood is a period for accumulating human capital. Whether or not one can develop a good constitution and learn useful knowledge has a decisive bearing on a person's state of living in adulthood. This consideration has made research on child poverty one of the most important topics in international academia. China has just begun its research on child poverty. This report presents the limited results to date in order to raise awareness of this issue.

As shown in Figure 2.5, compared with the entire rural population, the rate of poverty is higher among children. In 1998, the rate was 9.1 percent, which was 98 percent higher than that of the entire rural population. In 2005, although dropping to 4.9 percent, the rate was still 96 percent higher than that of the entire rural population. This suggests that children register a higher rate of poverty in rural areas at all times. Figure 2.6 reveals that in 2005, the rate of poverty among children from birth to age 6 was the highest of all age groups. The rate for children from 7 to 12 years old was higher than the average in rural areas by 24 percent and 32 percent, in 1998 and 2005, respectively.

In order to understand child poverty in depth, it is essential to introduce geographical distribution and regional structures. Table 2.5 sets out the country's child poverty indexes in 1995 and 2002. According to the official poverty line, the rate of subsistence poverty among children aged 15 years and below was 8.5 percent in 1995, which is 1.4 percent higher than the overall poverty rate in rural areas in the same year. In 2002, the rate in rural areas declined to 4 percent. Within the same period, the rate for the entire rural population was 3.1 percent, or 0.9 percent lower than the rate among children. Extrapolating from a sample survey in 2002, 7 million children were in subsistence poverty in rural areas that year.

Table 2.6 sets out the results of analysis on the geographical distribution of child poverty. In terms of poverty rate, children in western China are most likely to be impoverished. In 1995, the rate of poverty there was up to 12.5 percent, or 62 percent higher than in central China and 112 percent higher than in eastern China. In 2002, the rates for children in all three regions declined, but the incidence in western China remained the highest – 88 percent and 156 percent higher than in central and eastern China, respectively. This indicates that the decrease in the rate of poverty of children in western China is smaller than in the other two regions. But from the perspectives of the poverty gap, poverty gap square index and the changes thereof, the three major regions have demonstrated different characteristics.

Table 2.2 Geographical distribution and trends in subsistence poverty in rural areas of China from 1998 to 2005

		1998	2000	2001	2002	2003	2004	2005	Decrease from 1998 to 2005	Rate of decrease from 1998 to 2005 (%)
Size of the poor population (10,000 persons)	Nationwide	4,210	3,209	2,927	2,820	2,900	2,610	2,365	−1845	43.8
	Eastern China	622	487	393	465	448	374	324	−298	47.9
	Central China	1,559	1,091	996	888	1,030	931	839	−720	46.2
	Western China	2,030	1,632	1,537	1,468	1,422	1,305	1,203	−827	40.7
Rate of poverty (%)	Nationwide	4.6	3.5	3.2	3	3.1	2.8	2.5	−2.1	45.7
	Eastern China	1.7	1.3	1	1.2	1.2	1	0.8	−0.9	52.9
	Central China	4.8	3.4	3.1	2.7	3.2	2.8	2.5	−2.3	47.9
	Western China	9.1	7.3	6.8	6.5	6.2	5.7	5.2	−3.9	42.9
Percentage of the poor population in rural areas	Eastern China	14.8	15.2	13.4	16.5	15.4	14.3	13.7	−1.1	7.4
	Central China	37	3	34	31.5	35.5	35.7	35.5	−1.5	4.1
	Western China	48.2	50.8	52.5	52	49	50	50.8	2.6	−5.4
Poverty gap index	Eastern China	0.011	0.008	0.008	0.008	0.006	0.004	0.002	−0.009	81.8
	Central China	0.020	0.012	0.010	0.010	0.011	0.010	0.006	−0.014	70
	Western China	0.049	0.028	0.023	0.023	0.023	0.021	0.018	−0.031	63.3

Source: A background report provided by the Department of Rural Affairs of the National Bureau of Statistics of China.

Table 2.3 Rates of subsistence poverty across provinces from 1998 to 2005 (%)

	1998	*2000*	*2001*	*2002*	*2003*	*2004*	*2005*
Nationwide	4.6	3.5	3.2	3	3.1	2.8	2.5
Beijing	1.6	0.6	0.5	0	0	0	0
Tianjin	0.5	0.9	0.5	0.2	0.7	0.2	0
Hebei	2	1.9	1.8	2.9	2.3	1.9	1.5
Shanxi	6	6.8	6.6	5	3.9	3.1	2.3
Inner Mongolia	6.4	8.2	13.3	9.8	9.4	7.5	6.6
Liaoning	3.1	3.5	3.2	3.2	3.6	2.5	2.2
Jilin	4.2	4.1	3.1	2.6	3	2	1.5
Heilongjiang	8.2	5.6	4.6	3.4	5.6	3.6	3.2
Shanghai	0	0	0	0	0	0	0
Jiangsu	0.6	0.3	0.2	0.4	0.3	0.3	0.2
Zhejiang	1	0.2	0.2	0.4	0.2	0.3	0.2
Anhui	3.2	2.5	1.8	2	3.3	2.7	2.4
Fujian	0.7	0.3	0.2	0.4	0.3	0.2	0.1
Jiangxi	6.5	2.8	2.8	3.4	3.6	3.8	3.5
Shandong	1.4	0.7	0.7	0.7	0.7	0.3	0.3
Henan	4	3	2.1	1.7	2.4	2.1	1.9
Hubei	4.4	2.2	1.8	2	1.8	3.3	3.1
Hunan	5	2.3	2.1	1.9	2.1	1.9	1.8
Guangdong	0.5	0.1	0.1	0	0.1	0.1	0.1
Guangxi	5.5	5	3.4	2.7	3.6	3.5	3.2
Hainan	2.7	1.9	1.7	3	2.1	1.9	2.2
Chongqing	6.6	4.2	4	3	3	2.2	1.6
Sichuan	5.5	3.7	3.3	2.2	2.5	2.2	2
Guizhou	12.9	10.8	10.4	10.7	10.1	9.7	9
Yunnan	12.2	8.2	7.9	11.1	7.9	7.5	7
Tibet	19	19.8	15.2	15.6	14	8.8	7.2
Shaanxi	9	7.9	7.8	6.2	8.3	7.8	7.2
Gansu	11.5	9.7	9.6	9.2	8.6	8.4	8.1
Qinghai	14	18.6	16.9	16.1	15.6	13.6	11.5
Ningxia	12.6	14.5	13.6	8.9	8.4	3.8	3
Xinjiang	8.9	10	6.5	6.9	5.7	5.7	5.1

Source: A background report provided by the Department of Rural Affairs of the National Bureau of Statistics of China.

Compared to 1995, by 2002 child poverty in the three major regions had been alleviated to a large extent. The child poverty gap indexes posted in eastern China, central China and western China dropped by 65 percent, 72 percent and 56 percent, respectively. The pace of decline exceeded that of the overall rates of poverty in the three regions. This means that the average income levels of poor children in the three regions have risen. In 1995, the percentage of poor children in western China out of the national total of poor children in rural areas exceeded the total population of western China's percentage of the country's aggregate population. In 2002, the discrepancy between these two percentages was even bigger.

Table 2.7 enumerates the child poverty indexes and decomposition in

Table 2.4 Geographical distribution and evolution of the population in subsistence poverty in rural areas

	2001	2002	2003	2004	2005	2000–2005
Nationally designated poor counties						
Subsistence poor (10,000 persons)	1,812	1,752	1,763	1613	1,430	−382
Rate of poverty (%)	9.1	8.8	8.8	8.1	7.1	−2
Non-poor counties						
Subsistence poor (10,000 persons)	1,115	1,068	1,137	997	935	−180
Rate of poverty (%)	1.6	1.4	1.5	1.4	1.3	−0.3

Source: Data on nationally designated poor counties came from the *Report upon Surveillance of China's Rural Poverty 2006* compiled by the Division of Rural Socioeconomic Survey under the National Bureau of Statistics of China. The data for non-poor counties were estimated from the data on the total poor population in rural China and the poor population in nationally designated poor counties.

Note: Nationally designated poor counties are now termed 'major counties subject to poverty alleviation'.

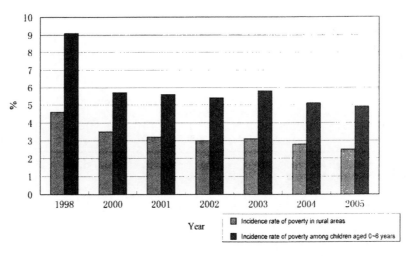

Figure 2.5 Incidence rate of poverty among children in rural areas of China from 1998 to 2005.

Source: Drawn from data in a background report provided by the Department of Rural Affairs of the National Bureau of Statistics of China.

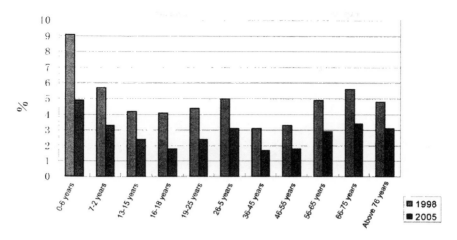

Figure 2.6 Incidence rates of poverty among people of different age groups in rural areas of China in 1998 and 2005.

Source: Drawn from data in a background report provided by the Department of Rural Affairs of the National Bureau of Statistics of China.

Table 2.5 Poverty indexes for children aged 15 years and below in rural areas of China in 1995 and 2002

	Rate of poverty (%)	*Poverty gap*	*Poverty gap square*
1995	8.5	2.6	1.4
2002	4	1	0.4

Source: A background paper from Yue Ximing ('Child Poverty in Rural Areas').

Note: The poverty index was calculated according to the official rural poverty line, namely RMB 530 yuan in 1995 and RMB 627 yuan in 2002.

nationally designated poor counties and other counties. The incidence of child poverty in poor counties is obviously higher than in other counties; such a difference has become more and more evident. In 1995, the incidence of child poverty in poor counties was 87 percent higher than in non-poor counties; in 2002, the former was four times higher than the latter. This means an increasing number of poor children in rural areas are from poor regions.

Other analyses have shown that the rate of poverty among children is positively correlated, to a strong extent, with their family size. Those families with more members are more likely to have their children living in poverty, because per capita income in a family often decreases with the addition of family members, especially multiple children. Furthermore, most poor children come from poorly educated families. Better educated families are less likely to have poor children.

Table 2.6 Subsistence poverty indexes and decomposition for children in different regions

	Poverty index			Decomposition of poverty index		
	Rate of poverty (%)	Poverty gap	Poverty gap square	Poverty rate	Poverty gap	Poverty gap square
1995						
Western China	12.5	3.6	1.7	41	38	35
Central China	7.7	2.5	1.4	38	40	43
Eastern China	5.9	2	1	21	22	22
Total				100	100	100
2002						
Western China	6.4	1.6	0.6	47	48	44
Central China	3.4	0.7	0.3	35	30	32
Eastern China	2.5	0.7	0.4	18	22	25
Total				100	100	100

Source: A background paper from Yue Ximing ('Child Poverty in Rural Areas').

Table 2.7 Child poverty indexes and decomposition thereof in poor counties and non-poor counties

	Poverty index			Decomposition of poverty index(%)		
	Rate of poverty (%)	Poverty gap	Poverty gap square	Rate of poverty	Poverty gap	Poverty gap square
1995						
Nationally designated poor counties	13.3	2.9	1.2	36	26	20
Non-poor counties	7.1	2.6	1.5	64	74	80
Total				100	100	100
2002						
Nationally designated poor counties	9.4	1.9	0.7	63	54	45
Non-poor counties	2	0.6	0.3	37	46	55
Total				100	100	100

Source: A background paper from Yue Ximing ('Child Poverty in Rural Areas').

In order to compare with international standards, this report, apart from adopting the Government's poverty line, also calculated and decomposed the poverty indexes pursuant to the US $1 poverty line of the World Bank. As the bank's standard was higher than the Government's poverty line in both 1995 and 2002, in the identical per capita income distribution scenario, the degree of child poverty in rural areas is greater under that measurement. To cite 2002 as an example, the rates of child poverty estimated according to the Government's poverty line and the World Bank's poverty line were 4 percent and 10.6 percent respectively. Poverty incidence was elevated by 40 percent, while child poverty went up by 1.65 times. This indicates that a majority of rural children have remained on the periphery of the poverty line. Even if the poverty line varies slightly, the rate of poverty will also undergo evident changes. In fact, the mixture and types of rural child poverty estimated with the World Bank's poverty standard, and by such factors as region, categorization between nationally designated poor counties and other poverty-stricken counties, family size, family educational background, etc., are roughly the same as the results from the Government's poverty line.

Familial characteristics of the poor population in rural areas

A comparison of poor and non-poor families reveals differences in familial characteristics that help in understanding the causes of poverty. Most of the data here come from the National Bureau of Statistics of China. According to its poverty definition, people in poverty fall into two categories: those in absolute poverty and those with low incomes. The population in absolute poverty corresponds with the population in subsistence poverty referred to in this report. The low-income population differs from the population below the developmental poverty line defined here, however.[7] Because no familial data are available for an analysis of the mixture and characteristics of that population below the developmental poverty line, we have adopted the results of estimates by the National Bureau of Statistics of China for the low-income population.

One characteristic of families in subsistence poverty is that they devote a higher percentage of their expenditures to food than low-income people do. This is confirmed by a relatively high Engel's coefficient. As shown in Table 2.8, compared to that of all sampled rural families, the Engel's coefficient for families in absolute poverty was 24 percent higher. It was nearly 11 percent higher than that of low-income families. The income and consumption levels of each of the two categories of poor people, when measured by a global standard, are low. Their average Engel's coefficients are higher than the definition of extreme poverty given by the UN's Food and Agriculture Organization (namely, with an Engel's coefficient of 60 percent or above).

The second characteristic of poor families is a low educational level and lack of human capital. The less-educated population has a higher incidence of poverty, and the percentage of illiterate and semi-literate people in the poor population has been higher than the average level. Table 2.9 presents the rates of subsistence poverty, from 1998 to 2005, for various groups of rural residents categorized by educational level. It is obvious that the rate for families whose members are illiterate or semi-literate is far beyond the average level. In 1998, the rate for such families was three times the average level; in 2005, this rate was 3.6 times higher than the average level. Likewise, the rate

Table 2.8 A comparison between poor families in rural areas and all rural families in China in terms of average indexes (2004)

	Families in absolute (subsistence) poverty	Low-income families	All rural families in China
Per capita net income (RMB yuan)	579	854	2936
Engel's coefficient (%)	71.3	66.5	47.2
Percentage taken up by illiterates and semi-literates in the total	18.3	14	7.5
Percentage taken up by wage income in the net income	19.9	22.7	34.1

Source: Division of Rural Socioeconomic Survey of the National Bureau of Statistics of China 2005.

Table 2.9 Rates of subsistence poverty of different groups of people with dissimilar educational backgrounds from 1998 to 2005 (%)

	1998	2000	2001	2002	2003	2004	2005
Rate of poverty in rural areas	4.6	3.5	3.2	3	3.1	2.8	2.5
By the educational backgrounds of family members							
Illiterates and semi-literates	14	11.9	9.5	9.3	10.1	10.9	8.9
Graduates from elementary schools	5.5	4.6	4.3	4.1	4.4	3.8	3.8
Graduates from junior high schools	3.3	2.6	2.3	2.3	2.2	1.8	1.6
Graduates from senior high schools	3	1.8	1.8	1.6	1.5	1.4	1.4
Graduates from secondary technical schools	2.5	1.8	2.1	1.7	1.1	0.6	0.5
Graduates from colleges or above	0	0.5	2.4	3	0.4	1.6	0.8

Source: A background report provided by the Department of Rural Affairs of the National Bureau of Statistics of China.

for families whose members are merely graduates from elementary schools is also higher than the average level. In 1998 and 2005, it was 20 percent and 52 percent higher, respectively.

To explore the discrepancy between the rural poor and non-poor in terms of educational background, this report has compared various groups of people with different levels of education (see Figure 2.7). Among the population aged 16 years and above that is not on a school campus, up to 23 percent of those who are poor are illiterates and semi-literates. This figure is only

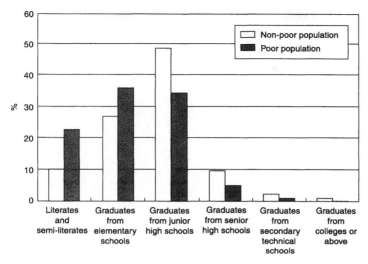

Figure 2.7 Discrepancy between the poor population and the non-poor population in rural areas in terms of educational background in 2005.

Source: Drawn from data in a background report of the Department of Rural Affairs of the National Bureau of Statistics of China.

10 percent for the non-poor population. Furthermore, the percentage of graduates from primary and high schools in the poor population is 22 percent higher than that of graduates from primary schools and high schools in the non-poor population. This means that the percentage of better-educated people in the non-poor population is higher than in the poor population. As indicated in Figure 2.7, the percentage of graduates from junior high schools in the population not in poverty is 42 percent higher than that of graduates from junior high schools in the poor population. The percentage of graduates from senior high school in the non-poor population is almost twice that of graduates from senior high schools in the poor population.

A third characteristic of poor families is a large family headcount and a heavy headcount burden. Data obtained from the surveillance of rural poverty, as set out in Table 2.10, show that the number of labourers in each family in absolute poverty in poor regions is 0.11 of a person more than the average level of all samples, but the number of children (aged 15 years and below) is 0.24 of a person more than the average level. The numbers of elderly and sick or disabled people are 0.05 and 0.02 of a person more than the average level, respectively.

The fourth characteristic of poor families involves their heavy educational and medical burdens. Table 2.11 sets out the percentages of medical and educational expenditures in the net incomes of each group of rural families, calculated according to 2004 data from poverty surveillance samples in six provinces selected by the National Bureau of Statistics of China.[8] The

Table 2.10 Headcount burdens of rural families[a] in poor regions

	Families in absolute poverty	Low-income families	All rural families
Number of children	1.21	1.18	0.97
Number of elderly people	0.26	0.26	0.21
Number of sick/disabled people	0.15	0.15	0.13
Percentage of families with no labourer	1.75	1.65	1.68
Percentage of the 'five guarantees' households[b]	0.36	0.17	0.25

Source: Results of a calculation from data obtained through rural poverty surveillance conducted by the National Bureau of Statistics of China.

Notes:
a The number of people in a family refers to residents; the number of labourers comprises those people from 16 to 65 years old with a capability for work; the number of children means those aged 15 years or below; the number of elderly people means those above 65 years old; and the number of sick or disabled people means those suffering major diseases, long-lasting chronic diseases or disability.
b The 'five guarantees' refer to those population groups targeted by the 'Regulations on Five Guarantees for Rural Areas', principally including elderly, disabled people and minors in rural areas who meet the following conditions: (1) they have no legally defined carer (as defined under the Marriage Law), or they do, but that person is unable to fulfil his or her maintenance obligations; (2) they have no ability to work; or (3) they have no income. The local governments guarantee them access to food, clothing, medical care, housing and burial expenses.

percentages are above 25 percent, making the medical and educational burdens of poor rural and low-income families far beyond the average level. In addition, the social expenses of these families have far exceeded their respective net incomes. Excessive burdens have resulted in compulsory overspending for necessary consumption expenditures, and caused a portion of rural families to survive by borrowing money (further discussion of this issue follows).[9]

The fifth characteristic of poor families is exposure to relatively poor natural and geographical conditions. Mountainous regions, and some places suffering a dry climate, arid land and poor natural conditions are particularly common in western China, which has a majority of the poor population. In 2004, 50 percent of the rural people in absolute poverty were in western China; 36 percent were in central China; and only 14 percent were in eastern China. In rural areas of western China, the rate of poverty was up to 5.7 percent. The highest rate of poverty, recorded in Qinghai, was close to 14 percent. In central China, the rate was 2.8 percent, and in eastern China it was only 1 percent (as per data provided by the Rural Survey Group of the National Bureau of Statistics of China 2005).

Table 2.11 Medical and educational expenditures of different groups of rural families, based on data from the surveillance of poverty in six provinces in 2004

	Families in absolute poverty	*Low-income families*	*All sampled families*
Personal consumption expenditures (yuan)	4,320	4,705	5,983
Medical expenditures (yuan)	298	302	448
Educational expenditures (yuan)	931	978	1,297
Ratio of medical expenditures to net income (%)	12.8	7.9	6.6
Ratio of educational expenditures to net income (%)	40	25.6	19
Percentage taken up by medical expenditures	79.9	82.8	85.5
Percentage taken up by educational expenditures	60.5	60	58
Number of sampled families	2,690	2,983	22,519

Source: Results of an estimate based on rural poverty surveillance data from the National Bureau of Statistics of China.

SIZE AND GEOGRAPHICAL DISTRIBUTION OF POOR POPULATIONS IN URBAN AREAS

Prior to the 1990s, urban poverty in China did not draw much attention because it affected few people due to the country's full employment policy and social security system at that time. China's reform of enterprises in urban areas since the mid 1990s, however, has triggered serious problems related to unemployment, even as the transformation of the social security system has reduced social safety nets (Li Shi and Hiroshi Sato 2004).

Research on urban poverty suffers from the lack of an official poverty line acknowledged by the Government. Therefore, estimates vary depending on the line selected for a certain point in time. But the variation trends in poverty incidence in a certain period, even when estimated with different poverty lines, are generally the same. Figure 2.8 shows an estimation of the variation trend of urban poverty from the mid 1980s to the late 1990s. From it, we can see that the rate of urban poverty measured by income level was around 2 percent before 1990; in 1990, the rate of poverty began to rise, topping 5 percent in 1993. It did not start to decline until the late 1990s.

Other studies have indicated that from 1995 to 2002, the rate of urban poverty fell. According to Khan (2007), if a relatively low poverty line is adopted, then the rate of urban poverty fell from 2.7 percent in 1995 to 0.8 percent in 2002. When a relatively high poverty line is adopted, then the rate fell from 8 percent in 1995 to 2.2 percent in 2002. As shown by the background report compiled by Zheng Feihu and Li Shi (2006), if the income

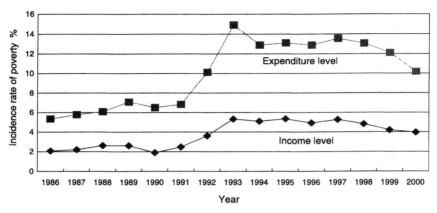

Figure 2.8 Variations in the incidence rate of urban poverty in China from 1986 to 2000.

Source: The data in this figure are from an estimate by Meng Xin et al. 2005.

concept of the National Bureau of Statistics of China is adopted, the rate of urban poverty was 5 percent in 1995. It rose to 6.7 percent in 1999 and slid to 3.1 percent in 2002. The alleviation of urban poverty in recent years is, in large part, inseparable from the effective implementation of the minimum livelihood security project in urban areas.

The rate of urban poverty is not only influenced by adjustments in the macroeconomic structure, but also correlates with the population mixture to a certain extent. Figure 2.9 shows the rates of poverty by gender and age group. Aside from the oldest age group, there is not much discrepancy between males and females in poverty incidence. The rate does demonstrate some lifecycle traits. At the age of childbearing, incidence begins increasing. Starting from the age when children are employed, incidence falls dramatically. Above the age of 70 years, the probability of being impoverished rises again.

Relative to the changes in population mixture, changes in economic structure have a more direct and greater impact on urban poverty. Figure 2.10 illustrates the relationship between unemployment and poverty. The unemployed people here include, besides the registered unemployed, laid-off workers and young people waiting for employment. It is not hard to observe that the rate of poverty of employed people is rather low (slightly above 2 percent). The rates for laid-off workers, youngsters waiting for employment and unemployed people are 2.5 times, 4 times and 5 times higher respectively. This means there is a strong positive correlation between unemployment and urban poverty. Unemployment is the most direct cause of urban poverty.

Figure 2.10 also suggests that physical health is a key factor influencing the rate of poverty. Even for employed people, the discrepancy in the rate between those in good health and those not in good health is quite large

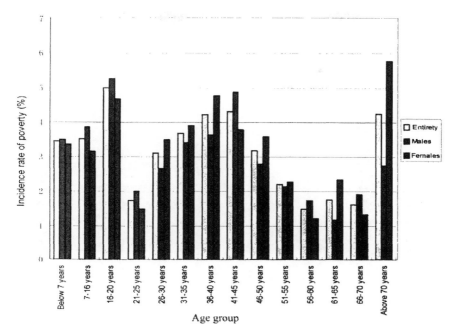

Figure 2.9 Incidence rates of urban poverty by gender and age group in 2002.

Source: Drawn from an estimate from Zheng Feihu and Li Shi 2006.

– sicker people have a rate six times higher than healthier people. Among retired people who are not in good health, more than 14 percent end up in poverty. The rate of unemployed people who are not healthy has exceeded 16 percent. While the overall incidence of poverty in urban areas is not high, it has been concentrated among certain groups of people who lack capabilities for earning money.

Notes

1 For relevant documentation, see Liu Chunbin 2006; Li Jing, Yang Guotao and Meng Lingjie 2006; and Wang Rongdang 2006.
2 The one-USD poverty line has been worked out according to the USD value and the purchasing power parity of different countries in 1985. Therefore, when determining the one-USD poverty line for a country, it is a critical to estimate the purchasing power of the national currency.
3 This coverage rate was calculated from a survey of urban residents that provides data on income, security lines for minimum subsistence, and actual population covered by the security lines. Wang Youjuan holds that the problems of missing data and concealing facts in the income data of the residential survey have caused the underestimation. On the other hand, the security lines for minimum subsistence provided by the Ministry of Civil Affairs may have overestimated the income level of those being surveyed. This factor helps explain the low coverage rate. Another

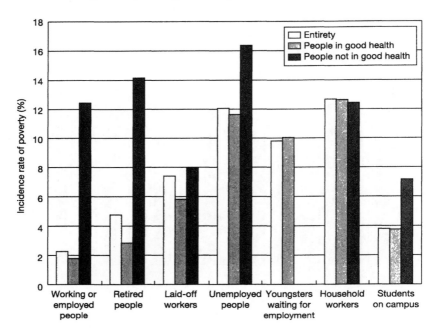

Figure 2.10 Poverty incidence rates among urban residents by personal capacity in 2002.

Source: Drawn from an estimate in a 2006 background report by Zheng Feihu and Li Shi.

element is that the Ministry of Civil Affairs has attached conditions besides income levels when determining who is entitled to benefits and has thus ruled out a portion of low-income earners.

4 When setting the developmental poverty line, we have deducted the expenditures of poor populations already accounted for in the subsistence poverty line, while adding the average expenditures in areas necessary for enhancing development capabilities, with an intent to avoid repetitive calculation.

5 This value is most probably underestimated. For in-depth discussions on this issue, please see Chapter 3.

6 This report has not considered the discrepancies among regions in terms of the variations in price levels. If increases in prices in eastern China exceed those in central and western China, utilizing the price index of all rural areas to set a uniform poverty line will cause an overestimation of the decrease in the size of the population in poverty in eastern China.

7 This report has estimated the developmental poverty line in rural areas in 2005 at RMB 1147 yuan; the low-income level defined by the National Bureau of Statistics of China was RMB 944 yuan.

8 The samples are 22,520 rural families in 242 poor counties inside Hebei, Hubei, Guangxi, Yunnan, Shaanxi and Xinjiang, excluding a small portion of those rural families with a net income that produces a negative value. An analysis of data found that characteristics other than income of this portion of rural families are the same as those of rural families with a relatively sound income level. They are mostly in temporary poverty due to business losses.

9 There are some other reasons why consumption expenditures far exceeded the incomes of poor rural families. An analysis of data reveals that a small portion of rural families under the income poverty line suffers temporary poverty. Their operating scales are big in relative terms, and their total incomes, expenditures and levels of living consumption are all obviously higher than those of other poor rural families. Their net incomes are low, however, and even produce negative values, which indicates that they have suffered temporary business losses or been affected by accidental factors such as natural disasters. Actually, this also indicates the instability of their incomes (some of them are perhaps herdsmen or fishermen). It is estimated that the population size of people in temporary poverty will not take up more than 1 percent of the country's total rural population size, and not more than one third of the poor population surveyed.

3   Analysis of the causes
of poverty

Economic analysis and historical experiences, both domestically and internationally, have shown that economic underdevelopment is the most important cause of poverty. But poverty results from many factors. Besides the level
of economic development, demographics, household structures, health and
education, employment, natural and geographical conditions, public policies,
income distribution and many other factors are likely to have positive or
negative effects on poverty occurrence. In different countries and regions, and
during different periods and under different circumstances, the impacts of
these factors may vary widely. Under certain conditions, some factors may
play a dominant role in poverty occurrence.

AN ANALYTICAL FRAMEWORK

Before delving into an analysis of the causes of poverty, this chapter offers an
analytical framework.

First, poverty is a familial phenomenon, not an isolated individual phenomenon. Because the means of livelihood in a family are shared, any family
member falling into poverty due to unemployment, sickness, injury or any
other reason will place all the other members at risk of poverty as well. In this
sense, it is more meaningful to treat the family, rather than the individual, as
the basic unit for analysing the causes of poverty in China.

Second, for families, the inability to obtain adequate resources for subsistence and development is the most direct cause of poverty. Resources mentioned here include income, and public services and public goods provided by
society. Inadequate income often results from one or more of the following
reasons: (1) the lack of the ability to work; (2) low-quality human capital;
(3) a shortage of employment opportunities; (4) a lack of sufficient physical
or financial assets; (5) a lack or aridity of land; (6) harsh natural conditions
and environment; or (7) the negative impact of an external shock (such as
natural disasters). These seven factors shape the relationship between productivity and the basic elements of labour, capital, land and natural
conditions.

The seven factors are at work in either a traditional natural economy or a market economy. For a rural family, the lack of a labour capacity increases the likelihood of poverty, because it will result in low labour income, given that families rarely have other sources of income. On the other hand, a family's possession of labour capacity does not necessarily mean that it is able to obtain a relatively high labour income, as this also depends upon the quality and effective allocation of that capacity. In economic terms, the quality of labour manifests in the volume of human capital, inclusive of education, working experience, skills and health conditions. In the past few years, researchers have emphasized the importance of health and education in poverty alleviation, affirming the essential role of human capital in labour capacity. The allocation of labour capacity has two aspects: labourers' employment choices among different economic activities and length of working time. These are linked with the amount of labour income.

In rural China, possession of labour resources alone is not enough. For engagement in either agricultural or non-agricultural industries, a certain quantity of physical and financial capital is also necessary. For rural families primarily engaged in agricultural production, land is a prerequisite, with the quality and quantity directly linked to the amount of income. Agricultural production is one of the few industries most likely to be influenced by natural conditions and the environment, so natural disasters and environmental deterioration will have a direct impact on agricultural output.

For low-income families, free public services not only supplement their limited income, but also constitute a part of their quality of living. Some of those families that would otherwise end up trapped in poverty are able to gain capabilities to pursue development on their own and escape poverty. If a society lacks necessary public services or provides them only in a commercial way, low-income families will have more limited access, and many will remain in poverty.

While all of the above factors are direct or indirect causes of poverty, that doesn't mean the occurrence of any single one of these will automatically result in poverty. The amelioration of some can help offset the negative influences of others. For example, a family that lacks land but owns adequate human capital, or lacks human capital but owns an adequate amount of financial capital, is unlikely to fall into poverty. From an anti-poverty perspective, eliminating any poverty-incurring factor or mitigating its negative influence will help alleviate poverty, although changing multiple factors will be more conducive overall.

Factors causing poverty are interlinked; one may cause another. A family that lacks human capital will hardly obtain a relatively high labour income, for instance, and may fall into poverty. This will in turn affect its accumulation of capital, which further entrenches it in poverty.

A vicious cycle exists between poverty and the factors that cause it, which gives rise to a long-lasting poverty state called the poverty trap.[1] Subsistence poverty is a state of living with poor income and/or less-than-necessary consumption. The income level suggests the volume of economic resources in one's possession. If a family can use its income for more than bare subsistence, for example, by channelling it into savings, capital or productive capital, or education, it will accumulate human capital. On the contrary, if a family does not have an adequate income for even bare subsistence, it will become utterly unable to make investments in human capital. The malnutrition that it suffers will give rise to more disease and result in a further loss of human capital, thus causing ever-deepening poverty.

In modern societies, due to anti-poverty measures employed by governments and practices adopted by people from all walks of life, the causes of poverty can be lessened, in relative terms. Social security systems and public services are known as among the best institutional arrangements for poverty alleviation. Although the absence of social policies and public services may not be a root cause of poverty, their existence, quantity and coverage will have a direct bearing on the scale and depth of poverty. For instance, prior to China's implementation of the minimum livelihood security policy, the incidence rate of urban poverty remained between 3 percent and 5 percent. After implementation, the rate fell to less than 1 percent. Comparing poverty in different regions reveals that incidence rates are lower in those that have effectively implemented the policy, so it is clear that policy discrepancy can foster poverty.

The following section analyses the major reasons for poverty in China in recent years, largely according to statistical data and pertinent surveys.

AGRICULTURAL DEPENDENCE AND NATURAL ENVIRONMENTAL CONSTRAINTS

Impacts of agricultural dependence

The income of rural populations in poverty comes mainly from agriculture. Their degree of dependence on this, especially farming, is higher than for other rural groups. At the same time, the per capita farming income of impoverished rural people is far below the per capita farming income level of rural residents (before 2005, the former was RMB 319 yuan and the latter was RMB 1098 yuan). In 2005, 57 percent of the net income of poor rural people came from farming. For rural residents as a whole, the percentage of income from farming was only 34 percent in 2005. Wage income and other income from household agriculture and non-agricultural industries have constituted about 59 percent of their net income (see Figure 3.1). This indicates that poor people are overly dependent on agriculture, especially farming. In some areas with poor conditions for agricultural production and limited production resources, and also owing to some reasons arising from the circumstances of individuals, agricultural productivity and income have remained particularly low, a major cause of poverty.

For years, due to an excessive supply of labour and the relative shortage of

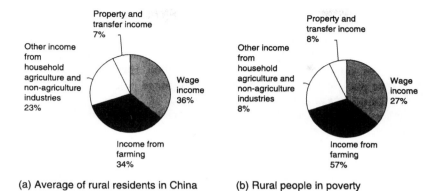

Property and transfer income 7%

Other income from household agriculture and non-agriculture industries 23%

Wage income 36%

Income from farming 34%

Property and transfer income 8%

Other income from household agriculture and non-agriculture industries 8%

Wage income 27%

Income from farming 57%

(a) Average of rural residents in China   (b) Rural people in poverty

Figure 3.1 Sources of income for rural people.

Source: Division of Rural Survey of the National Bureau of Statistics of China 2006.

land, productivity in agriculture was far below other industries, thereby giving rise to a huge income gap. This gap is, in large part, inseparable from the large number of redundant agricultural labourers. In order to mitigate this redundancy, over the last two decades, tens of millions of rural labourers have either migrated to urban areas or engaged themselves in rural industries other than agriculture. This has constituted the most important reason for increases in rural residents' incomes. For a relatively long period to come, the flow of rural populations into non-agricultural industries and urban areas will likely continue, and will serve as the most effective method for subsequent increases in rural incomes.

Poor people always face greater difficulties when it comes to moving into non-agricultural industries from agriculture (Du Ying 2006). This has been demonstrated by data on the discrepancies among rural residents at different income levels in terms of occupational engagement. As per the data from a rural family survey conducted by the National Bureau of Statistics of China, among rural families in the lowest 10 percent income bracket in 2004 (roughly tantamount to the total size of those rural families below the developmental poverty line and referred to here as poverty-stricken), 84 percent of labourers were engaged in agricultural production. In the second lowest 10 percent, 80 percent of labourers were engaged in agricultural production. The average among all income levels was 68 percent. Among rural families in the top 10 percent income bracket, only 43 percent of labourers were chiefly engaged in agricultural production. Compared to 2000, the percentage of agricultural labourers in the poorest group fell by less than 1 percentage point. The average level has decreased by 4 percentage points, and in the wealthiest group has declined by nearly 6 percentage points. As agricultural income is far below the income from other industries, the slow flow of labourers from agriculture into other industries is a significant reason for relative poverty.

Among the labourers most stricken by poverty, the percentage of those relocating to make a living is also lower than in other groups. In 2004, only 14 percent of the poorest people went elsewhere in search of work, which is lower than the average of 19 percent among all groups. In terms of the evolution of such an outflow, compared to 2000, the percentage increase among the poorest labourers was only 3 percentage points, with the average increase being 5 percentage points.

The survey in Box 3.1 shows the close correlation between poverty and dependence upon agriculture. According to the survey, 52 percent of the sampled rural families and 86 percent of poverty-stricken families said that they had livelihood difficulties. Both impoverished and other rural families listed 'too limited income from agriculture' as the foremost reason for financial hardships (see also Box 3.2).

Box 3.1 Three major causes of poverty: low revenue in agriculture, and high costs for medical services and children's schooling

Table 3.1 Ranking of causes of livelihood difficulties: a survey of 4,000 rural families in 15 provinces (districts, cities)

	Below the subsistence poverty line	*Below the developmental poverty line*	*Rural families not stricken by poverty*	*Percentage in the total*
Range of per capita net income (RMB yuan)	0–683	683–1147	>1147	
1. Too limited income from agriculture (%)	68	79.2	71.4	72
2. Heavy expenditures for access to medical services (%)	58	49.2	47.8	49.4
3. High cost of education for children (%)	30.3	32	39.2	36.8
4. Large family headcount or lack of labourers (%)	30.3	21.1	15.1	18.1
5. Shortage of funds for investment or business initiation (%)	24	25.4	25.2	25
6. Suffering of natural disasters (%)	24	19.1	18.5	19.4
7. Difficulty in finding employment opportunities (%)	16.7	24.8	25.2	23.9

8. Large expenses in erection of houses, holding of wedding ceremonies and funerals, etc. (%)	11	14.5	18	16.5
9. Limited compensation for expropriated lands (%)	2	2	3	2.7
10. Too heavy a tax burden (%)	1.3	1.3	1.7	1.6
11. Arrears of wages (%)	1	0.3	2.3	1.8
12. Loss of assets due to robbery or pilferage, or fraud (%)	0	0.7	0.8	0.7
13. Others (%)	2.7	3.3	2.1	2.3
Percentage of samples with livelihood difficulties in the total number of valid samples	85.5	74.6	45.5	52.1
Valid samples	351	406	3,191	3,950

Source: The survey was fielded by the Office for Fixed-Point Surveillance of Rural Areas under the Ministry of Agriculture, and Shanghai DataSea Market Research Company as commissioned by the China Development Research Foundation. It took place in the provinces of Shanxi, Anhui, Henan, Guangxi, Guizhou, Yunnan, Chongqing, Shaanxi, Gansu, Tianjin, Liaoning, Shandong, Jiangsu, Fujian and Guangdong. It covered 4041 sampled rural families in 72 villages (mostly affected by poverty).

Note: The data were calculated based on the answers to the question: 'What are the reasons that give rise to your livelihood difficulties?' Thirteen optional answers were offered; sampled rural families were allowed to select more than one. Families with livelihood difficulties made up 100 percent of the sample.

Analysis of the survey findings

According to the survey, all types of rural families have chosen 'too limited income from agriculture' as the foremost reason for livelihood difficulties; 72 percent of those sampled opted for this. This indicates, by and large, the income gap between agriculture and other industries, which has been a primary reason for rural poverty.

'Heavy expenditures for access to medical services' was the second most important reason for poverty, an unexpected finding. Among families in absolute poverty, 58 percent attributed their situation to this reason; about 48 percent of other families also listed it. This shows that the defects in the existing medical system and lack of social security for rural areas have placed a heavy burden on rural residents and gravely impeded poverty alleviation.

Other high-ranking reasons for livelihood difficulties among families in absolute poverty were the 'high cost of education for children' (30 percent), 'large family headcount or lack of labourers' (30 percent), 'shortage of funds for investment or business initiation' (24 percent), 'visitation by providence' (24 percent) and 'difficulty in finding employment opportunities' (17 percent). Some factors relate to human behaviour and institutions, including 'limited compensation for expropriated lands,' 'too heavy a taxation burden,' 'arrears of wages' and 'loss of assets from robbery or pilferage'; 4.3 percent of families in absolute poverty listed these, out of which two percent chose 'limited compensation for expropriated lands'. In comparison to previous surveys, the incidence rate of poverty incurred by 'too heavy a tax burden' fell dramatically (only 1.3 percent selected this reason). This proves that the country's cancellation of the agricultural tax has played a visible role in the alleviation of rural poverty.

'Heavy expenditures for access to medical services' and 'large family headcount or lack of labourers' have had a more visible influence on impoverished rural families than on those not stuck in poverty. Other factors have made no marked difference or have a lesser impact.

It has long been the case that as a result of surplus labour and the relative shortage of land resources in the agricultural sector, agricultural efficiency is far lower than that of the other sectors, which in turn leads to big income gaps between the agricultural and non-agricultural sectors. To perform an econometric analysis of the impact of agricultural labour, non-agricultural labour and a number of other factors upon the incomes of rural residents, the authors utilized data on 22,520 rural families in certain poverty-stricken regions that were sampled by the National Bureau of Statistics of China. These samples were drawn from six provinces and autonomous regions with a high concentration of poverty-stricken counties: namely, Hebei, Hubei, Guangxi, Yunnan, Shaanxi and Xinjiang. The 242 selected counties account for roughly half of the total number of counties most affected by poverty.

The results of the analysis indicated that when other conditions are identical, the per capita income discrepancy between rural labourers engaged in agriculture and their counterparts engaged in other industries in the same location is about RMB 300 yuan. The per capita income discrepancy between rural labourers engaged in agriculture and those relocating to work elsewhere is even greater. This means that families with labourers either able to work in local non-agricultural industries or to go elsewhere to make a living can basically emerge from poverty.

Such results accord with the fact that most impoverished rural families put 'too limited income from agriculture' as the first and foremost reason for their poverty in the survey in Box 3.1. Nationwide, the relative average pay for non-agricultural labour has remained at least three times that of agricultural labour for many years. In 2005, the per capita disposable income of urban residents in China and the per capita net income of rural residents were RMB 10,493 yuan and RMB 3,255 yuan, respectively, with the former 3.2 times the latter (National Bureau of Statistics of China 2006). In deducting the per capita net income of rural residents by their income from industries other than agriculture, this discrepancy is even bigger. According to the findings of a random survey of 3,288 samples in different Chinese cities in 2004, the average annual income of peasant workers in cities (including those who were self-employed) was RMB 9,288 yuan. On average, they remitted more than half of their income back to the rural area they came from. Such remittances have become a major source of incomes for rural residents in poverty-stricken regions and can even constitute the primary source of their incomes (Fan Gang, Wang Xiaolu and Zhang Hongjun 2005).

Impacts of market fluctuations

The poverty-stricken population in rural areas has not only been slowly flowing into industries other than agriculture, but has also been involved in market competition to a rather poor extent, especially in market segments for basic agricultural products, such as grain, oil-bearing crops, and vegetables. For the most impoverished rural families (that is, rural families with per capita incomes below the subsistence poverty line), the average rates of commodification of their grain, oil-bearing crops and vegetables in 2004 were 28.7 percent, 45.6 percent and 29.8 percent, respectively. In comparison, the rates for all rural families were 41.1 percent, 55.1 percent and 59.2 percent, respectively (Division of Rural Survey of the National Bureau of Statistics of China 2005a). Due to low yields for the most impoverished people, these products were mainly self-consumed. The degree of involvement in market competition can be measured through the ratio of poor people's cash income, other than their income-in-kind, in their net income. The average ratio of all rural families is 78.9 percent. For the most impoverished families in the poor regions, this figure is only 43.1 percent (according to data from rural poverty surveillance in some regions provided by the National Bureau of Statistics of China).

The greater part of agricultural products produced by the most impoverished populations are consumed to maintain bare subsistence. This income-in-kind constitutes a major component of their total income. They can depend on only a small quantity of products to satisfy all their needs for medical services, education, clothing and other daily necessities that require cash. Basic consumption needs are thus squeezed into a rather narrow space, or have been tackled through loans.

Excessive dependence on agriculture and a low degree of commodification mean that fluctuations in the supply and demand for agricultural products and their prices will have an amplified influence on poverty-stricken people. They may face formidable instability and a dire need for security. Once the price parity between agricultural products and non-agricultural products deteriorates (e.g., relative decreases in the prices of agricultural products or increases in the prices of agricultural inputs such as fertilizers, pesticides, etc.), or in a case where agricultural output is affected by a natural disaster, living conditions will markedly worsen. In this situation, some people close to the rural poverty line will fall into subsistence poverty, which indicates their vulnerability. Box 3.2 analyses the influence of grain price changes upon the living conditions of rural families in the 10 percent lowest income bracket. It shows that the sharp decrease in prices caused per capita income to fall below the subsistence poverty line between 2000 and 2003.

Constraints from geographical and natural resource conditions

Geographical and natural conditions have a direct bearing on the level of agricultural production and poverty occurrence. As per the surveillance data of the National Bureau of Statistics of China, in 2005, 60 percent of the population in absolute poverty in rural China was in the western parts of the country. According to a categorization by topography, 51.9 percent of the poorest people are in mountainous regions. Those regions suffering aridity and other inhospitable natural conditions have the highest incidence rate of poverty. For instance, the rate in Qinghai is above 10 percent. Rates in seven other provinces and autonomous regions (Inner Mongolia, Guizhou, Yunnan, Tibet, Shaanxi, Gansu and Xinjiang) are between 5 percent and 10 percent (Division of Rural Survey of the National Bureau of Statistics of China 2006). After making necessary adjustments for statistical omissions for some surveyed samples suffering poverty for health problems, the degree of geographical convergence of poverty-stricken regions is likely to fall to some extent; however, the basic feature of incidence rates of poverty being visibly higher in western China than eastern China will not be changed. This is chiefly because of discrepancies in natural and geographical conditions.

In a regression analysis of surveillance samples in six provinces, after controlling for a series of other influencing factors, this report discovered that location still has a marked bearing on the income of rural families. In two northwestern provinces, Shaanxi and Xinjiang, the per capita incomes of sampled rural families were more than RMB 400 yuan lower than the per capita income of sampled rural families in Hebei province, on average. The regression also scrutinized specific natural and geographical factors. Natural disasters and local topography (flat, hilly and mountainous regions) both have a marked influence on rural per capita income, giving rise to a discrepancy of nearly RMB 100 yuan and more than RMB 100 yuan, respectively. The area of arable land possessed by rural families also influences per capita income, although it does not constitute a decisive factor (as the difference of each one *mu* (= 666.6667 sq m) of arable land yields a discrepancy of less than RMB 100 yuan in per capita net income, after ruling out irrigation provisions). Irrigation has a heavier influence. When other conditions are

Box 3.2 The influence of foodstuff prices upon incomes in rural low-income populations

Since 1998, China has begun to see an oversupply of grain, which has caused market prices to dramatically decline, along with a sharp decrease in the cash incomes of people in poverty and those on the verge of poverty. The following figure shows that while the consumption price index (CPI) of rural residents has not varied in a big way, the grain production index (GPI) remained low from 1998 to 2003. Accordingly, the lowest-income rural families, which constitute 10 percent of the total rural population, have had their per capita factual income level (which is a result of the CPI of rural residents deflated to the constant price in 1985, and shown by LY in the figure below) fall short of the national poverty line (PL) from 2000 to 2003. This is apparently because of their overdependence on crop production and especially grain production. The trend did not shift until 2004.

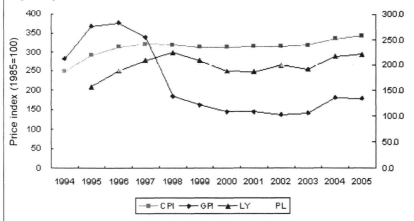

Source: Data came from a survey of rural residents conducted by the National Bureau of Statistics of China.

Note: The GPI is worked out according to the weighted mean of the price indexes of paddy rice, wheat and corn. The GPI and CPI are shown by the left vertical axis (1985 = 100). LY and PL are shown by the right vertical axis (with both based on the constant price in 1985).

identical, there is a discrepancy of more than RMB 300 yuan in per capita income between irrigated and non-irrigated land.

Economic geography is of greater importance than purely geographical factors. This is because the development of cities (especially big ones) tends to boost incomes in the surrounding rural region. Eastern China is better developed economically and hosts a relatively high density of cities. The development of rural areas in the vicinity of these cities has come from a 'spillover' effect generated by these economic hubs. The developing urban economy has supplied rural areas with marketplaces, employment opportunities, financing channels, and knowledge and information, which are all of great significance for alleviating poverty. Unfortunately, there are no data on geographical distances among the sampled rural families and their nearby large or medium cities. It is clear, at least, that the geographical distances between the sampled rural families and county towns have an obvious bearing on income level (the further the distance, the lower the income), if to a relatively small extent.

The impact of geographical conditions on per capita income and the incidence rate of poverty largely relates to transportation access. Many natural and geographical factors cannot be changed or are hard to change. From the angle of poverty alleviation, it is necessary to consider economically feasible improvements through infrastructure facilities such as roads and irrigation facilities where possible.

Constraints from infrastructure facilities and conditions

Among a variety of rural infrastructure facilities, transport deserves special attention. In 2005, 38,426 administrative villages in China still remained inaccessible by road, constituting 5.7 percent of the total number of administrative villages in the country. More than half of these are in western China (Ministry of Communications 2006). A small number had no access to power. In general, villages with a grave lack of infrastructure facilities are largely distributed in the western part of China, and especially in remote and mountainous areas far from cities and the main lines of communication. The discrepancy between poverty-stricken and other regions in terms of infrastructure facilities has impeded the growth of agricultural and non-agricultural activities, and been a key factor slowing the reduction of rural poverty.

As indicated by the findings of the quantitative analysis of the surveillance data on poverty in six provinces, the influence of road accessibility on income is up to RMB 160 yuan per person. The availability of telephone and television services also has an effect. Due to limited data, these influences may all be underestimated. According to a rough reckoning, the actual influence of such factors as the accessibility of roads, power and information services on per capita income is likely once or twice the result of this report's analysis.[2] Box 3.3 outlines the discrepancy between poorer villages and others in terms of infrastructure.

It will be a significant measure for the Government to keep investing in the construction of infrastructure to provide each and every village in the country with roads, power, telephones, television and radio services, including in impoverished regions to alleviate and even eliminate poverty there. It is also critical to keep investing in drinkable water and irrigation facilities in dry regions, both for productive activities and daily use.

Box 3.3 Survey of infrastructure facilities in central and western China

According to data from a survey of 3,500 rural families in nine provinces in central and western China, there is a close relationship between the income levels of rural families and local infrastructure. In the table accompanying this box, the samples are divided into five groups by per capita income level, with the comments collected by the survey listed by group. In the lowest-income villages, which comprised 20 percent of the total sampled, 38 percent of those surveyed said that 'bad roads, therefore traffic inconvenience' are a major infrastructure problem. In the highest-income villages, which made up another 20 percent of the total sample, only 18 percent of the surveyed rural families made the same comment. The discrepancy between the two types of village in terms of the unavailability of telephone service appeared even bigger (20 percent and 0.2 percent, respectively). A smaller number of villages suffer an unstable power supply and are not yet provided with television and radio services, but there are still discrepancies correlated to income (see background report of Ma Yongliang, Zhao Changbao and Wu Zhigang 2006).

Out of 58 sampled villages, 16 were listed as poverty-stricken. Only 7 of these are accessible by road or surfaced rural passageway (where automobiles can move in and out all year round), comprising 44 percent of the total. Out of the other 42 villages, 29 are accessible by road or surfaced rural passageway, comprising 69 of the total. This implies that transportation access is linked to poverty.

	Lowest-income villages (20%)	Below medium-income villages (20%)	Medium-income villages (20%)	Above medium-income villages (20%)	Highest-income villages (20%)
Number of those rural families that answered 'bad roads, therefore traffic inconvenience'	240	203	270	210	123
Percentage in the total number of surveyed rural families	37.7	35.2	39.9	33.4	18.5
Number of those rural families that answered 'no power supply, or power cut from time to time'	28	79	7	9	21
Percentage in the total number of surveyed rural families	4.4	13.7	1	1.4	3.2
Number of those rural families that answered 'no telephone service'	127	14	24	28	1

	Lowest-income villages (20%)	Below medium-income villages (20%)	Medium-income villages (20%)	Above medium-income villages (20%)	Highest-income villages (20%)
Percentage in the total number of surveyed rural families	20	2.4	3.6	4.5	0.2
Number of those rural families that answered 'no radio and television service'	53	6	13	21	18
Percentage in the total number of surveyed rural families	8.3	1	1.9	3.3	2.7

The survey found that the most impoverished villages not only suffer from relatively poor road conditions, but also are far from major traffic hubs and big cities. The average distance from poverty-stricken villages to the nearest railway station is 122 km, the average distance to the nearest city is 100 km, and the average distance to the provincial capital is 334 km. For villages that are not poor, these figures are 39 km, 42 km and 261 km, respectively. Relatively disadvantageous traffic conditions seem to have fed difficulties for impoverished villagers in agriculture and other industries through higher costs, including those related to redundant labourers seeking employment opportunities elsewhere. A relatively low percentage of labourers in poverty-stricken villages have left to work or do businesses elsewhere.

Source: Background report, Ma Yongliang, Zhao Changbao and Wu Zhigang (2006).

HUMAN CAPITAL CONSTRAINTS

The relationship between education and poverty

In recent years, the relationship between education and poverty has drawn increasing attention from academics in China and abroad. As indicated by theoretical research and empirical analyses, inadequate human capital is one of the root causes of high rates of poverty and the inability of the poor to escape poverty. Educational investment is therefore of great significance. But more often than not, poverty restricts investments by impoverished families in the education of their children. The results last a lifetime. After entering the labour market, poorly educated children cannot seize job opportunities and earn more money. They are more likely than better-educated peers to remain stuck in poverty. A vicious cycle, where poverty causes poor education and poor education causes more poverty, results in poverty passing from one generation to the next.

Some simple statistical data show the influence of education on rural poverty. In 2005, 9.9 percent of rural adults above age 16 were illiterate, compared to up to 22.5 percent of those in absolute poverty. Among youth between the ages of 18 and 24, 5.2 percent of those in absolute poverty were illiterate, compared to only 1.2 percent of all rural residents in the same age group (Division of Rural Survey of the National Bureau of Statistics of China 2006a).

The data on rural populations grouped by income level are helpful to explain the relationship between poverty and educational background. In 2004, the average length of schooling time of labourers in rural families in the bottom 10 percent income bracket was 6.1 years. The average length of schooling time of those in the top 10 percent income bracket was 7.7 years. The rates of illiteracy in these income groups were 14 percent and 4 percent, respectively (see Table 3.2). Because educational background here refers to adults, the correlation between educational background and income level reflects the influence of education on poverty, instead of the influence of poverty on education.

Although the educational level of the poverty-stricken population remains relatively low, from 1995 to 2004, the rates of illiteracy in different income groups all fell dramatically. The most impoverished group recorded the largest decrease (up to 9 percent); the wealthiest group recorded a decrease of 4 percent. In Figure 3.2, the uppermost curve in the figure is the rate of illiteracy of labourers in the poverty group; the rates of other income groups are all ranked below. The decrease in the number of illiterates and semi-literates among labourers not only correlates with the greater reach of education in rural areas in the past few years, but is also a consequence of the gradual withdrawal from the labour market of poorly educated people born in the 1930s and 1940s.

Table 3.2 Educational backgrounds of rural labourers in China by income group in 2004

Income group	Per capita net income (RMB yuan)	Rate of illiteracy of labourers (%)	Average length of schooling time (years)
The country's average	2,936	7.5	6.95
Group 1	730	13.6	6.15
Group 2	1,296	10.4	6.44
Group 3	1,670	9.3	6.62
Group 4	2,017	7.5	6.82
Group 5	2,381	7	6.92
Group 6	2,782	6.1	7.05
Group 7	3,279	5.9	7.14
Group 8	3,951	4.9	7.33
Group 9	5,051	4.6	7.46
Group 10	9,021	4.2	7.73

Source: Data from a survey of rural families conducted by the National Bureau of Statistics of China.

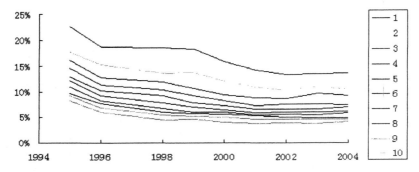

Figure 3.2 Rates of illiteracy among labourers in different income groups.

Source: Rural household survey data from the National Bureau of Statistics of China.

Note: The curves in the figure stand for the rates of illiteracy of labourers (namely, the percentages of illiterates and semi-literates) in 10 groups of rural residents ranked by per capita income. The first curve is associated with the poorest group and the tenth curve with the wealthiest.

Impacts of education on labour transfers and agricultural incomes

As stated above, the transfer of the rural population and labourers into non-agricultural industries is an effective means of rural poverty alleviation, particularly transfers to urban areas. Several factors have impeded this flow for people in poverty, however. The inadequacy of human capital, caused by a low level of education and a lack of occupational skills, is the most important restriction.[3] At present, rural labourers who migrate to urban areas to offer labour services or do business are mostly young or middle-aged people who have been better educated than average.

According to a statistical analysis of supply and demand in the labour markets of 99 Chinese cities in the second quarter of 2006, which was conducted by the Ministry of Labour and Social Security, 89.9 percent of employers have requirements related to the education of job applicants: 22 percent stipulate college diplomas or above; 48.3 call for graduates of secondary technical schools, vocational senior middle schools and technical schools; and only 27.6 percent need graduates from junior high schools or below[4] (Topical Research Group of the Ministry of Labour and Social Security. 2006). The average length of schooling time for rural labourers is only seven years, far less than needed to finish junior high school. People in poverty and those with low incomes have an even lower level of education (refer to Table 3.2 and Figure 3.2). The imbalanced supply and demand structure in today's labour market, which is demonstrated in terms of gaps in education and occupational training, constitutes a major barrier for the further transfer of rural labourers into urban areas.

In a 2004 survey of 3,200 rural labourers in different urban areas of China,

54 percent of the respondents put a low degree of education as the main reason for difficulties they have encountered in job-seeking, among eleven reasons listed on the survey questionnaire. The influence of education is also felt in income gaps. According to the same survey, the monthly wage gap on average between rural labourers who are graduates from elementary schools and those who are graduates from junior high schools was RMB 150 yuan or so. The gap between graduates from junior high schools and graduates from senior high schools was about RMB 300. That means the monthly wage of a graduate from senior high school was RMB 450 yuan more than that of a graduate from elementary school (Wang Xiaolu and Fan Gang 2005; and Fan Gang, Wang Xiaolu and Zhang Hongjun 2005).

Faced with even greater difficulties are those peasants who are so poorly educated that they are hardly able to land jobs locally or elsewhere. In 2005, the per capita wage income of rural residents in China was RMB 1174 yuan; that of people in absolute poverty was only RMB 148 yuan (Division of Rural Survey of the National Bureau of Statistics of China 2006a). This indicates a low degree of transfer into industries other than agriculture that is closely related to limited education.

Knight *et al.* (2006) used the data from a 2002 survey of rural families to discover that education can enhance peasants' income by two means: (1) for rural labourers, exposure to more education means obtaining more job opportunities in non-agricultural industries; and (2) the rates of return from education in industries other than agriculture are higher. Compared with illiterate and semi-literate labourers, those who are graduates from junior high schools have 10 percent more opportunities to enter local industries other than agriculture. Those labourers who are graduates from senior high schools have 15 percent more opportunities. As for opportunities for working elsewhere, a higher degree of education is also likely to bring in more options, even when other conditions are the same. The research also showed that the rate of return from education in non-agricultural industries is 50 percent to 90 percent higher than in the agricultural sector.

Education also influences income from agricultural production. Those labourers with a low degree of education are, more often than not, unable to grasp new agricultural techniques related to fertilizing, pest and disease control, or the use of improved plant varieties. They may not be able to get the latest market information. A quantitative analysis based on poverty data in six provinces, after controlling for a series of variables, found each additional year in the education of rural labourers in agriculture produces an income gap of RMB 20 yuan on average. The disparity of one rung in terms of the degree of education (i.e., between elementary school and junior high school, and between junior high school and senior high school) for the family member with the highest educational level produces a per capita income gap of over RMB 100 yuan. These data suggest that knowledge and skill discrepancies in agricultural labour result in income gaps.[5] This also shows the 'knowledge spillover' effect in a family, meaning the enhanced education of one person will have an income effect on his or her family as a whole.

Compulsory education and the continuance of poverty over generations

Compulsory education in rural areas plays a role not only in ensuring rural residents can be employed and helping people get out of poverty, but also in assisting the next generation to avoid poverty. While a low degree of education is a cause of poverty, poverty can also result in a low level of education if the educational cost is high, thus leading to continued poverty. In the past years, the high cost of education has remained an important factor impeding poor children's access to it. In 2005, the schooling rate of all children between the ages of 7 and 15 years in rural areas was 97.2 percent. It was only 90.1 percent for children from poverty-stricken families.

Figure 3.3 illustrates schooling rates for ten groups of rural families categorized by family income from 1995 to 2004. Obvious discrepancies exist. In 2004, the schooling rate for children in the highest-income and second-highest-income groups (comprising 20 percent of the total number of rural families) was up to 99 percent. The schooling rates of children from the two groups in relative poverty were 95 percent and 96 percent. In spite of that, in the past decade, the schooling rates of children from different income groups have significantly risen. The rate for children from rural families in the lowest 10 percent income bracket, mainly comprising those in

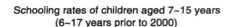

**Schooling rates of children aged 7~15 years
(6~17 years prior to 2000)**

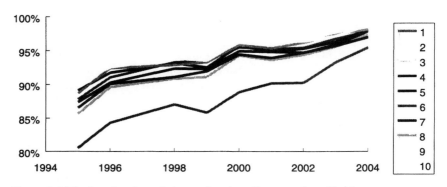

Figure 3.3 The in-school rate is increasing, but discrepancies still exist.

Source: National Bureau of Statistics of China.

Note: The curves in the figure stand for the percentages of children aged 7 to 15 years who are studying in schools and come from rural families in different income groups.

absolute poverty or considered low income, rose from 81 percent to 95 percent.

Knight *et al.* (2006) used data from a 2002 survey of rural families to analyse the cause-and-consequence relationship between poverty and education. When using family income to explain the schooling discontinuity rate of children aged 15 to 16 years, it was discovered that there is a strong correlation between family income level and children's opportunities in access to education. Among the five groups divided by income level, 48 percent of children in the lowest-income group did not finish the nine years of compulsory education; in comparison, only 26 percent of children in the highest-income group did not finish compulsory education. Furthermore, only 29 percent of children in the lowest-income group continued their education in senior high schools; but in the highest-income group, this percentage reached 55 percent. The analysis used a logistic model to discover that income level and poverty have a significant impact on the schooling discontinuity rate. When the income level goes up by 1 percent, the schooling discontinuity rate declines by 0.5 percent. When dummy variables are used for different income groups, it is found that the probability for schooling discontinuity in the lowest-income group is 80 percent higher than that of the medium-income group. The study also discovered that family income level and poverty influence not only access to educational opportunities, but also the quality of education received. Specifically, the scores recorded by those children from low-income and poverty-stricken families are lower than those of children from other types of families. On one hand, the lower degree of education of the parents in low-income and poverty-stricken families is a cause for lack of in-family education. On the other hand, financial difficulties increase working time for children from low-income and poverty-stricken families compared to children from other types of families. This reality shortens time for studying. Furthermore, the educational expenses of low-income and poverty-stricken families are generally below those of relatively wealthy families, even as the former must devote a substantially higher percentage of overall family expenditures to education.[6]

To stop the passage of poverty across generations, it is important for the Government to enable all children in rural areas to have equal access to the nine years of compulsory education. In order to improve basic education in western China and guarantee equal access there, the Government has formulated a series of relevant policies on the provision of compulsory education in state-specified poverty-stricken regions, the reconstruction of dilapidated school buildings, the construction of boarding schools in rural areas, etc.[7] The 'Two Exemptions and One Subsidy' policy has been implemented.[8] The Government has also initiated a programme for adjusting the layout of elementary and high schools, in an effort to consolidate educational resources. The 'Modern Remote Education by Elementary and High Schools in Rural Areas' programme aims to improve the quality of education.

In 2006, the Central Committee of the Communist Party of China and the State Council made a decision to exempt children in western China from all tuition fees and incidental charges in the course of their nine-year compulsory education, and further granted allowances to poor students to buy textbooks and cover their accommodation costs in boarding schools. This measure was adopted for the entire country in 2007. Meanwhile, more intensive efforts have been made to provide financial transfers and specific allowances to economically backward regions, with a view towards full coverage of the cost of compulsory education in rural areas by the public financial system. The national finance administration has also offered financial support to ensure that teachers in elementary and high schools in western China, central China and some parts of eastern China will receive their salaries in full and on time, according to national standards. In years to come, education for impoverished populations will hopefully improve and generate a visible influence on rural poverty alleviation. Expenditure on basic education is a long-term social investment that generates invaluable returns, including a well-developed, civilized and economically powerful nation in the future.

Some research indicates that the 2001 policy for adjusting the layouts of elementary and high schools in rural areas has boosted the effective utilization of educational resources and enhanced the quality of education, but has also increased the distance of rural children from their schools. According to surveys in Guizhou, Ningxia and Gansu, nearly a third of students in elementary and high schools in rural areas have to travel more than 3 km to reach their schools. An eighth of students have to travel 5–10 km. Some children in mountainous regions have to walk for several hours a day to go to school; a portion end up discontinuing their studying for this reason. Regression analysis also shows that the distance of children from their schools has a direct bearing on their scores (see the background report of Jin Lian 2006). The boarding school construction project, which was launched in 2004, will help alleviate this problem. From 2004 to 2006, the country saw over 7,000 boarding schools either built or under construction. These are, however, not enough to meet the needs of tens of millions of rural elementary and high school students. Erecting more boarding schools should be complemented with accommodation allowances for students.

While efforts are being made to expand compulsory education, it is essential to adjust the structure of secondary education, and boldly develop vocational schools and job training programmes. This is a key measure to rebalance supply and demand in today's labour market.

Health of the labour force and poverty

The health of the labour force constitutes an essential component of human capital, and an important factor influencing the incidence of poverty. Surveys indicate that a considerable portion of the rural population ends up in poverty due to sickness, disability or senility. This situation has not been fully reflected by the poverty statistics.

The rural household survey and poverty surveillance survey conducted by the National Bureau of Statistics of China and similar surveys on the incomes of rural residents fielded by other organizations have encountered difficulties in covering peole who are sick or have disabilities. The National Bureau of Statistics of China has not offered concrete descriptions of the health conditions of poverty-stricken populations in its rural household survey. The average number of labourers in the poor families sampled, however, does not vary largely from the average level, except for a slightly higher number of children and elderly people. In addition, as per the data from the 2005 surveillance of poverty in state-specified major counties subject to poverty alleviation, just 2.1 percent of the sampled people suffered serious or chronic diseases, while only 1.1 percent were disabled (Rural Department of the National Bureau of Statistics of China 2006b). Analysis of poverty surveillance data in six provinces in 2004 has found that the proportion of the sick and disabled in the population in poverty did not differ significantly from its proportion in the total population. Based on the calculation of the proportions, among the 23.65 million rural people in absolute poverty in China, the number of impoverished people with serious and chronic diseases was below 500,000; that of the disabled was about 200,000 in 2005.

A lot of evidence shows, however, that as a result of practical problems in statistical analysis, the percentages of sick and disabled persons in the sample of rural families and the poverty surveillance sample, or in the poverty-stricken families in both samples, are far below the actual proportions they account for in China's rural population. This is especially the case for poverty-stricken families. Using the two samples to estimate the total population in poverty in China would result in a serious underestimation of the number of sick and disabled people in poverty.

Evidence for this argument comes from some special surveys. A 2006 survey of China's disabled population – jointly conducted by sixteen government and social organizations (including the National Bureau of Statistics of China, the Ministry of Civil Affairs, the China Disabled Persons' Federation, etc.) estimated that the total size of China's disabled population is 82.96 million persons or 6.34 percent of the total population of China (Leading Group for the 2nd National Sample Survey of Disabled Persons and the National Bureau of Statistics of China 2006). This survey did not reveal the size of the disabled population in poverty, but an earlier survey in 1998 suggested that 12.06 million disabled people were living in rural poverty. The incidence rate of poverty among disabled people in China was estimated to be 20 percent, far beyond the rate among healthy people (Division of Poverty Alleviation, China Disabled Persons' Federation 1998).

People with chronic and serious diseases and their family members are also prone to poverty. According to a 2003 survey fielded in some regions of

China by the Ministry of Health, 9.9 percent of rural residents have suffered chronic diseases. The incidence rate is higher than the incidence rate of disability, and also far beyond the incidence rate of chronic and serious diseases discovered as a result of surveillance (which is only 2 percent). According to the second health service survey in 1998, the lack of labour capacity and sickness and injury are two major causes of poverty, accounting for, respectively, 23.1 percent and 21.6 percent of the poverty-stricken population in rural areas (see also background report, Han Jun 2006).

According to various survey data sources mentioned above, in 2006, the percentage of the disabled population was 6.34, and the percentage of the rural population with chronic diseases was 10.4 (Ministry of Health 2006; Leading Group for the 2nd National Sample Survey of Disabled Persons, National Bureau of Statistics of China 2006). Data from the 2005 surveillance of poverty in state-specified major counties subject to poverty alleviation indicated that the disabled population and the population 'suffering serious and chronic diseases' accounted for 1.2 percent and 2.1 percent, respectively, of the total sample population. The percentages were roughly the same for the poverty-stricken population in poor counties (Poverty Surveillance Data from National Bureau of Statistics of China 2006), which are far below the percentages obtained from the national topical surveys). It remains a puzzle as to the cause of the differences.

Numeric differences have resulted from variations in survey methods. In the survey fielded by the National Bureau of Statistics of China, the respondents were required to record their family income and expenses on a regular basis to provide accurate data on the income and expenditures of rural families. Rural families lacking the capability to record these data were not supposed to be surveyed. As a result, the survey excluded those falling into the following categories: disability in vision, hearing or language; intellectually and mentally retarded; incapacity to write due to physical disability; serious illness; elderly people with limited mobility and illiterates. These people are far more likely to end up in poverty than their healthy and literate counterparts. Some special surveys (for example, a survey fielded by the China Disabled Persons' Federation and the Ministry of Health) have adopted the method of sending interviewers to the household to conduct the survey. Respondents are not required to have the capability to record family income and expenses. This approach reduces the chance of overlooking the populations categorized above, and thus provides more convincing information on the size and distribution of the population with diseases and disabilities. The two different survey methods may explain the fact that the failure to account for people in poverty due to disabilities and diseases in the statistical calculations conducted by the National Bureau of Statistics of China means the size of the poverty-stricken population has been underestimated, along with the impact of disabilities and diseases on poverty.

Some surveys have also revealed that the percentage of the disabled population in poverty in the total poverty-stricken population differs by the degree of regional economic development. In the impoverished regions of central and western China, the disabled population in poverty comprises a relatively low percent of the total poverty-stricken population. In eastern China, where the economy has been better developed, the disabled population in poverty is quite a high percentage of the total poverty-stricken population. Within those regions that are not economically well developed, a large number of non-disabled people have not broken out of poverty. With economic development and poverty alleviation work, those with the capability to work gradually better their lives, thus cutting down the incidence of poverty. Most of the remaining people in poverty are those facing greater challenges, such as disabled persons without the capability to work. People suffering long-term diseases and old people without carers and lacking capability for work are faced with similar circumstances.

A survey conducted by the China Disabled Persons' Federation (Division of Poverty Alleviation 1998) looked at disabled people in Guizhou, which is not economically well developed; Heilongjiang, which has a moderately developed economy; and Jiangsu, which is relatively well developed. The lowest percentage of disabled people in the total poverty-stricken population was recorded in Guizhou (only 10.3 percent). In Jiangsu, this figure was up to 61.4 percent (see Table 3.3). This indicates changes in the mixture of the poverty-stricken population in rural areas. With the decrease in the number of people in poverty, the percentage of those stuck in poverty for health reasons will keep rising.

These results have been supported by data obtained from a 2006 random sample of 523 rural families in 11 poverty-stricken villages in five provinces and municipalities in eastern China. The families with patients who had been ill for more than half a year or with disabled persons together made up 36 percent of the total number sampled. In families in absolute poverty (each with a per capita income below RMB 683 yuan), these two types of families made up 49 percent of the total (see Table 3.4). Different from the statistical survey above, this survey did not request respondents to have a bookkeeping capability; instead, it dispatched certain survey specialists to pay random visits to respondents' families. Data on income and expenditures were provided by respondents according to their memory. This method has, undoubtedly, had a

Table 3.3 Percentages of disabled people in the total population in poverty (1998)

Province	The poverty-stricken population (10,000 persons)	Disabled population in poverty (10,000 persons)	Percentage of disabled in the total population in poverty
Jiangsu	28	17.2	61.4
Heilongjiang	60.5	17.3	28.7
Guizhou	603.4	62.4	10.3

Source: Division of Poverty Alleviation, China Disabled Persons' Federation 1998.

Table 3.4 Percentages of families with sick or disabled family members in the total number of families in some poverty-stricken villages in eastern China (2006)

	Rural families in absolute poverty	*Rural families below the developmental poverty line*	*Rural families not affected by poverty*	*Total*
Income range (RMB yuan)	0–683	683–1,147	>1,147	
Number of samples (families)	164	111	248	523
Percentage of those families with sick or disabled people in the total number of families	49.4	39.6	26.6	36.5

Source: Data were drawn from a rural poverty survey in eastern China conducted by DataSea Marketing Research Company. This survey constituted a component of the previously mentioned survey of rural poverty in five provinces and municipalities.

Note: 'Percentage of families with sick and disabled family members' refers to the number of families with disabled or chronically sick family members (for more than half a year) out of the total number of sampled families in each income group.

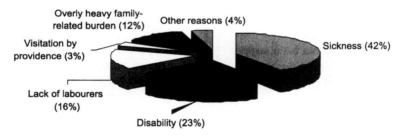

Figure 3.4 Distribution of families in absolute poverty in rural areas of Hefei City by causes of poverty.

Source: Huang Haili 2007.

certain bearing on the accuracy of the data, but has avoided missing data on sick and disabled people.

Hefei City in Anhui Province conducted a checkup on rural families in absolute poverty in 2005. According to the findings of this survey, 65 percent of families in nearby rural areas (totalling 27,000 families) are impoverished due to sickness and disability (see Figure 3.4). Anhui Province is located in central China, and its degree of economic development falls far behind those of the coastal provinces in the eastern region, but the rural areas near Hefei city have a higher development level than ordinary rural areas. The findings do not fully depict the situation of the vast rural areas in central China, but they do reflect the correlation between the high percentage of people in poverty because of sickness and disability and the degree of economic development.

Population burdens and poverty

As indicated by data from a survey of rural families, compared with other rural families, poverty-stricken families have a high dependency ratio (dependent family members per labourer). There is a negative correlation between income level and the family headcount burden coefficient; per capita income level decreases with the rise of the coefficient.

According to a 2004 survey of rural families conducted by the National Bureau of Statistics of China, the family dependency ratio of the 10 percent lowest income group was 0.58, but that ratio for the total rural population was only 0.45, and for the highest-income group was merely 0.32. Thus, there is a difference of 0.13 between the lowest income group and the average level. As the rural poverty surveillance data in Table 3.5 indicate, the average number of labourers in families in absolute poverty in the poverty-stricken regions is 0.11 greater than the average level of all samples; the average number of children (aged 15 years and below) in these families is 0.24 greater than the average level; the average number of elderly persons and sick and/or disabled persons is 0.05 and 0.02 greater than the average levels, respectively. The family dependency ratio of poverty-stricken families is 0.08 more than the average level. Table 3.5 also indicates the percentage of families entitled to receive the 'five guarantees' and the percentage without labourers out of all families in absolute poverty. Both percentages are slightly higher than the average level. Among these samples, however, the major difference between poverty-stricken families and the average family is that poverty-stricken families have a relatively high child burden coefficient.

A heavy dependency ratio in a family is usually incurred by factors including: more elderly people without the capability to work, more children, a lack of people of working age, and the existence of people who have lost their ability to work due to sickness or disability. According to a field survey for this report, some poverty-stricken families in rural areas mainly comprise the elderly, sick and (physically or mentally) disabled people, and children. A high dependency ratio and lack of labourers increases the chances of falling into or staying in poverty.

Overlooking those in poverty due to sickness or disability may produce a statistical artefact: the actual family headcount burden coefficient may be higher than the coefficient inferred from statistical estimation. The issue of overlooking the sick and disabled has been discussed earlier in this report. The following discussion approaches the family headcount burden based on statistical data only.

The effect of the family headcount burden coefficient on the per capita income of a family (without considering the non-labour remuneration) can be deduced theoretically:

Table 3.5 Family headcount burdens of rural families in poverty-stricken regions

	Rural families in absolute	Rural families in relative poverty	Low-income families	Lower middle-income rural families	Middle-income rural families	Uper middle-income rural families	High-income rural families	Average
Family size	4.78	4.79	4.52	4.25	4.01	3.74	3.49	4.38
Number of labourers	2.93	2.95	2.85	2.78	2.73	2.65	2.51	2.82
Dependency ratio	0.63	0.62	0.59	0.53	0.47	0.41	0.39	0.55
Number of children	1.21	1.18	1.07	0.91	0.76	0.57	0.51	0.97
Number of elderly people	0.26	0.26	0.23	0.20	0.15	0.16	0.14	0.21
Number of sick/disabled people	0.15	0.15	0.13	0.12	0.11	0.12	0.13	0.13
Percentage of families without labourers in the total	1.75	1.65	1.54	1.52	1.60	2.41	2.76	1.68
Percentage of those families entitled to receive the 'five guarantees' in the total	0.36	0.17	0.28	0.21	0.11	0.51	0.16	0.25
Number of samples	2,800	2,968	6,494	5,247	2,821	1,574	616	22,520

Source: Rural poverty surveillance data of the National Bureau of Statistics of China.

Note: The family size refers to the number of resident persons in a family. The number of labourers refers to those aged 16 to 65 years with the capability to work. The number of children refers to those aged 15 years and below. The number of elderly people refers to those persons above 65 years old. The number of sick or disabled people refers to those suffering serious diseases, long-standing chronic diseases and disabilities. In addition, the classification of five groups of rural families, from those in relative poverty to those with high incomes, were calculated according to per capita incomes from the five-quintile rural household survey data of the National Bureau of Statistics of China.

$$I = LR*L/N = LR/(FDR + 1)$$

In the equation, I is the per capita income of a family; LR is the average remuneration of labourers; L is the number of labourers in a family; N is the number of persons in a family; and FDR refers to the family headcount burden coefficient, namely the number of non-labour family members on average supported by each labourer.

According to data on the income and expenditure of rural residents obtained from a 2005 survey conducted by the National Bureau of Statistics of China, the average remuneration for an agricultural labourer (assuming that he or she is solely engaged in agricultural labour, without considering familial discrepancies) is RMB 2972 yuan. According to the above formula and data on sampled families in rural areas, it can be derived that the per capita income gap incurred by the difference between the family headcount burden level of poverty-stricken families and the average level is RMB 177 yuan. The result indicates that without taking into account poverty factors caused by sickness and disability, the discrepancy in terms of the family headcount burden level is indeed a factor causing poverty, but it is not a crucial factor.

According to a calculation based on poverty surveillance data in six provinces, the per capita discrepancies resulting from the differences in the family headcount burden coefficients is even smaller: an estimated RMB 82 yuan. This is apparently owing to the relatively low per capita agricultural income and the relatively high family headcount burden level in the poverty-stricken counties. In addition, in impoverished rural regions, statistics show that most non-labourers (i.e., elderly people above 65 years old and children below 16 years old) are actually involved in labour, which might be a factor that suppresses the magnitudes of the family headcount burden coefficients.

According to another questionnaire survey of 4,000 sampled rural families in 15 provinces (districts and municipalities), the 'surplus of family headcount or lack of labourers' ranked as the fourth leading cause of poverty among families in absolute poverty in the sample, and the seventh among all sampled families. The results have indicated that such a factor does not have a substantial effect on poverty (see Box 3.1 in this chapter).

The above analysis has demonstrated that the discrepancies in the family headcount burden coefficients have an impact on the occurrence of poverty. Among others, a large number of children is a crucial factor. Leaving out the issue of poverty occurrence due to sickness or disability, compared with other factors, the discrepancies in family headcount burden coefficients do not have a decisive impact on the occurrence of poverty.

PUBLIC SERVICES CONSTRAINTS

Poverty alleviation beyond livelihood subsistence

The criterion for poverty is primarily income-based in China. Some rural residents cannot be defined as poor by per capita income or per capita consumption level, but nevertheless live in poverty. This population has spent too much on basic subsistence and capability development, such as education and medical care, which has severely reduced other necessary expenditures.

The traditional theory of poverty construes poverty as a state in which income is not enough to satisfy a family's minimum needs for bare subsistence. In the past, when circumstances were characterized by low social productivity, such a belief was tenable. The poverty concept has been constantly expanding, however. Some researchers in the twentieth century have brought the needs for clothing, housing, medical care, education and basic cultural activities into the scope of the basic needs of human beings (see Chapter 1). Amartya Sen (Sen 2002) has proposed that poverty is a deprivation of humankind's basic capabilities and should not be measured by income alone.

Such changes in thinking are the inevitable results of the development of human beings. Today's China has stepped into a development stage featuring wholehearted efforts to create an affluent society. In an overwhelming majority of China's rural areas, the basic needs of rural people can no longer be simply summarized as having enough clothing and food. For the sake of survival and also the development of themselves and the next generation, education and medical care have become an indispensable part of their basic needs. Health care chiefly meets their need for subsistence, while education helps them embrace self-development. In today's fast-evolving society, a person without a basic education may even lose the capacity to survive.

One element worth cherishing in China's traditional values is that Chinese families always put their children's education first, even when parents' investments in children's education cannot produce returns for them. Faced with skyrocketing educational expenses, most rural residents have opted for keeping their children in school, even if that means reducing expenditures on food and clothing, or even asking for loans.

For many years, when the Chinese people lacked adequate food and clothing, the rural poverty line was designed to capture the basic need for food for the sake of bare subsistence, while taking into account other needs for basic consumer goods. Although this poverty line is adjusted according to the consumption price index for each year, it has not been adjusted for the sharp increase in medical and educational expenses since the 1990s, the steep rise in expenditures for daily necessities, and the consequent impact on low-income rural residents. If no burdensome medical and educational expenses are incurred, rural residents whose per capita income exceeds the poverty line can satisfy their basic needs for bare subsistence. But since medical and educational expenses have become regular expenses for families, and continue to increase, most rural residents below the poverty line have seen their expenditures go beyond their income. This leads to worsening poverty. Some are unable to obtain medical services or send their children to school. A portion will fall below the poverty line and end up trapped in poverty.

In a survey of 4,000 rural families in 72 villages (mostly poverty-stricken) in 15 provinces and municipalities, which was conducted by a research group in 2006, two-thirds of families stated they have suffered financial difficulties. Sixty-one percent said it was hard to cover medical expenses and the tuition of children. This was far beyond the 12 percent who said it was hard to have enough clothing and food. Among families in absolute poverty, up to 66 percent noted problems in covering medical expenses and the tuition of children; only 31 percent stated the same for clothing and food (see Table 3.6). This indicates that enough clothing and food have become an almost omnipresent fact. Rural residents today are in more evident need of care for their physical health and better development of their offspring.

Demands for medical services and education

Given the classification between the subsistence and developmental poverty lines, this report used 2004 data on poverty surveillance samples in six provinces provided by the National Bureau of Statistics of China and the 2005 survey data of some rural areas in nine provinces and municipalities offered by the Ministry of Agriculture[9] to calculate the medical care and educational expenditures of rural residents within different groups (see Table 3.7 and Table 3.8). The two surveys were conducted independently and by different methods. Despite some discrepancies, they reflect the same basic conditions (the grouped samples in the latter survey are on a low side; in relative terms, the accuracy of the samples of the former survey may be higher).

The data in Table 3.7 and Table 3.8 indicate in a rather clear way that, owing to high educational and medical costs, the consumption needs of poverty-stricken rural families have gone far beyond their net incomes. They reflect the fact that overspending on medical care and education has resulted in compulsory over-expenditure on living consumption, which forces a large number of rural families to incur debts.[10]

Among the two samples, medical and educational expenditures together comprised around an average of 25 percent of the net family income of all sampled rural families. The percentages for families below the subsistence poverty and developmental poverty lines far surpassed this average, however. According to data from poverty surveillance samples, the per capita net income of rural families in absolute poverty was RMB 483 yuan, and their educational and medical expenditures were RMB 265 yuan, taking up more than half of their per capita net income. The percentage for the other sampled poverty-stricken population was even higher. These two groups of data have both indicated that when food expenditures were included, total living consumption expenditures far exceeded net incomes, averaging out at

Table 3.6 The main financial difficulties encountered by rural families at present

	Rural families below the subsistence poverty line	Rural families below the developmental poverty line	Rural families not stricken by poverty	Total
Income range (RMB yuan) In which respects have you suffered difficulties (percentage in the total number of those rural families answering 'difficulty in any respect')?	0–683	683–1,147	>1,147	
1. Difficulty in receiving medical service and sending children to schools (%)	66	59.2	60.3	60.9
2. Difficulty in covering the costs of daily necessities (%)	65.4	68.8	51.6	55.7
3. Difficulty in buying fertilizers and pesticides (%)	59.9	58	39.8	44.9
4. Difficulty in investment and business operation (%)	37.5	46.2	58	53.7
5. Difficulty in having food and clothing (%)	31.4	21.6	7	12.2
Percentage of rural families answering 'difficulty in any respect' in the total number of effective samples	94	90.7	61.8	67.8
Percentage of rural families answering 'no difficulty in any respect' in the total number of effective samples	6	9.3	38.2	32.2
Number of effective samples	332	367	2,869	3,568

Source: Data were drawn from a survey of rural poverty in 15 provinces and municipalities in 2006 that was fielded by the Office for Fixed-Point Surveillance of Rural Areas under the Ministry of Agriculture and the Shanghai DataSea Marketing Research Company, as commissioned by the China Development Research Foundation.

Note: This table was compiled based on surveyed rural families' answers to the question: 'Does your family suffer financial difficulties in the following respects?' Six optional answers were offered, and multiple options were allowed. The ranking of financial difficulties in the table has been done in conformity with the options chosen by rural families below the subsistence poverty line.

Table 3.7 Medical and educational expenditures of rural families: poverty surveillance in six provinces (2004)

	Rural families below the subsistence poverty line	Rural families between the subsistence poverty line and the developmental poverty line	Other rural families	All sampled rural families
Income range (RMB yuan)	0–668	668–1,046	>1,046	
Average number of people resident in the family	4.79	4.73	4.16	4.35
Per capita net income (RMB yuan)	483	863	2,127	1,668
Per capita living consumption (RMB yuan)	936	1,066	1,655	1,452
Per capita expenditures on food (RMB yuan)	555	627	857	775
Per capita expenditures on education (RMB yuan)	198	212	344	300
Per capita tuition and incidental fees and textbook costs (RMB yuan)	96	104	175	149
Per capita medical expenditures (RMB yuan)	67	71	131	112
Educational expenditures/ net income (%)	41	24.5	16.2	18
Medical expenditures/net income (%)	13.9	8.2	6.1	6.7
Number of samples	2,690	4,460	15,260	22,520

Source: Poverty surveillance data of the National Bureau of Statistics of China.

RMB 936 yuan. This report's definition of rural families in absolute poverty is different from that of the National Bureau of Statistics of China. In Box 3.4, we discuss how to distinguish the two definitions, and their impacts on identifying families in poverty.

Medical burdens and poverty

High medical expenses explain why many rural families, including some with a relatively high income, have suffered subsistence difficulties. From 1980 to 2003, the per capita net income of rural residents, calculated by the price of the concerned year, rose 12.7 times. Per capita living consumption rose

Table 3.8 Medical care and educational expenditures for rural families in different income groups: poverty surveillance in nine provinces and municipalities (2005)

	Rural families below the subsistence poverty line	*Rural families between the subsistence poverty line and the developmental poverty line*	*Other rural families*	*All sampled rural families*
Income range (RMB yuan)	0–683	683–1,147	>1,147	
Average number of people resident in the family	3.82	3.98	4.14	4.11
Per capita net income (RMB yuan)	449	943	3,187	2,843
Per capita living consumption (RMB yuan)	919	1,154	2,163	2,007
Per capita expenditures on food (RMB yuan)	389	470	765	721
Per capita expenditures on education (RMB yuan)	207	309	535	499
Per capita tuition and incidental fees and textbook costs (RMB yuan)	188	220	422	402
Per capita medical expenditures (RMB yuan)	123	108	195	185
Educational expenditures/net income (%)	46.1	32.8	16.8	17.5
Medical expenditures/net income (%)	27.4	11.4	6.1	6.5
Number of samples	187	295	2,943	3,427

10.9 times. But per capita medical expenditures rose 32.9 times, far beyond increases in income and consumption. Many rural residents have given up seeking medical treatment even when they are sick. According to one survey, from 1998 to 2003, the percentage of rural residents who did not see a doctor after having been ill for two weeks increased from 33.2 percent in 1998 to 45.8 percent in 2003. The rate of hospitalization in the same period dropped from 4 percent to 3.3 percent, while the average number of hospitalization days fell from 12.6 days to 10.2 days. This indicates that high medical charges have gravely affected the health conditions of rural residents (see background report, Han Jun 2006).

Box 3.4 The methods for defining the subsistence poverty line

Some calculations in this chapter (such as Tables 3.4 and 3.5 employed the income poverty line given by the National Bureau of Statistics of China, and defined a family in absolute poverty as one with a per capita net income between RMB 0 yuan and RMB 668 yuan (2004) and 683 yuan (2005). This scope may include a small number of rural families that used to earn a relatively high income, but have sustained business losses even as they maintain a relatively high consumption level. The National Bureau of Statistics of China adjusted its poverty calculation in 1998, and has, in reality, adopted two poverty standards (income and consumption) at the same time. Under the first, income is below the poverty line, and consumption is lower than 1.5 times the poverty line – later adjusted to 1.2 times the poverty line. For the second, consumption is below the poverty line, and income is lower than 1.5 times (later 1.2 times) the poverty line. Such an adjustment has, on the one hand, slightly broadened the income poverty standard according to actual consumption and, on the other hand, ruled out those rural families whose income level is relatively high under normal circumstances and has been reduced temporarily. As far as these circumstances are concerned, the adjustment is rational. A problem that remains unsolved is the failure to differentiate necessary and unnecessary consumption. A considerable number of people who earn an income lower than the poverty line, but have to maintain a relatively high consumption level, have been ruled out. A few cases found in a field survey can serve as evidence.

Case 1: Peasant Zhang, who lives in Chadia Village in Wuding County of Yunnan Province, has a family of four persons. In 2005, his family recorded a per capita net income of RMB 500 yuan or so and per capita food expenditures in excess of RMB 400 yuan. His wife suffers from kidney stones and incurred a medical charge of RMB 2,000 yuan due to hospitalization in 2005. Zhang spent RMB 500 yuan in buying drugs and nutritional supplements for his wife, which was all from a loan he asked for from relatives and friends. According to this family's actual income and living conditions, it is in a state of severe poverty. The per capita consumption expenditure of this family is RMB 1,200 yuan (including the medical charge), however, which is far beyond the standard of '1.2 times the poverty line'. Accordingly, this family will not be defined as poor.

The Director General for the Health Board of Wuding County notes that only a very small number of rural families in poverty-stricken townships and villages within the county can afford their medical charges. Poverty incurred by sickness is an evident problem.

Case 2: Peasant Wu, who lives in Taigu County of Shanxi Province, has a family of three persons. In 2005, his family recorded a per capita net income of about RMB 600 yuan, which was below the poverty line. In the vicinity of his home, there is no high school. So his son has to study in a junior high school in Taigu County. Due to a long distance between his home and school, his son has to live in the school. The total tuition and incidental fees, accommodation costs and meal expenditures total more than RMB 4,000 yuan. Wu has to ask for loans to cover the expenses. The per capita consumption expenditure of this family exceeds RMB 1,600 yuan (including the educational expenditure); according to the above poverty standard, this family cannot be defined as living in poverty.

Case 3: Peasant Zhu, who lives in Qijing Township of Shitai County in Anhui Province, has a family of four persons. In 2005, his family recorded a per capita net income of about RMB 1,000 yuan. His son suffers falling sickness, requiring medical care costing more than RMB 10,000 yuan in that year. His elderly mother is ill. Her medical care totalled RMB 4,000 yuan. Zhu paid most of these charges through loans from relatives and friends; he also managed to secure a small loan from the local credit cooperative. This family cannot be defined as poverty-stricken when measured by either income level or consumption level. In particular, its consumption level (including the medical charge) exceeded RMB 4,000 yuan. But heavy medical burdens mean this family actually remains in a state of poverty and has incurred large debts that it can hardly repay.

The Director General of the Health Board of Shitai County notes that a survey of 2,000 poverty-stricken rural families found 59 percent had ended up in poverty through sickness.

These cases indicate several issues. First, the ongoing method for defining the poverty line may cause some poor people suffering subsistence difficulties to be ignored by statisticians. It is essential to conduct further research upon how to make adjustments accordingly. An optional method is to differentiate necessary and unnecessary consumption.

Second, medical and educational expenditures constitute an important component of expenditures for rural residents' subsistence and the development of the capabilities of their offspring. The ongoing subsistence poverty line cannot capture these issues. Therefore, it is necessary to establish a developmental poverty line.

Third, the most important step to alleviate poverty is to stem the excessive increase in medical and educational expenditures, and mitigate the burdens on low-income people through public services.

According to a survey of 4,000 rural families in China, 49 percent of those in financial difficulties listed excessive medical charges as the second most common reason for their subsistence hardship, after only too limited an income from agriculture. Among rural families in poverty that claimed to have suffered financial difficulties, 58 percent listed excessive medical charges as a reason for their poverty (see Box 3.1 in this chapter).

According to an analysis of samples from the Ministry of Agriculture, if medical charges are excluded from the calculation of per capita net income, the number of rural families whose per capita income falls below the poverty line will increase exponentially. The incidence rate of poverty will increase from 5.4 percent to 8.6 percent.[11] As a whole, the absolute amount of medical expenditures for rural families below the subsistence poverty line and developmental poverty line is lower than that of relatively high-income families, but the percentage required of their net income is obviously higher. Figure 3.5 shows the percentage of expenditures required for medical care among rural families by income (see background report, Ma Yongliang, Zhao Changbao and Wu Zhigang 2006; the data not otherwise annotated and some analysis on the following pages are extracted from this report).

According to the findings of one survey, in the past five years, the living standards of most rural families have increased; however, growing medical charges have caused living standards for some to remain stagnant or drop. When asked, 'Has your family been leading a better or worse life in the past five years', 75 percent of surveyed rural families answered 'better', 6 percent answered 'worse', and 19 percent answered 'no change'. The analysis by income group suggested that the major reason for decreased living standards for some rural families has been relatively large medical charges. Figure 3.6 shows that those rural families that answered 'better in the past five years'

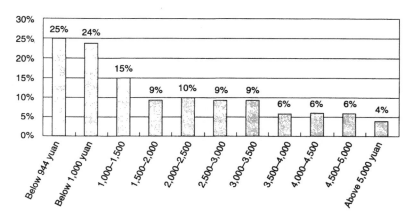

Figure 3.5 Percentage of medical expenditures in the net income of rural families by income groups (%).

Source: A 2006 background report by Ma Yongliang, Zhao Changbao and Wu Zhigang.

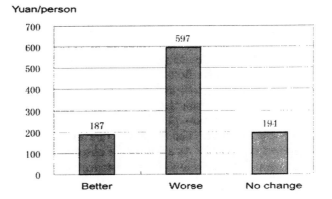

Yuan/person

Figure 3.6 Relationship between changes in living standards and per capita medical expenditures among rural families in the past five years (2005).

Source: A 2006 background report compiled jointly by Ma Yongliang, Zhao Changbao and Wu Zhigang.

recorded a per capita medical charge of RMB 187 yuan; those that answered 'worse' had a per capita medical charge of RMB 597 yuan; and those that answered 'no change' had a per capita medical charge of RMB 194 yuan. The per capita medical charge recorded by families answering 'worse' is 3.1 times that recorded by those answering 'better'. This underscores how excessive medical charges have become an important cause of poverty in recent years.

In addition, according to data on 22,520 rural families in six provinces obtained from a 2004 poverty surveillance survey conducted by the National Bureau of Statistics of China, 14.7 percent of surveyed rural families have encountered problems in receiving medical services for their family members due to financial hardship. Among those rural families in absolute poverty, this percentage is as high as 29.7 percent.

This suggests that excessive medical charges now constitute a major cause of rural poverty. In the 1980s, with the abolishment of the people's commune system, the original rural cooperative medical system was also disaggregated. Subsequently, market-oriented reform was implemented in the health sector, causing substantial increases in the prices of medical services and drugs, and making public medical and hygiene services unavailable. This has negatively affected rural residents. During the initial stage of the economic reforms, the rapid growth of living standards compensated for some negative impacts in the rural areas. But with the slowdown of growth in income and the soaring price of medical expenses, many negative consequences have arisen. There is an urgent need to fully establish a rural social security system and a public medical and hygiene service system. This has become indispensable to poverty alleviation efforts.

The burden of high medical service charges faced by rural residents stems not only from the lack of basic public services or a social security system, but also from a distorted pharmaceutical market. The examination, approval and circulation of drugs is chaotic, causing drug prices to severely deviate from normal market prices. Authorities have pointed out that an old drug may be advertized as a new drug bearing dozens of brand names and prices by simply switching it into different packages. For example, Roxithromycin is a drug in common use that comes in 50 varieties priced from RMB 1 yuan to over RMB 30 yuan (according to the *Yangtze River Daily* in 2006). The pharmaceutical market is a special market, with information asymmetry dominating the relationship between doctors and patients. It is impossible to reach equilibrium and the optimization of resource allocations by merely relying on spontaneous market competitions. Government supervision and guidance is necessary along with the function of market mechanisms. In early 2007, Zheng Youyu, former Director General of the State Food and Drug Administration, was prosecuted for being corrupt, auguring a good start towards straightening out the pharmaceutical market (xinhuanet.com, 2007). In the long run, the rectification of the pharmaceutical market and the separation of the processes of dispensing and prescribing drugs, along with intensified regulations, may be as important for poverty alleviation as the establishment and improvement of rural social security and medical services systems.

Educational burdens and poverty

The data in Tables 3.7 and 3.8 indicate the financial burden from education borne by rural families. The data on per capita educational expenditures in the two tables were the averaged results of the entire sampled population. If the calculation were based on only those rural families that have incurred educational expenditures, the average result would be higher. Among the surveyed surveillance samples in six provinces and municipalities, nearly 60 percent of the over 20,000 sampled rural families in 2004 had children in school. On average, each family was paying RMB 646 yuan for tuition and incidental fees and textbook costs. The total educational expenditure was as high as RMB 1,297 yuan. The average educational expenditure for families in absolute poverty was RMB 970 yuan, accounting for 45 percent of net family income (RMB 2,165 yuan).

According to the fixed-point surveillance data of rural families in nine provinces and municipalities, expenditure on children's schooling in 2005 (including tuition and incidental fees, textbook costs, accommodation, living expenses and transportation) was RMB 2,050 yuan per rural family and RMB 499 yuan per capita. This was higher than per capita medical expenditures (see Table 3.8). Generally speaking, the per capita educational expenditures of low-income families are lower than those of high-income families. But the percentage of educational expenditures in per capita net income is higher for low-income families. Low-income rural families spend RMB 148 yuan or 24.3 percent of their per capita net income. Rural families in the highest-income group, with a per capita net income in excess of RMB 5,000 yuan, spend RMB 424 yuan or 5.5 percent of per capita net income. Figure 3.7 demonstrates that with the decrease in income, the percentage of per capita educational expenditures increases, indicating their rigidity.

The survey reveals that a major reason for the excessive burden of education is the high cost of accommodation, meals and transportation expenses related to schooling (such expenses are not listed as educational expenditures in conventional statistical surveys). In recent years, many rural elementary schools and high schools with a relatively small number of teachers and students have been either closed or merged to adjust the school layouts. This has, on the one hand, integrated and enhanced the efficiency of educational resources. On the other hand, it has brought inconvenience for an enormous number of rural children of school age. Those from remote villages have to walk one or more hours to go to school every day, and a majority end up boarding in schools or taking school buses, which dramatically increases living expenses. This has demonstrated that the policy design and implementation of some departments is reasonable, but lack of a deep understanding and comprehensive evaluations of the advantages and disadvantages of circumstances at the grass-roots level may lead to unexpected side effects.

Field surveys in Shanxi, Anhui and Yunnan provinces carried out for this study have found that children's educational expenses for a minority of poor rural families almost exhaust their total annual family income. A significant number of poor families are in debt after paying their children's school expenses.

The increase in educational expenditures is another important factor that has led to a drop in living standards for some rural families. In Figure 3.8, the

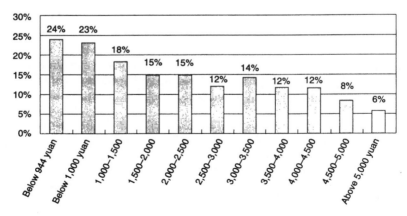

Figure 3.7 Percentages of educational expenditures out of net incomes for families in different rural income groups (2005).

Source: A 2006 background report compiled jointly by Ma Yongliang, Zhao Changbao and Wu Zhigang.

Yuan/person

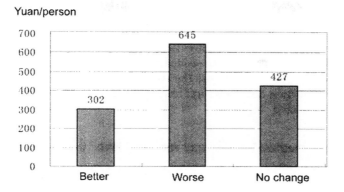

Figure 3.8 Relationship between the changes in living standards of rural families in the past five years and their per capita educational expenditures (2005).

Source: A 2006 background report compiled jointly by Ma Yongliang, Zhao Changbao and Wu Zhigang.

per capita educational expenditures of those rural families that said they have a 'better life in the past five years' was RMB 302 yuan; those that answered 'worse' were spending RMB 645 yuan; and those that answered 'no change' were spending RMB 427 yuan. The per capita educational expenditures of families that answered 'worse' is 2.1 times that of those answering 'better', and 1.5 times that of those answering 'no change'.

Excessive educational expenditures are one of the main causes of subsistence hardship for many rural families, including some high-income rural families. In the 2006 survey on the causes of poverty in 4000 rural families in 15 provinces (districts and municipalities), 37 percent of those in financial difficulties listed the 'high cost of education for children' as a cause of their poverty (see Box 3.1).

The survey also showed that the educational burden of rural families has been mitigated. Despite the fact that the per capita educational expenses in 2005 were higher than the per capita medical services expenses, the sampled rural families in 2006 still ranked educational expenses as the third cause of poverty, just below medical services expenses. That year, the policy of 'two exemptions and one allowance' (i.e., exemption of incidental fees and textbook costs, and provision of living allowances to boarded students) for students in financial difficulties in central and western China promulgated by the State Council was implemented, along with the 2006 legislation of the Central Committee of the Communist Party of China and the State Council to waive tuition and incidental fees for the nine-year period of compulsory education in rural areas of western China. After splitting the survey samples in central and western China from those in eastern China, the data revealed that the 'high cost of education for children' dropped to the sixth ranked cause of poverty among sampled poverty-stricken rural families in the central and western regions, while it is still ranked in third place for all rural families (see Table 3.9). As the country has already exempted rural students from their tuition and incidental fees for compulsory education, and the policy of granting subsidies to poverty-stricken students for textbooks and accommodation expenses was implemented across the country starting in 2007, the financial burden for education borne by rural residents, especially those in poverty, will be further alleviated.

Educational, medical burdens and rural residents' indebtedness

Data analysis confirms that the medical and educational burdens now borne by rural families in subsistence and developmental poverty have taken up more than half of their extremely low net income, leading to a sharp decrease in their most fundamental consumption expenditures for bare subsistence or severe indebtedness. This is a major reason for the deterioration in the living conditions among a portion of the rural population in poverty as well as severe indebtedness among a large number of rural families in recent years.

Based on survey data on 3,500 rural families in nine provinces (districts and municipalities) in central and western China, among rural families in absolute and relative poverty, 48 percent have borrowed money from private parties or taken loans in the past three years; two-thirds had not repaid their loans at the time of the survey. Only a small portion of these borrowers had asked for loans to purchase agricultural products or make investments. Most

Table 3.9 Causes of livelihood difficulties in rural families in nine provinces and municipalities of central and western China (2006)

	Rural families in absolute poverty	All rural families
1. Too limited income from agriculture	71.6%	70.9%
2. Heavy expenditures on medical services	54.7	49.2
3. Suffering from natural disaster	41.9	20.2
4. Shortage of funds for investment or business initiation	30.4	25.8
5. Large family headcount or lack of labourers	24.3	15
6. High cost of education for children	18.9	36.8
Number of samples in financial difficulties	148	1,623
Total number of valid samples	187	3,427

Source: Data obtained from a survey on rural families in nine provinces and municipalities conducted by the Office for Fixed-Point Surveillance of Rural Poverty under the Ministry of Agriculture.

Note: The entirety of sampled rural families in financial difficulties is 100 percent.

borrowed money to cover their daily consumption expenditures, pay tuition fees for their children or pay medical charges (a total of 53 percent for the three items). Medical and educational expenses were the two major sources of loan expenses (see Table 3.10). Compared with this type of rural family, the incidence rate of borrowing money among other types was lower, and the percentage of repayment was higher. Most of these families used loans for investments or business operations. But even among high-income families, 24 percent had borrowed money to pay tuition fees and medical charges. This speaks volumes for the enormous influence of medical and educational expenditures on the lives of rural residents.

Heavy medical and educational expenditures have caused poverty-stricken people to suffer greater financial difficulties in everyday life, and have forced more people who were not poor to fall into and remain in poverty. This phenomenon manifests not in the decrease of their income and consumption level, but in the increase of their consumption expenditures. Neither per capita income nor per capita consumption measures can explain such an impact. It demonstrates the crucial importance of the developmental poverty line as proposed in this report.

Serious consequences have resulted from previous reforms that failed to distinguish between the public services sector and ordinary competitive industrial sectors, attached excessive importance to commercialization, and abandoned the duty of providing public services for all members of the society. These tendencies have been the main underlying causes of the deterioration of living conditions among rural populations in absolute and relative poverty, the deceleration of poverty alleviation efforts and even the expansion of the population in actual poverty. The construction of a rural public service system is an important task for tackling rural poverty.

In 2006, the Central Committee of the Communist Party of China and the State Council decided to exempt students in western China from all tuition and incidental fees for the nine years of compulsory education, and confer subsidies to boarded students from poor families to pay for their textbooks and accommodation. In 2007, this measure was widely implemented in eastern and central China, which will relieve the financial burdens on farmers and be of great significance for poverty alleviation.

Institutional deficiencies and poverty

Besides public medical and educational services, the public service system in broad definition includes administrative management and public services provided by the public security and justice departments. The nature and structure of this system is significant in anti-poverty efforts. The survey finds that a proportion of the rural poor have ended up in poverty due to negative institutional factors, primarily including: (1) expropriation of lands and limited compensation; (2) heavy taxes; (3) arrears in wages; and (4) loss of

Table 3.10 Loans incurred by families in relative poverty and other types of rural families (sample: 3427 families)

	Incidence rate of loan (%)	Incidence rate of failure in in repayment of loans (%)	Average amount of loans	Purpose of loan			
				Coverage of everyday expenditures	Payment of tuition fees	Access to medical services	Sub-total
Families that have incurred loans/total number of sampled families	Families that have not repaid their loans/total number of families that have incurred loans	RMB yuan	Percentage of the total number of borrower families	Percentage of the total number of borrower families	Percentage of the total number of borrower families	Percentage of the total number of borrower families	
Families in relative poverty	47.9	66.4	4,088	15	16.8	21.4	53.2
Low- and medium-income families	41.7	63.4	7,483	9.8	22.3	18.1	50.2
Medium-income families	40.7	67.8	7,273	9.2	21.1	18.4	48.7
Medium- and high-income families	33.7	61.4	7,357	5.6	20.8	10.4	36.8
High-income families	35.5	57.6	13,041	4.7	18.7	5.6	29

Source: A portion of the samples surveyed by the Office for Fixed-Point Surveillance of Rural Areas under the Ministry of Agriculture.

Note: The loans in this table include private loans, microcredit loans granted by credit cooperatives to rural residents, interest-subsidized loans granted by the Agricultural Bank of China for poverty alleviation and other commercial loans of various types. The loans in the term 'average amount of loans' do not include commercial loans. The five income groups have been defined by the National Bureau of Statistics of China according to the results of a national survey of rural residents.

assets due to robbery, pilferage or fraud. In total, 4.3 percent of rural families in absolute poverty and 6.8 percent of rural families with livelihood hardship have become impoverished due to these factors (see details in Box 3.1). Table 3.11 presents the percentages of rural families influenced by each of these factors out of the total number of surveyed rural families.

Two percent of families in absolute poverty and 2.7 percent of all rural families with livelihood hardship suffered because their lands were expropriated and the compensation fees were small. Although these families do not constitute a large percentage in the total number of samples, considering only a small percentage of rural families have had their lands expropriated, the incidence rate of poverty resulting from such a reason is rather high. For many rural families, losing lands means the loss of their primary source of income, which will cause serious social problems. It is necessary to continue to seriously address the issue of rational compensation for the appropriation of lands for farmers.

The arrears in wages for rural migrant workers have drawn the attention of the State Council, which has repeatedly issued legislation to resolve the problem. This practice still happens from time to time, however, affecting 1.8 percent of the rural households with livelihood hardship in the survey sample. The survey was fielded in rural areas, and those rural workers

Table 3.11 Rural poverty and livelihood hardship incurred by institutional factors (2006)

Reasons resulting in livelihood hardship	*Percentage of the total number of rural families in absolute poverty*	*Percentage of the total number of rural families with livelihood hardships*
Expropriation of lands and limited compensation	2	2.7
Heavy taxes	1.3	1.6
Arrears in wages	1	1.8
Loss of assets due to robbery, pilferage or fraud	0	0.7
Total	4.3	6.8
Total number of sampled rural families in livelihood hardships	300	2,057
Total number of sampled rural families	351	3,950

Source: The survey was fielded by the Office for Fixed-Point Surveillance of Rural Areas under the Ministry of Agriculture and DataSea Marketing Research Company, as commissioned by the China Development Research Foundation. It took place in the provinces of Shanxi, Anhui, Henan, Guangxi, Guizhou, Yunnan, Chongqing, Shaanxi, Gansu, Tianjin, Liaoning, Shandong, Jiangsu, Fujian and Guangdong, covering 4,041 rural families in 72 villages (mostly affected by poverty).

working in urban areas were not directly surveyed. This percentage may be underestimated.

Compared to some previous findings, the incidence rate of poverty from heavy taxes has dropped substantially, affecting only 1.3 percent of poverty-stricken rural families and 1.6 percent of rural families in the sample. This indicates that the lifting of agricultural taxes has resulted in obvious positive effects in alleviating rural poverty. But in the meantime, some regions have not yet lifted these taxes, suggesting the need for continued efforts to fully implement this policy.

Only 0.7 percent of rural families with livelihood hardship have suffered from the loss of assets due to robbery, pilferage or fraud. Although these are not important causes of poverty, public security problems do exist in rural areas. It is necessary to continue to enhance security protection, to improve the social ethos, to promote social harmony, and to reduce crimes and social conflicts.

CAUSES OF URBAN POVERTY

Underemployment

Research has concluded that the foremost and fundamental cause of urban poverty is unemployment. Figure 3.9 illustrates the mixture of poor urban residents who received minimum livelihood subsidies in 2004. Those laid-off and unemployed together accounted for 40 percent of recipients. The retired and the 'three-NOs' (those with no capability for work, no income sources and no legal supporters or carers, mostly the elderly) together accounted for 7 percent. Only 6 percent were currently employed. The remaining 47 percent were most likely family dependants of people who had been laid-off or were unemployed (see background report, Cai Fang and Wang Meiyan 2006).[12]

In addition, among those employed in some cities, there are some who receive no income despite their nominal employment (or 'kept idle'). For

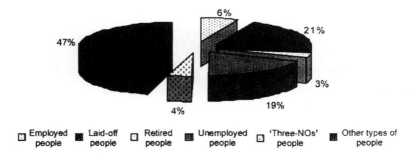

Figure 3.9 Mixture of urban residents receiving security benefits for bare subsistence.

Source: Huang Haili 2007.

example, in Beijing in early 2006, among the 67,400 families receiving minimum security subsidies, 42,900 families had no employed family members; 20,100 families had employed family members. The employed people were receiving no income despite nominal employment, earning extremely low wages or facing arrears in their wages (see background report, Wang Zhenyao 2006).

The particular importance of employment in urban poverty is also manifested in the geographical distribution of urban poverty. In 2006, there were nine provinces in China that had over 1 million people receiving minimum security subsidies. In total, 12 million people in these provinces were receiving minimum security subsidies, accounting for 54 percent of the total subsidized population of 22.41 million people nationwide. The provinces included Liaoning, Jilin, Heilongjiang, Anhui, Jiangxi, Henan, Hunan, Hubei and Sichuan. Most of them used to have concentrations of large state-owned industrial enterprises. A large number of workers were laid off or became unemployed during the restructuring of state-owned enterprises in the 1990s. Various research on urban poverty problems in some regions has shown that a majority of impoverished people in urban areas have low educational credentials and skills, are older or were employed by the state-owned enterprises (see Zhang Lu and Jiao Weidong 2005; Wei Jinsheng 2004; Teaching and Research Division of Sociology, Party School of Beijing Municipal Party Committee 2002).

Besides the restructuring of state-owned enterprises and shrinkage of traditional industries, the differential development in the non-state-owned sectors is an important factor. The nine provinces with acute urban poverty all lag behind coastal provinces in eastern China such as Guangdong, Shanghai, Zhejiang and Jiangsu provinces in the development of non-state-owned sectors. The lack of adequate job opportunities is a looming problem for them. On the other hand, in the eastern coastal regions, the development of the non-state-owned economy has created a large number of job opportunities for most workers laid off from state-owned enterprises.

The above analysis has shown the link between unemployment and urban poverty. Policies and measures aiming to increase job opportunities in urban areas can therefore be seen as having the potential to alleviate urban poverty. Since small enterprises are usually labour intensive and flexible in employment, they play a particularly important role in providing job opportunities. Generally, regions with well-developed small enterprises have a better outlook for employment and distinctive achievements in poverty alleviation.

Impacts of education and health

Econometric analysis of large survey samples reveals that besides household employment status, the total number of years of education of the household head and his/her spouse are key in determining the incidence of poverty (measured by per capita income below the security line for minimum subsistence) for urban families. The effects are significant in all samples. The self-evaluation of health conditions by the respondents is of equal importance. Essentially, a person with a low education or poor health conditions has a higher probability of poverty (see background report, Du Yang 2006). Much other research on urban poverty also shows that most poverty-stricken families have a low degree of education, relatively poor professional skills, a high average age and relatively poor average health conditions.

The impact of education on poverty has two aspects: (1) the degree of education has a direct effect on income level; and (2) a low level of education is a principal factor leading to layoffs, unemployment and the impeding of reemployment, and hence affects family income by its indirect impact on employment status. For a family in absolute poverty, the latter aspect, namely the effect of education on employment, may be a more important cause of poverty. As the educational factor affects urban poverty through its impact on employment, it is hard to strictly differentiate their respective impacts on poverty. But some case studies confirm the importance of education.

Survey findings reveal that health conditions are another important factor affecting poverty, primarily through their impact on employment. Under certain circumstances, poor health is a leading cause of severe livelihood hardship for a small portion of urban families. According to a survey conducted by Hefei City in Anhui Province in 2005 on the causes of livelihood hardship among all urban families receiving minimum security subsidies and other urban families with livelihood hardship, one third of those reliant on subsidies have become impoverished because their family members have suffered diseases, injuries or disabilities. The percentage is smaller than that of families in poverty due to unemployment (41 percent). Figure 3.10 illustrates the results of this survey.

Surveys in some other places have produced similar results. For instance, a survey of workers in severe financial difficulties in the large cities of Hubei Province found that among the 460 sampled families, 162 persons were

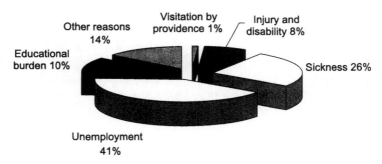

Figure 3.10 Distribution of causes of poverty among urban families receiving minimum security subsidies in Hefei City.

Source: Huang Haili 2007.

mentally or intellectually retarded, and 280 had suffered serious diseases. Up to 96 percent of the families had disabled persons or sufferers of serious diseases (Huang Guoqing 2002). Disability and sickness have caused victims to lose job opportunities, prevented the employment of their family members, and caused heavy medical expenses. Another survey of poor families in Beijing receiving minimum security subsidies discovered that among the 1,033 sampled families and 2,959 persons, only 41 percent were in good physical health; 33.8 percent were in poor health or suffered from various diseases at different degrees of severity; and 19.8 percent were disabled (Teaching and Research Division of Sociology, Party School of Beijing Municipal Party Committee 2002).

The survey research and case studies have confirmed that besides unemployment, adverse education and health conditions are the two most important causes of urban poverty. They both not only have a direct effect on the income level of urban residents, but also an indirect effect on poverty by their effects on employment. Generally speaking, if a low degree of education and the poor health of a labourer only affect his or her income levels without leading to unemployment, they may cause relative poverty but the probability of absolute poverty is rather small. When the two factors affect unemployment, however, they are likely to cause absolute poverty.

Social security and public services

Due to the important influence of employment, education and health on urban poverty, the social security and public service systems play a key role in reducing the incidence of urban poverty. Since the late 1990s, China has gradually established a social security system comprising such modules as basic medical insurance, unemployment insurance, the minimum security line for bare subsistence for urban residents, etc. Each of these programmes has played an important role, but the social security system is not yet fully developed.

By the end of 2005, the number of workers in China that had joined the unemployment insurance, basic medical insurance and basic pension insurance systems was 106 million, 100 million and 175 million respectively, accounting for 39.5 percent, 37 percent and 64 percent of the total employed population in urban areas (calculated with data provided by the National Bureau of Statistics of China in 2005). This indicates that the coverage rates of these three types of insurance have been far from enough. The population that have not been covered are mostly those who have not reached the labour age, have no capability to work, have been unemployed, have worked in non-regular sectors or are migrant labourers. They are in fact mainly the low-income and poverty-stricken populations in urban areas who are most in need of the assistance and protection offered by the social security system.

According to a 2005 survey of urban residents at all social strata, as far as the reimbursement of basic medical charges is concerned, the per capita medical charges of the medium- and high-income populations were greater than those of the low-income population. The percentage of reimbursed medical charges in the total medical charges incurred by the medium- and high-income population is also higher than for the low-income population. Low-income groups have to bear a majority of their medical charges, which confirms the fact that the low-income population has not been able to enjoy basic medical insurance (Wang Xiaolu and Fan Gang 2005). A similar situation applies to unemployment insurance and basic endowment insurance.

The social security system tends to fail to cover the low-income population for a few reasons. First, due to fiscal constraints and other challenges of the Government, the system itself is not fully functional. For example, there are no concrete methods to provide security for unemployed personnel. Even existing measures have not been widely applied. Second, there are no obligatory measures defining employers' responsibilities, especially in small enterprises and informal sectors where employees are recruited and fired frequently. This consequently leads to extremely low coverage. Third, the high insurance premiums borne by individuals have prevented the low-income population from accessing the insurance. To improve the social security system, the emphasis should be placed on expanding its coverage, allowing more people to access the system, ensuring its function in a simple and convenient way, and reinforcing the legal responsibilities of employers.

Rural labourers currently working in urban areas have been largely ignored by the social security system. They lack sufficient financial backup and interpersonal networks in urban areas. Once they suffer from disease, injury, disability or unemployment, they are vulnerable to poverty. The improvement of the social security system must take into account the protection of rural migrant labourers.

As for education, the migrant population and particularly the children of rural migrant labourers have been largely overlooked. The fact that public educational services have, in fact, excluded the children of rural labourers has resulted in an extra educational burden for them. This has made it harder for the rural population to settle in urban areas. It has also caused a series of problems, such as discontinuity in education, lack of parental care, and physical and mental health problems among the children of rural migrant labourers.

A BRIEF SUMMARY OF THE CAUSES OF POVERTY

Economic development is the most important means of fighting poverty. With rapid economic development in China in the last three decades, the size of the rural population in poverty has dropped dramatically, and by and large the severity of poverty has been alleviated. But past experiences have also proved that economic development does not automatically eliminate poverty.

A number of factors affecting poverty occurrence are worth highlighting, as discussed below.

First, low income from agriculture, poor geographical and natural conditions (remote and mountainous regions, aridity and weather-related disasters), and inadequate infrastructure (no access to roads, power, telephone service, drinkable water, etc.) remain fundamental causes of rural poverty. The most effective means of poverty alleviation is to enable rural labourers to switch into non-agricultural sectors in rural and urban areas, especially in the urban areas. But it is equally necessary to continue to improve infrastructure in impoverished areas.

Geographical and natural conditions are hard to change within a short period of time. Improvement in infrastructure in rural areas can to a great extent compensate for those disadvantages. It helps boost rural development as well as alleviate poverty. Empirical analysis has pointed out that infrastructure changes may first benefit the non-poor population and enable them to earn more. With the development of an entire region, however, the population in poverty will gradually drop and they will eventually benefit from development as well. The past efforts to construct roads, reconstruct power grids, put irrigation systems in place, and establish radio, telephone and television services for every village have contributed to the alleviation of rural poverty. The present policy of 'village-wide poverty alleviation' will continue to help make progress in this direction.

Second, surveys and analysis show that inadequate human capital has loomed increasingly large as an impediment to poverty alleviation. Most poor people in rural areas have a low degree of education and limited occupational skills, hence inadequate human capital, which prevents them from switching into industries other than agriculture or to urban areas. It also hinders their ability to grasp agricultural technologies and enhance the technological value of their productions. Analysis has shown that efforts to provide farmers with occupational training, to facilitate labour force transfers and to disseminate agricultural technologies have effectively helped them to switch into non-agricultural industries and earn more, thus contributing to poverty alleviation. These efforts are worth pursuing on a larger scale.

Inadequate education will result in poverty; poverty will in turn hinder the education of offspring. When the children of poverty-stricken rural families end up receiving no or little education, poverty will likely pass from one generation to another. To break the vicious circle, there should be greater efforts to strengthen compulsory education in rural areas so that the children of all rural residents have equal opportunities to receive education.

Investment in rural education and human capital is not only a powerful anti-poverty weapon, but also brings enormous social benefits and returns in the long run. The Central Committee of the Communist Party of China and the State Council are now implementing the 2006 legislation on the exemption of rural students from tuition and incidental fees for the nine years of compulsory education, which will play an important role in alleviating rural poverty. In the future, it is necessary to continue to improve the quality of rural education, including the quality of teaching, and to expand and enhance vocational education.

Third, health is an important component of human capital. With economic development and a large number of rural people equipped to work their way out of poverty, the causes of impoverishment have increasingly included poor health, especially when it involves disability or sickness that causes loss of capability for work. In some economically more developed regions, health problems have become the leading causes of absolute poverty. With the advancement of economic development, the percentage of people unable to make a living without assistance in the overall population in poverty will continue to increase. Present statistical data and estimation have not captured the actual status of this population. Adjustments to poverty alleviation policies are required to shift from the past emphasis on productive and developmental poverty alleviation to the establishment and improvement of a rural social security system, and a public medical and hygiene system.

Recent years have witnessed a slow increase in the incidence rate of sickness and disability among rural residents. The health conditions of rural residents are worrying. This has been closely related to such factors as medical and sanitary conditions, disease control and epidemic prevention measures, environmental safety, housing conditions, access to drinkable water, etc. It is also directly related to the chaotic pharmaceutical market and the shortage of public medical services. More efforts need to be made towards the prevention and control of diseases, the provision of drinkable water, the management of the environment in rural areas, etc. At the same time, it is also essential to regulate the pharmaceutical market and counteract corruption in the medical services areas. Close attention should also be paid to widowed or single elderly people and poverty-stricken children in rural areas.

Fourth, the basic demands of living for rural residents are no longer at the subsistence level of clothing and food, but instead extend to ensuring the development of self and offspring, including through basic health care and children's education. Research has found that excessive medical and educational charges have become the most severe problems faced by rural families in poverty and those at the low- and medium-income levels in the past decades. This trend has aggravated the degree of poverty and caused some rural families above the subsistence poverty line to actually fall back into poverty. This report's analysis has demonstrated that it is essential to set up a developmental poverty line distinct from the subsistence poverty line to reflect the change. It is also necessary to adopt practical measures to alleviate medical and educational burdens on rural residents, and to establish and improve a social security and public service system for rural areas (including the widespread use of a new type of rural cooperative medical system and a medical rescue system).

The latest survey has shown that the policy to exempt students in western

China from tuition and incidental fees for compulsory education, which was formulated by the Central Committee of the Communist Party of China and the State Council in 2006, has already taken effect in alleviating the financial burdens of farmers in that region. With the implementation of this policy in eastern and central China in 2007, excessive educational charges will be mitigated nationwide. The efforts of subsidizing children from poor rural families with textbooks, accommodation and meal expenses need to be further implemented. At present, farmers are more concerned about the alleviation of medical service charges.

Fifth, due to the restructuring of state-owned enterprises and the massive layoff of workers since the mid 1990s, urban poverty has become an important poverty issue. Unemployment is the primary cause of urban poverty, particularly in former industrial bases with a concentration of state-owned enterprises. The degree of development of non-state-owned sectors has become key to resolving unemployment. In regions with underdeveloped non-state-owned sectors, urban poverty problems have become particularly acute. Besides employment, two other key factors behind urban poverty are education and health. A low degree of education leads to fewer job opportunities and negatively affects income, for example.

To alleviate urban poverty incurred by such factors as unemployment, limited education and poor health, the social security and public services system must be fully functional. The social security system must be expanded and easy to access, with simplified operational modes. The legal responsibilities of employers must be reinforced. Low-income and migrant populations must be included in the social security system so that it covers the entire society.

Lastly, survey analysis has revealed that the quality of services offered by the public administrative management and the justice divisions has to some extent affected the incidence rate of poverty. What is discussed in this report mainly refers to institutional factors. As far as rural residents are concerned, these include expropriated lands, arrears of wages, excessive tax charges in certain regions, rural public security and social order problems, etc. All these concerns have to be addressed by enhancing institutional structures and improving the institutional environment in rural areas. For urban residents, fair, transparent, incorruptible and effective legal and administrative management will help ensure the normal functioning of the social security and public services systems.

Notes

1 For the latest literature on the poverty trap, refer to Bowles, Durlauf and Hoff 2006; Banerjee, Benabou and Mookherjee 2006; and Bowles and Gintis 2002.
2 One administrative village consists of about seven natural villages on average. First-hand information about accessibility by road, availability of power and telephone services, etc. at the natural village level was not available. Corresponding indexes on the average of administrative villages was substituted. The so-called 'index of village accessibility by road' refers to the ratio of those natural villages

accessible by road to the total number of natural villages in the same administrative village where the surveyed rural families are situated. The other indexes are defined likewise. In fact, having a high index of village accessibility by road does not necessarily mean that those natural villages where the surveyed rural families are situated are accessible by road, but simply that they may be closer to some roads, and thus perhaps enjoy greater traffic convenience. This has reduced the actual influence of infrastructure facilities.

3 De Brauw *et al.* (2002) show the degree of education has a rather apparent influence on rural labourers' options for working elsewhere. Each additional year of schooling raises the probability of getting hired elsewhere by 16 percent.

4 The latter two types of employers may be partly superimposed.

5 As shown by Deng Quheng (2007), the impact of China's rural education on agricultural production has increased. For instance, the impact of the average degree of education of family members on their net income from agriculture in 2002 was nearly 80 percent stronger than in 1988 and nearly 55 percent stronger than in 1995. Prior to that, Li and Zhang (1998) analysed the data from a survey of 3856 families in Sichuan Province conducted in 1990, and found that each additional year of schooling increased the family's net income from agriculture by 2.7 percent. Yang (1997) analysed data obtained from a survey of 197 rural families in Sichuan Province conducted in 1991, discovering that each additional year of schooling can increase the net income from agriculture by 3.9 percent to 5.8 percent.

6 For those school children aged 7 to 12 years, the per capita educational expenditure of the richest third of their families is 1.79 times that of the poorest third. For those aged 13–15 years, the former is 1.67 times the latter. For those aged 16–18 years, the former is 2.31 times the latter. The percentage of educational expenditures in total family expenditures in the richest 20 percent of families is only 7 percent, but in the poorest 20 percent of families it is up to 25 percent (see Knight *et al.* 2006).

7 In 2004, the Ministry of Education formulated the 'Programme for Reinvigorating Education from 2003 to 2007', and continued to implement the 'National Project for Compulsory Education in Poverty-Stricken Regions' and the 'Project of Reconstruction of Dilapidated Houses in Elementary and High Schools'. In the same year, the Government initiated a 'Two Bases' plan for western China. Implemented through 2007, it covered 83 million persons in 372 counties.

8 The 'One Fee System' is a reform policy adopted initially in 2004. It stipulates that 'all the administrative educational fees shall be made public and collected at one go; and it is prohibited to levy any extra educational fee'. The 'Two Exemptions and One Allowance' policy was implemented initially in 2005, and stipulates that in compulsory education for rural areas, 'it is necessary to exempt those children, who hail from poverty-stricken families, from textbook costs and incidental fees; and also gradually put into force the policy of granting living allowances to those students who are boarded; and also step up the pace in alleviating the poverty scene in those state-specified major counties subject to poverty alleviation'.

9 The former includes 22,520 sampled rural families in 242 poverty-stricken counties in Hebei, Hubei, Guangxi, Yunnan, Shaanxi and Xinjiang; the latter includes 3518 sampled rural families in 61 sampled villages in Shanxi, Anhui, Henan, Guangxi, Guizhou, Yunnan, Chongqing, Shaanxi and Gansu. These two sample groups have both ruled out a small number of sampled rural families with a negative net income. It was discovered by data analysis that characteristics other than income (including consumption expenditures, savings and investment scale, etc.) of these rural families conformed to those of rural families on a relatively high-income level. They are mostly in a stage of temporary poverty incurred by business losses. This rules out temporary poverty, for the sake of logical consistency.

10 Other reasons can cause consumption expenditures to exceed family incomes in

poverty-stricken rural families, but they are not as major. Data analysis also shows that a small number of rural families below the poverty line are in temporary poverty. Their production and operation scales are big in relative terms, and their total incomes, total expenditures and living consumption levels are obviously higher than those of other poverty-stricken rural families. Their net income is rather low, however, and even shows a negative value, which demonstrates that they are in temporary poverty incurred by business losses. This also reveals the instability of their income. According to a rough estimation, the number of these poverty-stricken people does not comprise more than 1 percent of the country's total rural population, and is likely to constitute a third (or less) of the population under the income poverty line. In the data in Tables 3.7 and 3.8, we have already ruled out those sampled families whose net income level is lower than 0 because these people are apparently in temporary poverty. Only a small quantity of these families has been considered poverty-stricken.

11 Other research indicates that once medical charges are deducted from the net income of rural families, the rate of subsistence poverty in rural areas (estimated according to the official poverty line) would rise by 1 percent in 1998 and 2.2 percent in 1995 (Gustafsson and Li 2004).

12 As indicated by Li Shi (2004), at the end of the past century, layoffs and unemployment caused the incidence of poverty among urban residents to go up three to four times. By 2002, with other factors unchanged, the incidence among unemployed people and those kept idle was four to five times that of employed people, and three times for laid-off people (background report, Zheng Feihu and Li Shi 2006).

4 China's poverty alleviation policies

Goals and impacts

Fast economic growth has been a decisive factor in the massive reduction of poverty in China. In addition, the Chinese Government has formulated and implemented poverty alleviation policies and measures targeting certain regions and groups of people, both in rural and urban areas. In recent years, other reforms, while targeted towards the entire rural population, have also contributed to poverty reduction through improvements related to agricultural taxation and subsidization, basic education, environmental protection, and medical and sanitary services.

This chapter will describe the evolution, goals and impacts of poverty alleviation policies. An assessment of impacts chiefly looks at the degree of implementation in terms of target populations and whether or not policies have reached the poor. Where data permit, the degree of benefits for people in poverty is also analysed.

MAIN POVERTY ALLEVIATION POLICIES AND THEIR CHARACTERISTICS

Table 4.1 sets out the major poverty alleviation policies for rural and urban areas that have had an important influence on the poor population. China implemented these in rural areas far earlier than in urban areas, so the policy course varies between the two. The focus in rural areas has been mainly on developmental poverty alleviation and in urban areas on social security.

China's two-tier system for poverty alleviation: developmental poverty alleviation in rural areas and social security in urban areas

China's targeted poverty alleviation policies began in the mid 1980s in rural areas. Urban poverty did not receive much attention until the mid 1990s, when the reform of state-owned enterprises started and many employees were laid off. In China at that time, rural and urban areas were separated from each other by the residency registration management system, which had featured a

Table 4.1 China's poverty alleviation policies

Categorization of policies		Major policies	Time of implementation	Targets
Developmental poverty alleviation policies	**Rural areas**	Immigration and resettlement	1983	Poor counties
		Food for work	1985	Poor counties
		Interest-subsidized loans	1986	Poor regions
		Budgetary development funds	1986	Poor counties
		Poverty alleviation through scientific and technological advancement	1986	Poor regions
		Poverty alleviation through social efforts	1986	Poor regions
		Compulsory education projects in poor regions	1995	Western China
		Microcredit	1996	Poor regions
		Integrated village development plan	2001	Poor villages
		Labour training for migration	2004	Poor counties
		Poverty alleviation through development of agribusiness	2004	Poor regions
		'Two Basic Education Plans' in western China	2004	Poor regions
	Urban areas	Re-employment project	1995	Laid-off workers
Social security policies	**Rural areas**	Welfare for those households entitled to the 'five guarantees'	People's commune period	'Three-NOs' population in rural areas
		Rural medical rescue	2002	Poor population in rural areas
		Minimum living standard for bare subsistence in rural areas	2003	Population in absolute poverty in rural areas
		Rescue for rural households in extreme poverty	2003	Population in absolute poverty in rural areas

Table 4.1 Continued

Categorization of policies		Major policies	Time of implementation	Targets
	Urban areas	Childbirth insurance	1988	Employed women in urban areas
		Unemployment insurance	1993	Workers in enterprises and public institutions in urban areas
		Endowment insurance	1995	
		Minimum living standard for bare subsistence in urban areas	1997	Workers in urban enterprises
		Medical insurance	1998	Poor households in urban areas
		Industrial injury insurance	2003	Workers in urban organizations
				Workers in urban enterprises
Pro-peasant policies	Rural areas	'One Fee System' reform	2001	Elementary and high schools in rural areas
		Consolidation of elementary and middle schools	2001	Elementary and high schools in rural areas
		Compensation for poor eco-efficiency in forests	2001	Ecological protection areas
		Conversion of croplands to forests and conversion of range lands to grasslands	2002	Mountainous and pastoral areas
		Crop, fine-breed and agricultural machinery subsidies for primary crop-producing areas	2003	Primary crop-producing areas and crop producers
		New cooperative medical system	2003	Rural population
		Reform of taxes and fees levied in rural areas	2004	Rural population
		Reform of compulsory education in rural areas	2006	Rural children of school age in compulsory education

Source: Calculated based on data provided by the World Bank and the Rural Survey Group of the National Bureau of Statistics of China.

strict division of the agricultural and non-agricultural populations since the 1950s. For many years, urban residents enjoyed a wide range of social services and social security in terms of housing, medical care, education, retirement pensions, etc. offered by the Government and employers. In contrast, social services and security for rural residents originated from households and communities, and were unstable and inadequate. After the people's commune system was rescinded, certain basic social services for the rural population (such as medical care) deteriorated further (Han Jun 2006).

In view of its financing power and the discrepancies between rural and urban areas in terms of their degree of economic development, the Chinese Government has applied different policies and systems to reduce poverty in the two areas. Rural poverty alleviation policies focus on boosting economic growth within poor regions and the income growth of the poor population, constituting developmental poverty alleviation (see Box 4.1). Urban poverty alleviation policies have emphasized providing minimum livelihoods for bare subsistence, namely through the minimum living standard system and a few other compulsory insurance systems.

Why has developmental poverty alleviation been emphasized in rural areas?

China's adoption of developmental poverty alleviation in rural areas correlates with the development degree of the rural economy. Compared to urban areas, most rural areas have a relatively low degree of economic development, and the economic gap between the two has been widening since China's reform and opening-up process began. The direct consequence of slow rural economic growth is that an overwhelming majority of the poor population (as per a comparable standard) lives in rural areas. As per the latest estimation by the World Bank, the percentage of the poor population in rural areas in 2003, measured by the absolute poverty line or the low-income line of the National Bureau of Statistics of China or the US $1 per person per day poverty line, exceeded 99 percent. Even if urban migrants, who generally come from rural areas, are included in the urban poor population, the percentage of the poor in rural areas still exceeds 91 percent (World Bank 2006). Since urban residents had a wide range of employment security and social welfare options in the 1980s, the percentage of the poor in rural areas was unlikely to be less at that time.

Since so many rural residents are poor, offering income subsidies for poverty alleviation is not feasible as it is in urban areas. A major obstacle to a social security system in rural areas is that the financing capabilities of local governments are not enough to ensure the provision of basic education and medical services, so a social security system with income subsidies would be impossible. Local governments are also faced with technological and institutional difficulties in identifying which households and individuals should be entitled to such a system, along with administrative challenges. It has been two decades since the developmental poverty alleviation policy was initially employed, but there is still no effective method for identifying the poor. Furthermore, a social security system featuring broad coverage is prone to reverse incentives, which reduce individual motivations to work and are not conducive for a developing country.

The rural poor are relatively concentrated in certain regions of western China that struggle with an inhospitable natural environment, limited resources and remote geography. It has therefore been appropriate for the Government to adopt a developmental poverty alleviation strategy that emphasizes regional development. First, regional development focuses on poor regions, instead of poor households and individuals, thus making it much easier to identify the targets. Second, the key point of developmental poverty alleviation is to improve living conditions in poor regions, and enhance the efficiency of agricultural and non-agricultural productivity through better infrastructure and public services. This enables rural households to earn more and emerge from poverty. Financing infrastructure and providing public services also requires a manageable quantity of resources. In the meantime, the Government can encourage financial institutions to give direct support to productive activities in poor regions and by rural households. Third, developmental poverty alleviation practices addressed to certain regions can make full use of the existing administrative management system instead of setting up a big poverty alleviation institution, hence reducing management costs.

Box 4.1 The evolution of China's developmental poverty alleviation policies for rural areas

The Chinese Government initially adopted rural poverty alleviation policies in the early 1980s, with continued development and improvements in the ensuing two decades. The evolution can be roughly divided into four stages:

(1) Rural economic reform and regional poverty alleviation on a small scale (1979–1985)

Due to the immense impact of the 10-year Cultural Revolution and the restrictions of the planned economy system, the 1970s left China's national economy in a state of utter stagnancy (Zhou Binbin 1991). Starting from 1979, the Chinese Government set out to reform the rural economic system, mainly through a household contract responsibility system with remuneration linked to output. Due to the transformation of the production and operation system, the partial opening of the Chinese market and the sharp increase in the prices of agricultural products, agricultural production and the rural economy began to grow at an unprecedented speed, spurring rapid growth in incomes. This benefited almost the entire rural population, thus dramatically reducing rural poverty.

While gradually carrying forward rural reforms, the Government also set out to propel the economic development of some regions particularly affected by absolute poverty. For instance, in 1980 it launched a fund specifically for boosting the development of economically underdeveloped regions. In 1983, it implemented a 10-year-long 'Agricultural Construction Programme' that covered 47 counties in the Dingxi and Hexi regions of Gansu Province, and the Xihaigu region of the Ningxi Autonomous Region (Li Zhong 2000 and Liu Yaqiao *et al.* 2005). In September 1984, the State Council and Central Committee of the Communist Party of China worked together to issue a 'Notice with Regard to Helping Poor Regions Emerge from Poverty as Quickly as Possible', and in the same year, they set up specific loans for old revolutionary bases, regions hosting a high density of people of national minorities, and remote regions. They also put into force a 'Food for Work Plan' to improve infrastructure and conditions in poor regions (Department of National Land Development and Local Economics under the (former) State Planning Commission 1991). These polices not only directly boosted economic development in some impoverished regions and bettered production and living conditions, but also generated experiences to inform the implementation of larger-scale rural poverty alleviation and development plans.

(2) Implementation of a targeted poverty alleviation plan on a large scale (1986–1993)

In the mid 1980s, the pace of rural economic reform and growth began to decline, and the growth of peasants' incomes slowed. Income gaps among rural residents began to widen quickly, making poverty prominent in certain regions. Changes in macroeconomic circumstances pushed the central Government to carry out a national rural development plan for poverty alleviation. In 1986, the fourth session of the 6th National People's Congress made it clear that 'it is an important task to help the four types of regions (namely time-honoured revolutionary bases, regions housing a high density of people of national minorities, remote regions and poor regions) out of their economic and cultural backwardness as soon as possible, under the country's "7th Five-Year-Long National Development Program (1986–1990)"'. Also in 1986, the State Council set up the Leading Group for Poverty Alleviation and Development, which symbolized the initiation of China's customized poverty alleviation plan on a large scale.

Subsequently, the Government formulated policies and measures to expedite poverty alleviation in rural areas. First, it opted to resort to developmental poverty alleviation in rural areas. Second, it focused its efforts on certain regions, and also conducted work from one county to another. The Leading Group for Poverty Alleviation and Development under the State Council determined a number of state-specified poor counties, according to the per capita incomes of peasants, per capita grain output and other factors, and adopted these counties as the main targets for development to reduce poverty. Third, on the basis of small-scale poverty alleviation investment plans formed in the early 1980s, the Government chose three major investment plans, including loans for poverty alleviation, food for work and a budgetary development fund. Fourth, favourable taxation was granted to state-specified poor counties. Fifth, all social forces were mobilized to participate in rural poverty alleviation.

(3) 'Eight-Seven Poverty Alleviation Plan' (1994–2000)

In the late 1980s and early 1990s, the pace of rural economic development and the increase in peasants' incomes remained slow. Despite the large-scale development plan for poverty alleviation, certain undesired changes in rural economic circumstances meant the decrease in the size of the rural poor population was far below that of previous periods. The poverty alleviation campaign seemed to have reached an impasse. To boost rural development in poor areas, in 1994, the Government launched the 'Eight-Seven Poverty Alleviation Plan'. The objective was to help the remaining population in absolute poverty (totalling 80 million persons) to secure enough food and clothing between 1994 and 2000. This underscored the growing determination of the Government to address rural poverty.

The main measures under the 'Eight-Seven Poverty Alleviation Plan' included: (1) to help poverty-stricken rural households improve their lands and ploughing practices, plant more fruit trees and cash crops, and enhance their production efficiency in animal husbandry, and to create many more job opportunities in non-agricultural industries; (2) to make most townships and towns accessible by roads and furnish them with power facilities, and improve the quality of water for humans and animals in poor villages; (3) to spread compulsory education, disease control and prevention, and medical care services at primary levels; (4) to readjust the distribution of poverty alleviation funds among regions, and focus more on central and western China; (5) to intensify the management of poverty alleviation funds, reduce the leakage of such funds and enhance the sustainability of poverty alleviation investments; and (6) to mobilize various party and political organs at all levels, including coastal provinces and major cities, and other types of organizations at home and abroad to take an active part in the poverty alleviation campaign (Poverty Alleviation Group of the State Council 1993). When the 'Eight-Seven Poverty Alleviation Plan' was implemented, the

Government re-specified poor counties, and strengthened the responsibility system for local government leaders for the poverty alleviation work in their regions. Since 1997, the amount of poverty alleviation funds has substantially increased (the amount was up by 50 percent in 1997 alone), thus stopping the trend in declining funds of the previous decade.

(4) Implementation of the 'Scheme for Rural Development for Poverty Alleviation' (2001–2010)

After the 'Eight-Seven Poverty Alleviation Plan' was achieved as a whole, the Government implemented the 'Scheme for Rural Development for Poverty Alleviation' (2001–2010). In the late 1990s, with the decrease in the size of the poor population in rural areas overall, the remaining population was distributed across the country in a more scattered manner. According to the poverty standard of the National Bureau of Statistics of China, in 2000, the size of the poor population in state-specified poor counties comprised 54.3 percent of the country's total population in poverty, with a poverty incidence rate of 8.9 percent (Rural Survey Group of the National Bureau of Statistics of China 2001). As indicated by the findings of a survey sponsored by the World Bank (2001), the incidence rate of poverty in poor counties was 16 percent (Wang *et al.* 2006). If poor counties were to continue as the basic focus of poverty alleviation, however, nearly 50 percent of the rural poor would not benefit, and there would be a decrease in the utilization ratio of poverty alleviation resources.

In 2001, the 'Scheme for Rural Development for Poverty Alleviation (2001–2010)' was introduced. This plan makes adjustments in the counties targeted for poverty alleviation, focuses more efforts on western China and designates poor villages as the basic units of development. It stipulates that poverty alleviation investments can cover poor villages in counties other than those targeted for poverty alleviation. The scheme attaches importance to developing the scientific, technological, educational, cultural and sanitation capacities of poor regions. It emphasizes a participatory mode of poverty alleviation, village-based integrated development and integrated village development (Leading Group for Poverty Alleviation and Development under the State Council 2001 and Gao Hongbin 2001). Lastly, it acknowledges the flow of the population between rural and urban areas as an important means of poverty alleviation by underscoring the need for new policies and measures to make it easier for rural residents to seek work in urban areas.

Productive development and human capital development: which is more important?

Rural poverty alleviation strategies in previous years have laid excessive stress upon productive development conducive to the growth of short-term income. But they have neglected the development of human capital and the enhancement of human capabilities that have a major bearing on the long-term development of the poor population. The main focus has been on pouring material capital into rural areas to pursue productive development. Only a small percentage of resources has been poured into human capital development. According to data from a survey of 519 poor counties conducted by the National Bureau of Statistics of China from 1998 to 2001, 46 percent of poverty alleviation funds went into agriculture (mostly credit funds for poverty alleviation); 20 percent was spent on infrastructure; 14 percent went towards industries; and only 4 percent supported the cultural, educational, health care and technical training sectors in developing human capital (see Figure 4.1). The unevenness in spending and approach is a significant matter that needs to be addressed.

The extra prominence given to productive development may be due to the following reasons. First, rural poverty defined by China refers to absolute poverty measured by income. When measuring the size of the poor population, the National Bureau of Statistics of China does not take account of social development indicators. In the short term, investments in material capital (road construction, irrigation, croplands, etc.) and direct productive activities are more likely to enhance the productivity and income level of rural households, thus generating more visible impacts on poverty alleviation. Second, the Chinese people have not become fully aware of the role played by human capital. It has been customary to deem educational and medical expenses as consumption expenditures, instead of long-term investments. In reality, developmental funds for poverty alleviation are not in the consumption domain. Third, education and medical services are mainly provided by public education and health departments, which have not had a big say in the formation of poverty alleviation policies and management of poverty alleviation funds and projects.

To achieve good results, poverty alleviation investments have to meet the actual demands of poor rural households. As indicated by an assessment of the investment requirements of 719 rural households in poor regions in Hebei, Yunnan and Gansu provinces by use of a participatory assessment method, 46 percent of the total investment demands was related to human capital, including a reduction in children's educational expenses, the provision of training on agricultural technologies, a reduction in medical expenses, an increase in investments in educational facilities and an increase in the number of medical services outlets (see Figure 4.2). For rural households, human capital investments are clearly as important as investments in material capital and productive activities.

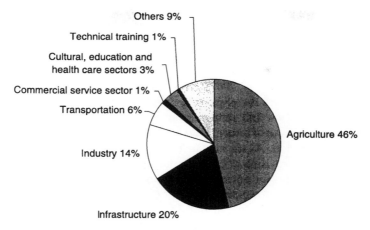

Figure 4.1 Spending of poverty alleviation funds allocated to poverty-stricken counties (1998–2001).

Source: Wang Sangui *et al.* 2004.

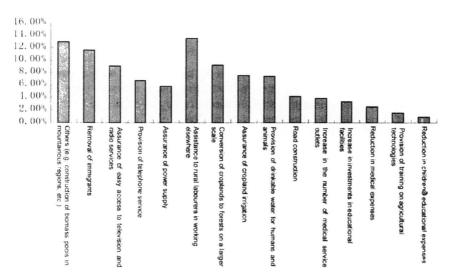

Figure 4.2 The investment demands of rural households in poor regions.

Source: Wang Sangui *et al.* 2004.

Investments in human capital are of great importance not only for reducing poverty in the long run, but also for economic development as a whole. In a developing market economy, the rates of return from educational investments are high for individuals and society. In China, as the country's labour market has not been well developed, the rate of return for individuals prior to the mid 1990s was relatively low, being approximately only 4 percent. With the growth of the labour market, increasing numbers of rural labourers have poured into industries and regions where the rate of return for individuals has gone up considerably, having exceeded 7 percent by the late 1990s (Heckman 2003). As indicated by the findings of pertinent research, increased inequality in China is in large part due to the enhanced rate of return on human capital (Benjamin *et al.* 2006; Yue Ximing *et al.* 2007). Investments in spreading the coverage of educational services will therefore be a decisive factor in alleviating poverty for the next generation and reducing income inequalities. Medical services also generate a high rate of return, because they guarantee basic capabilities in production and action. As an increasing number of labourers move among regions, the public provision of educational and medical services in particular will yield better results for poverty alleviation.

Investments in human capital should not be viewed merely from the angle of income and economic growth. In fact, education and health are the most fundamental demands of humans, and are as important as food and clothing. Wholesome educational and health conditions will not only contribute to the growth of household income and the national economy, but will also greatly enhance people's freedom of action. They are the objectives pursued by people to improve the quality of their choices and lives (Sen 1999).

Developmental poverty alleviation alone is inadequate

Developmental poverty alleviation has to be combined with a rural social security system to alleviate rural poverty in a more effective way. Developmental poverty alleviation is still a major strategy appropriate to the current level of economic development in rural areas of China, but this does not mean it will solve the issue of rural poverty alone. To benefit from developmental poverty alleviation, people in poverty must acquire the potential to develop, particularly a labour capability. If all the members of a household have lost their labour capabilities for various reasons, any form of poverty alleviation oriented around development will not be of assistance to them. Further, the development of human resources with a focus on basic education will generate an immense influence on the future living and welfare conditions of the minors in this household. But in the short term, it will still be necessary for them to be supported by social security policies in order to avoid falling into poverty.

The inability to access social security has caused a portion of the rural population to remain mired in absolute poverty. This group includes people who are physically or mentally disabled, elderly, orphaned, or have lost the capacity to work due to sickness, and are not supported or fostered by anyone else. In 2003, the Ministry of Civil Affairs carried out a national survey of those households suffering special difficulties in rural areas. Respondents were mainly 'three-NOs' rural households (whose members have no work capability, no source of income, and no legal supporter or foster parent) and those entitled to receive the 'five guarantees' (whose incomes fall short of the local minimum income levels). As indicated by this survey, the total size of the rural population in special difficulties in China is 25.42 million persons. Out of these, 19.72 million persons are in a state of absolute poverty and in dire need of assistance, and 5.7 million persons are in rural households entitled to receive the 'five guarantees' (Ministry of Civil Affairs 2004).

Since the National Bureau of Statistics of China used a bookkeeping approach for the survey, country survey departments would have avoided sampling those households lacking any bookkeeping capability or production activity, aiming to minimize the percentage of these special households in the total number of sampled households. As a consequence, a majority of the poor people who need social security assistance to get out of poverty, as per the statistics of the Department of Civil Affairs, was not categorized as part of the rural population in absolute poverty estimated by the National Bureau of Statistics of China.[1] In fact, these people all need to receive direct livelihood support.

The lack of necessary social security support has constrained the effects of developmental poverty alleviation. A majority of the people already helped out of poverty are vulnerable in economic terms, and often return to poverty after suffering even a single disaster or sickness period. This is chiefly because when their income falls, they have no cushion. Some may remain in poverty for a long time. Recognizing that it is no longer enough to conduct developmental poverty alleviation alone, the Government has agreed to establish a social security system covering both rural and urban areas by 2010, and has emphasized gradually establishing a minimum living standard system for rural residents (Ministry of Civil Affairs 2006b).

Background of the social security system for urban areas and evolution of relevant policies

Urban poverty did not loom large in China until after the 1990s. As a result of economic restructuring and particularly the reform of state-owned enterprises, which caused many workers to end up unemployed, the incidence rate of poverty rose by 10 percent from 1995 to 1999, and the poverty gap widened by 36 percent (Li Shi 2003). As urban poverty worsened, the Government began to implement anti-poverty policies in urban areas, and established an urban anti-poverty system chiefly comprising a minimum living standard system (see Box 4.2 for a description).

Box 4.2 The evolution of China's urban minimum living standard policies

China's minimum living standard system for urban residents has evolved in four stages.

Stage 1 was the exploration stage. From 1993 to the first half of 1997, China put into force minimum living standard policies for urban areas first in Shanghai and then in a couple of other coastal cities. In June 1993, Shanghai implemented a minimum living standard system that set a subsidy standard of RMB 120 yuan per person per month on average. In May 1994, the Ministry of Civil Affairs officially announced: 'it is one development objective of the civil affairs work in the future and even until the end of this century to gradually grant subsidies to qualified urban residents according to the local security line for bare subsistence' (Duoji Cairang 2001). In November 1996, the Shanghai Municipal Government took the lead in the country by promulgating the 'Shanghai Municipal Measures for Social Welfare', under which 'social welfare refers to a social security system in which governmental departments and other pertinent organizations jointly bear the responsibility of providing those urban residents in the concerned city, whose living standards fall short of the minimum living standard line, with necessary material assistance'. In some places, most of the people receiving such subsidies were those who had already received financial assistance from civil affairs departments for years.

Stage 2 involved the formation of minimum security policies (1997 to the first half of 2001). In September 1997, the State Council officially released the 'Notice with Regard to the Establishment of a Minimum Living Standard System for Urban Residents in China', and unambiguously underscored the need for a minimum living standard system for urban residents during the 'Ninth Five-Year-Long National Development Plan'. This would enable urban residents to receive a guarantee for their bare subsistence. The notice also specified who would be entitled to receive minimum security – namely, those urban residents whose per capita household incomes fall short of the local minimum living standard lines and whose domiciliary registries are kept within urban authorities. These people are in three categories: (1) urban residents who have no source of income, no work capability and no legal supporter or foster; (2) urban residents who are unable to get employment while receiving unemployment subsidies or after the expiry of the period of unemployment subsidies, and whose per capita household incomes fall short of the minimum living standard lines; and (3) urban residents who are employed or laid-off, and whose per capita household incomes still fall short of the minimum living standard lines after withdrawing their wages or minimum wages and basic living subsidies, or are retirees whose per capita household incomes still fall short of the minimum living standard lines after withdrawing their retirement pensions. This notice also stipulated that the security lines should be determined by the local people's governments; the country would not implement a uniform security line for bare subsistence. In September 1999, the State Council officially promulgated the 'Regulations on Minimum Living Standards for Urban Residents'. That year, the Government poured RMB 400 million yuan into subsidies for people with financial hardships. In 2000, the amount of such subsidies was increased to RMB 800 million yuan.

Stage 3 was the implementation of minimum security policies (the second half of 2001 to 2002). In this stage, the size of the population entitled to the minimum living standard system rose rapidly from 4.02 million persons to 20.64 million persons. In 2001, because the country quickened the restructuring of state-owned enterprises, laid-off workers and their household members faced greater livelihood hardships, which caused some social instability. In August 2001, the Government decided to invest another RMB 1.5 billion yuan, in addition to the budgeted RMB 800 million yuan, to boost the implementation of the minimum living standard system in urban areas. In early 2002, the budget was increased to RMB 4 billion yuan, most of which has been used for minimum livelihood subsidies.

Stage 4 entailed the reinforcement of minimum security policies. In this stage, the size of the population entitled to the minimum living standard subsidies has remained largely the same since 2003. Nevertheless, the Government has continued investing more funds for implementation, with the amount increasing by up to RMB 1 billion yuan on an annual basis, thus rising to 11.2 billion yuan in 2005. Fund management practices have been standardized. Since 2002, many local governments have begun to manage the minimum security system by the categorization of targeted groups. This mainly involves separating those youngsters with a capability for work from those people without this capability, in order to help the former find employment. So far, the minimum livelihood subsidies cover medical care, employment, schooling and housing (Wang Zhenyao 2006).

Unavailability of social security for circulating populations in rural areas

With the speedy economic growth of China and her accelerating drive towards urbanization, more rural residents and labourers have left their homes and arrived in urban areas and developed regions to seek job opportunities. According to a sample survey of rural households and villages conducted by the National Bureau of Statistics of China across the country, the number of outgoing rural labourers has been rising annually, and reached 132 million persons in 2006. According to a quick survey in May 2005 conducted by the Ministry of Labour and Social Security, the total number of rural labourers in urban areas is about 89.07 million persons. Allowing a 5 percent omission, the actual number of rural labourers in urban areas may approach 100 million persons (Topical Research Group of the Ministry of Labour and Social Security 2006).

Owing to a public management system that segregates urban and rural areas, and also because urban residents have fewer sources of income than rural residents do, it was essential to consider the demands of urban residents when initially establishing the urban livelihood security system. But within a market economy mechanism that features an increasingly mobile population, a poverty alleviation system characterized by a segregation of urban and rural areas has demonstrated an increasing number of defects. The nearly 100 million rural residents in urban areas have no access to any social welfare or security, but they cannot turn alternatively to the poverty alleviation policies for rural areas. They are, in short, a group ignored by policy makers.

Most rural labourers in urban areas are engaged in high-labour, high-risk jobs. They receive no guarantees at work, their accommodation and sanitation conditions are poor, and they do not have equal access to educational and medical services. Many suffer discrimination. When they fall into poverty, they cannot receive social assistance, in normal circumstances. Such grave disparities have given rise to crime and other social problems.

THE EFFECTS OF POVERTY ALLEVIATION POLICIES IN RURAL AREAS

An overall assessment of developmental poverty alleviation

China's investments in rural poverty alleviation

The central and local governments have devoted vast funds to implement poverty alleviation policies based on rural development. Some international organizations, non-governmental organizations and other types of social organizations have also made investments. In the past two decades, the total investment made by the central Government in production related to poverty alleviation has topped RMB 150 billion yuan, taking up 2 percent to 3 percent of its total fiscal expenditures. Governmental financial institutions have issued credit for poverty alleviation totalling over RMB 160 billion yuan. The central Government has invested more than RMB 10 billion yuan in poor regions to boost education and health care. In the same period, local governments have contributed over RMB 70 billion yuan to poverty alleviation, while the amount from international and social organizations is estimated to be upwards of RMB 100 billion yuan.

Since the early 1980s, the central Government's poverty alleviation investments have primarily involved three areas: (1) construction funds invested in the Dingxi and Hexi regions of Gansu Province, and the Xihaigu region of Ningxi Province since 1983, the budgetary development fund added in 1986 and the newly added poverty alleviation fund in 1997 (to be shortened as 'budgetary development funds'); (2) food for work funds since 1985; and (3) interest-subsidized loans for poverty alleviation initiated in 1986 and managed by the Agricultural Bank of China.[2]

From 1986 to 2005, the poverty alleviation investments in these three areas, calculated according to their current values, totalled RMB 322.8 billion yuan, including interest-subsidized loans of RMB 167.1 billion yuan, food-for-work funds of RMB 83.4 billion yuan and budgetary development funds of RMB 72.3 billion yuan. According to a calculation based on the constant price in 1986, the total amount of poverty alleviation funds for all three areas grew from RMB 4.3 billion in 1986 to RMB 12.1 billion yuan in 2004, representing an annual average growth rate of 6.1 percent.[3] Due to high inflation, the amount of poverty alleviation funds calculated according to the constant price actually fell annually before 1990. From 1991 to 1994, this amount rose due to a sharp increase in the amount of food-for-work funds. Compared to 1986, the actual amount of poverty alleviation funds in 1996 fell by 5 percent. The increase in the amount of poverty alleviation funds invested by the central Government mainly happened after 1996, when investments until 2004 recorded an annual growth rate of 14.9 percent on average (see Figure 4.3). The central Government increased its investments in poverty alleviation under the 'Eight-Seven Poverty Alleviation Plan'.

In most periods, more than half of poverty alleviation funds have been interest-subsidized loans, making them the main source of financing for poverty reduction. After a sharp increase from 1997 to 2002, however, the amount of interest-subsidized loans started to fall in 2003, and dropped by 56 percent by 2005. This caused a steep dive in the total amount of poverty alleviation funds. The amount of food-for-work funds reached an apex in the mid 1990s. Only budgetary development funds increased at a stable pace after 1996 (see Figure 4.3).

Apart from the three types of poverty alleviation funds just described, specific government departments have implemented poverty alleviation plans

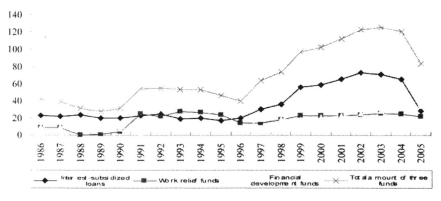

Figure 4.3 Trends in the three kinds of poverty alleviation investments made by the central Government (constant price in 1986, RMB 100 million yuan).

Source: Calculated by the authors of this report according to data offered by the Poverty Alleviation Office under the State Council, the Ministry of Finance, the National Development and Reform Commission, and the Agricultural Bank of China.

and investments directly targeted to poor regions. The largest current project is the national effort to provide compulsory education in poor regions, which is being implemented by the Ministry of Education. This project is mainly targeted to state-specified and province-specified poverty-stricken counties. Phase I began at the end of 1995. In 2000, the central Government invested RMB 3.9 billion yuan, and Phase II was initiated under the 'Tenth Five-Year-Long National Development Plan' for 2001 to 2005. The Government invested an additional RMB 5 billion yuan (Jin Lian 2006).

In conformity with regulations for the management of poverty alleviation funds, the Government requests local governments to offer counterpart funding when poverty alleviation funds other than credit loans are involved. In previous years, the required ratio for such funding was 1:1, but as the governments in poverty-stricken regions mostly face severe financial constraints, they generally cannot comply. In the beginning of this century, when the scheme for rural poverty alleviation began, the central Government did not put forward any specific requirement for counterpart funding; however, it still requests local governments to invest more funds in poverty alleviation. According to surveillance data on 523 poor counties provided by the National Bureau of Statistics of China, from 1998 to 2001, up to 34.6 percent of all food for work funds and 16.1 percent of the total amount of budgetary development funds came from local governments at all levels. Local government funding has been falling from year to year, however (Li Wen and Wang Sangui 2004).

Based on the average percentage of counterpart funds contributed by local governments between 1998 and 2001, the poverty alleviation funds contributed by local governments from 1986 to 2001 were estimated to total about RMB 26.8 billion yuan. In addition, in each year, provincial, municipal and prefecture or county-level governments allocated some financial funds for poverty alleviation in poor counties. According to the same data source, from 1998 to 2001, those funds comprised approximately 33 percent of the total amount of budgetary development funds of the central Government.

Projects for compulsory education in poor regions have a higher percentage of their funds supplied by local governments. According to data from the Ministry of Education, the counterpart funds contributed by local governments in the two phases of work under the compulsory education project in poor regions are 1.22 times the amount of financial allocations by the central Government on average. The percentage of such counterpart funds contributed by local governments in the total amounts of centrally allocated financing has dropped from 223 percent in Phase I to 20 percent in Phase II (Jin Lian 2006).

Apart from poverty alleviation investments made by the central Government, local governments and state-owned financial institutions, other funds from various channels have been raised by social organizations formed to reduce poverty and encouraged by the central Government. As estimated by researchers, the amount of these funds comprised about one quarter of overall financing. Since the mid 1990s, funds invested in poverty-stricken regions by these organizations have totalled RMB 113.7 billion yuan (Li Zhou and Cao Jianhua 2006).

Distribution and delivering of funds

The central Government's poverty alleviation funds have been primarily distributed to central and western China, as well as major counties with relatively grave poverty. Credit funds for poverty alleviation, however, have deviated from poverty-stricken counties. As noted above, while investments from the central Government have constantly increased, those made by local governments have been falling.

According to surveillance data from the National Bureau of Statistics of China, although the central Government largely enhanced its poverty alleviation investments from 1998 to 2001, the amount of funds directly invested in poor counties has decreased on a yearly basis, principally because an increasing amount of funds specified for poverty alleviation has failed to arrive in poor counties. From 1998 to 2001, the total amount of loans for poverty alleviation issued by the central Government was up by 21.99 percent, but the amount ending up in poor counties fell by 27.51 percent. The amount of budgetary development funds directly poured into poor counties was up by 61 percent, far beyond the average growth rate of 16 percent for the country's total amount of budgetary development funds, which indicates that budgetary development funds have played an increasingly important role in poor counties. The amount of food for work funds sent into poor counties increased by 6.98 percent. The percentage of food for work funds contributed by local governments out of the central Government's total dropped from 42.92 percent to 25.86 percent, and the percentage of budgetary development funds contributed by local governments out of the central Government's total fell from 27.67 percent to 9.79 percent (Li Wen and Wang Sangui 2004).

With the increased focus on poverty alleviation in central and western China under the 'Eight-Seven Poverty Alleviation Plan', a larger portion of poverty alleviation funds was distributed to these two regions. From 1998 to 2001, the average sums allocated by the central Government and distributed to rural residents in poor counties in western, central and eastern China were RMB 92 yuan, RMB 63 yuan and RMB 7 yuan per person, respectively. Adding on local government and other sources of funds, the amounts come to RMB 130 yuan, RMB 101 yuan and RMB 43 yuan, respectively. On average, the per capita amount of poverty alleviation funds distributed by the central Government to those residents in time-honoured revolutionary base regions, those regions populated by national minorities and remote regions was 37 percent more than funds distributed to other poor counties.

A quantitative analysis shows the distribution of poverty alleviation funds among poor counties mainly relies on their degree of poverty and population size, with extra consideration for regions with time-honoured revolutionary bases or national minorities, or that are remote. When the incidence rate of poverty in a poor county rises by one percentage point, the per capita amount of poverty alleviation funding from the central Government will go up by RMB 0.9 yuan. This indicates that both the central Government and the provincial governments have taken full account of the degrees of poverty in poor counties when distributing poverty alleviation funds. When the size of a rural population in a poor county expands by 10,000 people, however, the per capita amount of poverty alleviation funding from the central Government will fall by RMB 2.44 yuan. Counties with a larger population face a disadvantage because of inadequate consideration being given to population.

The per capita amount of funds distributed to counties with national minorities is RMB 14 yuan more than that distributed to other counties with the same conditions in other respects. The per capita amount of funds for remote counties is RMB 67 yuan more. The per capita amount of funds for time-honoured revolutionary bases was RMB 26 yuan less, mainly because loans for poverty alleviation and food for work funds are made available there in relatively small amounts. Disparities exist among provinces in the distribution of poverty alleviation funds (Li Wen and Wang Sangui 2004).

Selection of targets for poverty alleviation

One of the most striking characteristics of poverty alleviation in rural China is 'regional targeting' – all public poverty alleviation plans and investments are targeted to certain regions, instead of the poor population directly. For many years, poor counties were the basic units targeted by poverty alleviation investments. Following 2001, poor villages have become the basic units. Box 4.3 describes the determination of poor counties and villages.

Box 4.3 Determining poor counties and villages

Poor counties

In 1986, the Leading Group for Poverty Alleviation and Development of the State Council determined there were 258 state-designated poor counties. The main yardstick was a per capita net income in 1985 of less than RMB 150 yuan. The standard for revolutionary base regions and autonomous counties populated by people of national minorities was increased to RMB 200 yuan. For certain time-honoured revolutionary base regions that have contributed heavily to China's revolution and a small number of autonomous counties with special financial hardships in Inner Mongolia, Qinghai and Xinjiang, the standard was increased to RMB 300 yuan (Poverty Alleviation Office of the State Council 1989). Among the counties determined as poor, 83 had peasants earning a per capita net income below RMB 150 yuan; 82 had incomes between

---

RMB 150 yuan and RMB 200 yuan; and 93 had incomes between RMB 200 yuan and RMB 300 yuan. Only one third of these counties had a per capita net income of RMB 150 yuan (the lower limit). This indicates that the choices of poverty-stricken counties had strong political consideration. In 1987, 13 counties that were formerly revolutionary bases and two other counties were listed as state-designated poor counties. In 1988, 27 counties in pastoral or semi-pastoral areas were designated. Adding in the poor counties in the Dingxi and Hexi regions of Gansu Province, and the Xihaigu region of Ningxi Province, which have received extra financial assistance from the central Government since the early 1980s, the total number of state-specified poor counties reached 328 in 1988. Shaanxi, Gansu, Yunnan, Guangxi and Sichuan provinces hosted the largest numbers of poor counties; while the provinces with the highest percentages of poor counties were Gansu, Ningxia, Shaanxi, Qinghai and Guangxi. Provincial governments also designated their own poor counties to assist with funds from local governments. As of 1988, there were 379 provincial-level poor counties. In 1989, Hainan was taken out of Guangdong Province and defined as a province; the Government then designated three poor counties in Hainan. Up to 1993, the number of state-specified poor counties remained the same (Wang Sangui and Li Wen 2005).

Considering the changes since 1986, when the state first determined poor counties, during the 1993 formulation of the 'Eight-Seven Poverty Alleviation Plan', the Leading Group for Poverty Alleviation and Development of the State Council made adjustments to the state-specified poor counties. Specifically, it determined the new yardstick for defining poor counties as a per capita net income in 1990 of RMB 300 yuan. Only 326 counties qualified. Even so, the number of state-specified poor counties grew from 331 to 592, although the size of the rural population in poverty dropped from 125 million persons in 1985 to 80 million persons in 1993. As poor counties enjoy various subsidies and favourable resources, fierce opposition greets attempts to remove counties from the list of state-designated poor counties. As a consequence, very few poor counties lost their status, and many new counties were granted this status.

In 2001, the basic unit for targeting poverty alleviation investments was changed to poverty-stricken villages under the 'China Schema of Rural Development for Poverty Alleviation', but the Poverty Alleviation Leadership Group of the State Council still re-determined 592 national key poor counties as the main targets of poverty alleviation. Adjustments to the list of poor counties have taken place mainly through the subtraction of counties within the economically well-developed coastal regions, and the addition of some poor counties in central and western China, without changing the total number overall. To date, there are still 592 counties in certain regions populated by national minorities, time-honoured revolutionary base regions, frontier regions and some regions in special financial hardships within 21 provinces (municipalities and autonomous regions) in central and western China that are designated as the key poor counties targeted by poverty alleviation endeavours. Furthermore, thirty-three poverty-stricken counties in five provinces (Liaoning, Shandong, Guangdong, Fujian and Zhejiang) have been listed separately as subject to funding arrangements made by their provincial governments. Tibet was made a principal unit for funding, and had those five poor counties originally on its territory listed separately and placed under a separate fund allocated by the central Government. Other provinces in central and western China have warranted extra attention. Among others, Hunan and Sichuan provinces recorded a relatively big increase in the number of poor counties. Yunnan, Guizhou and Shaanxi provinces each host more than 50 poor counties. Guizhou, Yunnan and Gansu provinces have more than 50 percent of their counties under the special designation.

Poor villages

Due to the lack of comparable village-related data nationwide, local governments (especially county governments) are liable for determining poor villages. This requires first ranking all the villages in the county. According to the method recommended by the Project Experts Team of the Asian Development Bank, poverty alleviation departments at the county level have adopted the weighted poverty indicator (WPI) to rank the administrative villages. The WPI is worked out mainly through the combination of eight weighted indicators that reflect the basic living conditions of rural households and their community. These include livelihood poverty indicators (per capita grain output per annum, per capita cash income and ratio of un-refurbished housing); infrastructure poverty indicators (percentage of those households with limited access to drinkable water, percentage of natural villages with a stable power supply, and percentage of natural villages accessible by roads throughout all four seasons), and human resources indictors (the percentage of women who have suffered health problems for a long period, and the percentage of children of school age who have discontinued their studying). Except for the first two indicators, which are continuous, the other six are discrete indicators.

After the indicators are selected, the value and weight of each is determined with a participatory method. Because the conditions in poor regions in the country vary largely, the Poverty Alleviation Office of the State Council has allowed local poverty alleviation departments to make adjustments to recommended indicators when necessary, so as to reflect local circumstances. Within the same county, the indicators and their weights for the calculation of the WPI are identical, but they may vary across counties. Therefore, the ranking of poor villages will be comparable in the same county, but not across all counties. This may produce disparities among different poverty-stricken villages in different regions in terms of the degree of poverty, and further cause the accuracy of targeting interventions according to comparable indicators to drop dramatically.

It takes a great deal of time and energy, along with support from certain experts in participatory assessment, to determine poor villages by use of the participatory method. Local governments have not strictly followed the procedure recommended by the Poverty Alleviation Office of the State Council and the Asian Development Bank. Some local governments have employed easier and simpler methods. For example, Jiangxi Province first had its Provincial Poverty Alleviation Office determine the percentage of poor villages within its territory, and then had each poor township select its poor villages through voting by local cadres.[4]

The accuracy of the determination of poor counties and villages

China has designated most poor counties and poor villages as targets for poverty alleviation using an income measurement.[5] A portion of low-income counties and villages have not been designated, however, while certain high-income counties and villages have received this status. This indicates some deviation in the selection of poverty alleviation targets.

Figure 4.4 sets out the distribution of poor counties in different income groups in 1986. The figure makes clear that many counties with a low-income level have not been specified as poor counties. For instance, 50 percent (99 counties) in the lowest 10 percent income group were not determined as poor counties; and 62 percent (185 counties) in the lowest 15 percent to 25 percent income group were not considered poor counties. This indicates major gaps in coverage, an issue largely mitigated in 1993 through the re-determination of poor counties under the 'Eight-Seven Poverty Alleviation Plan'. Only 9.7 percent (18 counties) in the lowest 10 percent income group were not determined as poor counties, while 35 percent (96 counties) in the lowest 10 percent to 25 percent income group were not determined as poor counties. In 1993, however, a growing number of high-income counties were dubbed poverty-stricken counties. While 96 counties in the second lowest income group were not designated as poor counties, 124 counties and 39 counties were determined as poor counties in the third and fourth highest income groups, respectively, comprising 32 percent of the total number of poverty-stricken counties (Figure 4.5).[6]

To look at whether the 2001 decision to make poor villages the basic units targeted by poverty alleviation investments has proven a more accurate

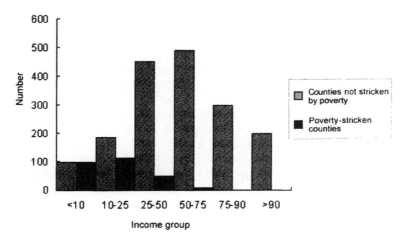

Figure 4.4 Distribution of poor counties in different income groups in 1986.
Source: Both the data and figure were provided by Park, Wang and Wu 2002.

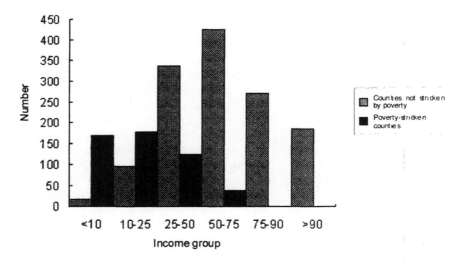

Figure 4.5 Distribution of poor counties in different income groups in 1993.
Source: Both the data and figure were provided by Park, Wang and Wu 2002.

approach than the designation of counties, Figure 4.6 sets out the distribution of designated poor and non-poor villages by different income groups. The data suggest that the lower the income level, the higher the percentage of poor villages: 55 percent of the poor villages were distributed in the lowest 20 percent income group, and 75 percent were in the lowest 40 percent income group. If income is the exclusive means of measurement, however, issues

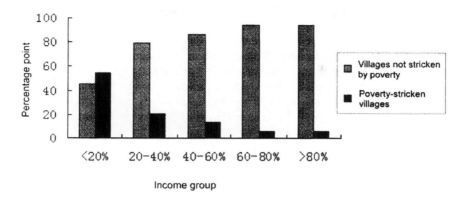

Figure 4.6 Distribution of poor villages by different income groups in 2001.

Source: Calculated according to data from the World Bank and the Rural Research Team of the National Bureau of Statistics of China.

related to incomplete coverage and omission still arise. Although a higher percentage of villages in lower-income groups were determined as poor, the lowest-income group still has 45 percent of villages not designated as such, suggesting that poverty alleviation investments have not yet reached a large portion of villages in a state of relative poverty. On the other hand, a large number of villages in the higher-income groups were designated as poor villages, e.g., 11 percent in the highest 40 percent income group were designated as targets of poverty investment, indicating poverty alleviation resources may leak into the pockets of high-income populations.

The reasons for these tendencies are clear. First, developed regions will employ a higher yardstick for determining poor villages than poor regions; therefore, the poor villages in developed regions might be categorized as a relatively high-income group. Second, the determination of poverty-stricken villages is not wholly conducted according to income level. A high-income village may have other indicators turn out on the low side, so it can still be considered a poor village under the weighted average method. Third, political and non-economic considerations may cause some low-income villages not to be determined as poor villages, even as some high-income villages are designated as such. Nevertheless, it is important to focus on the fact that a number of low-income villages are not classified as poor villages and do not benefit from the state's poverty alleviation policies and investments. In the case of a prolonged lack of support, they are likely to lag increasingly behind other villages.

Quantitative analysis indicates that those counties with a low-income level, low per capita grain output and a low degree of industrialization are more likely to be determined as poor counties. After other factors are controlled, those counties populated by national minorities or that are time-honoured revolutionary bases are much more likely to be determined as poor counties compared to others within the same province. Discrimination in poor county designation is also evident among provinces. Compared to their counterparts in Hebei Province, those counties in such provinces as Sichuan, Guizhou, Yunnan, Guangxi, Inner Mongolia, Gansu and Henan were 50 percent less likely to be determined as poor counties in 1986. By contrast, those counties in Fujian, Shandong and Hubei provinces, and the former Hainan region of the Guangdong Province were 30 percent more likely to be determined as poor counties. Although this situation shifted slightly in 1993 when the adjustment was made to the list of poor counties, provinces in southwestern China such as Sichuan, Guizhou, Yunnan and Guangxi, and other provinces such as Qinghai, Anhui and Hunan were still at a disadvantage (Park *et al.* 2002). As indicated by one study, villages with a low-income level, a high incidence rate of poverty, a remote location and a lack of social service facilities, and populated by national minorities or considered time-honoured revolutionary bases, are more likely to be determined as poor villages. Those villages with easy access to drinkable water and roads, and relatively high agricultural productivity are much less likely to be classified as poor (Wang *et al.* 2006).

What portion of the poor population is in poor counties and villages?

About half of the population in poverty resides in poor counties and villages. At present, the size of the poor population in counties targeted for poverty alleviation is larger than the size in poor villages. There have been different estimations of poverty coverage in poor counties. Data from the National Bureau of Statistics of China show that in 1992, 57 million poor people were living in poor counties, or 71 percent of the total poor population of 80 million persons. A small-scale survey of rural households, however, found a larger percentage of the poor population lives in counties not designated as poor.[7] According to a study conducted by the World Bank, nearly 50 percent of the poor in four provinces in southwestern China do not live in poor counties. By the end of 1998, only 21 million poor people were in state-specified poor counties. According to the latest World Bank estimate, based on data from a survey of households conducted by the National Bureau of Statistics of China in 2001, poor villages contained about 60 percent of the population in absolute poverty and 52 percent of the population below the low-income level, nationwide. Key poor counties contained 71 percent of the population in absolute poverty and 67 percent of the population below the low-income line.

One of the many reasons why poor counties have covered a larger percentage of the poor population is that the percentage of poverty-stricken counties in the national total (24.7 percent) is higher than the percentage of poor villages in the country's total number of villages (20.7 percent). Poor counties cover a larger segment of the rural population. Another important reason is that the error rate for determining poor villages in 2001 was far higher than that for designating poor counties in the same year. Analysis shows that the higher the poverty line, the lower the percentage of the poor population that poor villages and poor counties can cover out of the country's entire population in poverty (Wang *et al.* 2006).

Non-poor population in poor counties and villages

At present, more than four-fifths of the total population in poor counties and villages does not suffer absolute poverty. Therefore, implementing poverty alleviation projects still involves a second round of targeting. As China's poverty alleviation endeavours focus on certain regions, the population not stricken by poverty will likely benefit. Experience shows that the higher the percentage of the population not in poverty in poor counties and poor villages, the higher the probability of the leakage of poverty alleviation resources. To ensure the poor benefit, the blunt targeting of certain regions is inadequate.

The poor counties determined by the Government in the mid and late 1980s covered a rural population totalling about 100 million persons. According to a widely acknowledged estimation, about 60 percent of the poor population lived in poor counties; their wealthier neighbours comprised less than half the total population. With the increase in the number of poor counties and the sharp decrease in the size of the poor population, the situation shifted. Although the size of the population in absolute poverty fell from 125 million people in 1985 to 75 million people in 1993, when the country increased the number of poor counties to 592, the size of the benefited population rose from 106 million persons to 199 million persons (Wang Sangui and Li Wen 2005). Today, most of the households and people in poor counties are not below the poverty line. According to the latest World Bank calculation, based on data on households from the National Bureau of Statistics of China, when measured by the absolute poverty line, up to 84 percent of people in poor counties and villages in 2001 were not in poverty. When measured by the low-income line, 69 percent of people in poor counties could not be considered low income, and 72 percent of people in poor villages were not poor (Wang *et al.* 2006).

Making poor villages the major targets of poverty alleviation in 2001 seemed not to visibly enhance the accurate targeting of poverty alleviation investments. As the figures show, the size of the poor population in poor villages was less than that in poor counties, and the percentage of the non-poor population was higher. The decision to target poor counties only in central and western China was intended to enhance the accuracy of targeting and increase the population covered by poverty alleviation in poor counties. But not all poor villages are in central and western China – the figures are 46.8 percent, 33 percent and 20.2 percent in western China, central China and the coastal region of eastern China plus northeastern China, respectively (see Figure 4.7).

Since poor villages in eastern China can cover only a small fraction of the poor population, the accuracy of the country's targeting through poor

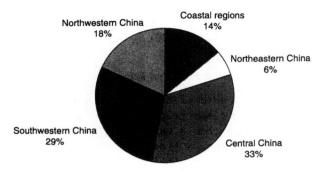

Figure 4.7 Geographical distribution of poor villages.

Source: Poverty Alleviation Office under the State Council.

villages has decreased. As indicated by an analysis conducted by the World Bank using data on households from the National Bureau of Statistics of China, the error rate in determining poor villages in non-western regions and non-poor counties was far higher than in western regions and poor counties, thus reducing the accuracy of village targeting (Wang *et al.* 2006).

Effects of poverty alleviation investments

China's rural development strategies to reduce poverty have accomplished important results. According to surveillance and survey data, from 1997 to 2001, 30.73 million households in state-specified poor counties received poverty alleviation support (for 124.69 million person-times). The total volume of the labour force employed by poverty alleviation projects reached 17.24 million person-times, and these projects formed fixed assets worth RMB 26.9 billion yuan in total. The total volume of the labour force that relocated to other regions was 83.43 million person-times. The total acreage of new forests amounted to 3.25 million hectares. The 592 state-specified poor counties constructed croplands with a total area of 60.12 million *mu* in total, built 320,000 km of new roads, erected 360,000 km of power transformation and transmission wires, and provided 53.51 million persons and 48.36 million animals with drinkable water. By 2000, administrative villages had been supplied with power (95 percent), radio and television (95 percent), roads (89 percent), mail services (69 percent) and telephone services (67 percent), respectively – these indicators have come close to the country's averages (Press Office of the State Council 2001).

After 2001, most poverty alleviation investments went into poor villages. In recent years, evident changes have taken place in infrastructure and public services. From 2002 to 2005, the percentages of natural villages furnished with road, power, telephone and television services within poor villages rose by 8.1 percent, 4.1 percent, 26.7 percent and 6.8 percent, respectively. The percentage of administrative villages furnished with a medical care outlet out of all poor villages rose by 8.4 percent. The changes in infrastructure and public service facilities in state-specified poor villages have been more apparent than those in designated poor counties, and also far more evident than average changes in the country (see Figure 4.8).

Assessing the major economic growth indicators of poor counties in terms of grain output, agricultural production and the per capita net income of peasants shows these are higher than the country's averages. From 1994 to 2000, the total value-added of farms in state-specified poor counties grew at an annual average of 7.5 percent, higher than the country's average of 7 percent. Grain output had an annual average growth rate of 1.9 percent, 3.2 times the country's average of 0.6 percent. The per capita net income of peasants grew to RMB 1,337 yuan from RMB 648 yuan, posting an annual average growth rate of 12.8 percent, which was 2 percentage points higher than the country's average (Press Office of the State Council 2001 and the National Bureau of Statistics of China 2001). From 2002 to 2005, the growth rate of per capita net income in poor villages was higher than that in poor counties and the country's average. On top of that, the growth rates of the per capita consumption and food consumption expenditures in poor villages also turned out higher than those in state-specified counties, but lower than the country's averages (Figure 4.9).

After controlling for various factors, one study finds that the growth rates of peasants' incomes and consumption in designated poor counties are markedly higher than those in non-poor counties. The World Bank researchers used data from a survey of households in four provinces (namely Guizhou,

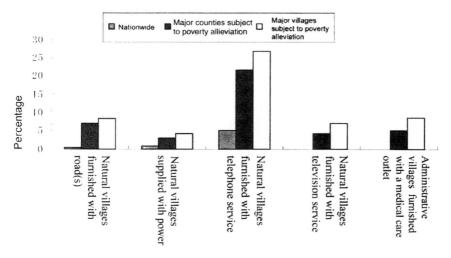

Figure 4.8 Changes in infrastructure and public service facilities from 2002 to 2005.

Source: Department of Rural Affairs of the National Bureau of Statistics of China 2006 and the Rural Survey Group of the National Bureau of Statistics of China 2003.

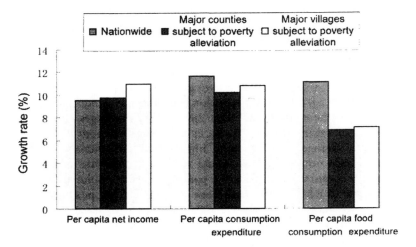

Figure 4.9 Comparison between income growth and consumption growth from 2002 to 2005.

Source: Department of Rural Affairs of the National Bureau of Statistics of China 2006 and the Rural Survey Group of the National Bureau of Statistics of China 2003.

Yunnan, Guangxi and Guangdong) in southwestern China to estimate the impact of poverty investments, and found that from 1985 to 1990, the growth rate of consumption among rural households in state-designated poor counties was 1.1 percent higher than that of households in non-poor counties, although such a trend was offset by other factors. The estimated rate of return generated by poverty alleviation investments was 12 percent (Ravallion and Jalan 1999).[8] By using county level data between 1981 and 1995 from the Ministry of Agriculture, some scholars analysed income growth in poor counties and non-poor counties, and discovered the growth rate of the per capita net income of peasants in the former was 2.2 percent higher than in the latter between 1986 and 1992, and 0.9 percent higher between 1992 and 1995. The rate of return generated by poverty alleviation investments, reckoned on the basis of such data, was 15.5 percent in the first stage and 11.6 percent in the second stage (Park, Wang and Wu 2002).[9]

In studies on the effects of poverty alleviation funds in various sectors, some scholars have concluded that agricultural investments directly granted to rural households had a markedly positive bearing on their income growth. Investments made in township enterprises and county enterprises had no influence on per capita income. Some agricultural infrastructure (such as terraced fields, etc.) do not generate a marked influence on agricultural output (Rozelle *et al.* 1998).[10] An analysis using household survey data and poverty investment data from poor counties from 1998 to 2001 collected by the National Bureau of Statistics of China found that poverty alleviation investments had a strong influence upon rural households' incomes in the short run. Further analysis showed that each extra RMB 1 yuan invested in agriculture can push up the per capita net income by RMB 0.17 yuan. When the per capita investment in small scale non-agricultural activities increases by RMB 1 yuan, per capita net income will go up by RMB 0.76 yuan. Investments in infrastructure did not generate a heavy influence on rural households' incomes in the short run (Wang Sangui,, Li Wen and Li Yun 2004). Since 2002, the influence of poverty alleviation investments in various sectors has been increasingly inconspicuous in terms of people in absolute poverty (Li Yingxing 2006).

The research results cited here suggest that China's poverty alleviation investments have, by and large, produced benefits for poor regions, and enabled the average growth rates of income and consumption in designated poor counties to climb higher than in non-designated poor counties with identical conditions. Among poverty alleviation investments, those directly related to agriculture and the productive activities of rural households (such as small business and services), when compared with investments in industry and infrastructure, generate greater income growth at least in the short run. Due to the limited availability of data, the findings of the surveys described here were all estimations of the average income and consumption levels in concerned counties. Although they indicated faster growth in state-specified counties, it is not clear to what extent the benefits were evenly distributed among the poorer and wealthier groups. Considering the mode of regional targeting and the existence of a large proportion of non-poor population within poor counties, it is necessary to further analyse internal distribution in both poor counties and poor villages. The following section will discuss in detail the influence of poverty alleviation investments on poor villages and different groups of people living there.

Major developmental poverty alleviation measures and their effects

Integrated village development: participatory community development practices

Progress of integrated village development

Integrated village development, as one of the key strategies in China's current focus on rural development based on poverty alleviation, is designed to use a relatively large amount of funds and other resources to enable supported villages to significantly improve their infrastructure and public services, production and living conditions, industrial development, etc. within a relatively short period. It also facilitates the coordination of various projects to collectively generate benefits adequate for allowing all poor people to emerge from poverty. There is an emphasis on enhancing the capacity of poor communities and populations to be productive in a comprehensive way, with a balanced approach to potential risks.[11]

According to the results of a mid-term review conducted by the Poverty Alleviation Office under the State Council on the 'Scheme for Rural Development for Poverty Alleviation,' among the 106,000 poor villages in 21 provinces in central and western China,[12] 83 percent have already accomplished their respective planning for poverty alleviation. Ten provinces and autonomous regions, namely Hebei, Heilongjiang, Jiangxi, Hubei, Guangxi, Chongqing, Guizhou, Sichuan, Yunnan and Qinghai, have accomplished their poverty alleviation plans for all those poor villages on their respective territories. However, Shanxi Province has accomplished poverty alleviation plans for only 9 percent of the poor villages on its territory; Gansu Province has done so for only 34 percent; and Jilin Province for only 41 percent (background report, Wang Sangui 2006a).

Overall, integrated village development based on village poverty alleviation plans has made obvious progress in terms of formulating plans, but implementation has been comparatively slow. The pace of implementation varies largely from one province to another, so the discrepancies need to be reduced. According to statistical data on 21 provinces and autonomous regions, the number of poor villages that took the lead in 2005 to initiate integrated village development work comprised only 32 percent of all poor villages in the country, and made up 43 percent of the poor villages that have already accomplished their village poverty alleviation plans. So far, half of the decade for implementation of the 'Scheme for Rural Development for Poverty Alleviation' has passed, but nearly 70 percent of the tasks involved still need to be achieved. If no effective measures are taken soon, it will be quite difficult to complete the scheme by 2010 (Wang Sangui 2006a).

Demands for funds and paid-in investments

As per statistical data in 70,000 poor villages in 16 provinces,[13] the total demand for poverty alleviation funds planned by each of the poor villages is RMB 2.28 million yuan, on average. In these 16 provinces, 12 saw the average demand turn out to be between RMB 1 million yuan and RMB 3 million yuan. Only Guangxi and Heilongjiang had this figure exceed RMB 3 million yuan, with it reaching over RMB 13 million in Guangxi in particular. The figure fell short of RMB 1 million yuan only in Hunan and Yunnan. According to a field survey, Hunan Province re-did its village-level poverty alleviation plans for poor villages in 2004 and determined funding according to pre-set quotas. The amounts were far below those worked out in 2001 based on actual demands.

According to the same statistical data, by mid 2005, the average poverty alleviation investment in each poor village was RMB 340,000 yuan, constituting only 15 percent of the requested amount. Even assuming that all funds have already been used in poor villages that have initiated the integrated village development work (in reality, only 32 percent have done so), the average amount invested per village was merely RMB 960,000 yuan. This falls far short of the planned investment and actual demand. Only Jilin, Jiangxi, Henan, Guangxi, Ningxia and Xinjiang recorded an average investment in excess of RMB 500,000 yuan. In Hubei, Hunan, Hainan and Qinghai, the amount was less than RMB 200,000 yuan. The findings of a survey conducted for this report on role-model villages were more worrying. A majority of poor villages, except for a few receiving support from certain institutions directly under provincial governments and also taken care of by major cadres, have either failed to garner any poverty alleviation investment or have secured only a small amount. Owing to its shortage of funds, Xiangxi Autonomous Prefecture in Hunan Province had to scale back village-level poverty alleviation plans for each poor village on its territory in 2004, and required each village not to request more than RMB 400,000 yuan. The relevant poverty alleviation department pointed out that it is still hardly possible to furnish each village with RMB 400,000 yuan. It appears impossible to enable an entire village to eliminate poverty without additional resources.

Pingyu county of Henan Province planned about 500 development projects for poverty alleviation over a period of seven years. These would require funding in excess of RMB 100 million yuan (including food for work funds), along with RMB 100 million yuan in credit. The credit was to go towards industrial development and loans for rural households. But this county can only collect funds of about RMB 50 million yuan. Even if all available poverty alleviation funds are used in a centralized way, only two to three villages each year can receive funds out of all those that have already initiated the integrated development work. And only some projects can be implemented. In addition, a shortage of counterpart funds means that the financing projects receive in reality is often less than the planned funds, causing the project to shrink, fail to operate properly or make up the shortfall by various means.

A primary reason for funding shortages is the failure to integrate available poverty alleviation funds in integrated village development strategies, plus the fact that loans for poverty alleviation, which comprise more than half of poverty alleviation funds, are not used in poor villages or for poor households. Finally, only a portion of food for work funds ends up in poor villages. Most funds for integrated village development come from budgetary allocations for poverty alleviation and some of the food for work funds, but shortages clearly have a negative influence.

Effects of integrated village development

Though integrated village development has progressed slowly due to funding shortages, the implementation of various poverty alleviation projects has visibly improved production and living conditions in poor villages. Incomes have increased. As indicated by a survey conducted for this report, poor villages that have fully implemented integrated village development have seen the per capita net income of peasants go up by more than 50 percent within one or two years. Due to improved roads and communications, many poor villages can explore new means of production and build upon their comparative advantages. Better infrastructure has also boosted the transfer of labourers from poor villages, increasing rural incomes.

To better structure analysis of the influence of integrated village development upon poor villages and rural households, this report has used data on poverty alleviation investments from a survey of sampled villages and rural households provided by the National Bureau of Statistics of China and the World Bank. Table 4.2 shows statistics on income growth for rural households in poor villages, non-poor villages, poor villages that have initiated the integrated village development work,[14] and those villages that have not. From 2001 to 2004, among all the samples, the increase of per capita income in non-poor villages was 27 percent higher than in poor villages. The increase in absolute income for wealthier villages in poor counties was 10 percent higher than in poor villages. A comparison of villages that have initiated the integrated village development work and those that have not reveals that, among all the samples, the increase in absolute income in the former was equal to that of the latter. But when the former are located in poor counties, the income increase is 22 percent higher than for other poor villages.

From 2001 to 2004, the income growth rates of poor villages exceeded those of non-poor villages, and the income growth rates of villages that have initiated integrated village development work exceeded those in villages that have not implemented it. The total income growth rate of all sampled poor villages in the country was 6 percent higher than for non-poor villages, and

Table 4.2 Income growth rates for different categories of villages (2001 to 2004)

	Growth of net income (RMB yuan/person)	Total growth rate (%)	Annual average growth rate (%)
All poor villages	367.79	20.58	6.86
All non-poor villages	467.76	14.54	4.85
Poor villages in poor counties	292.42	22.1	7.37
Non-poor villages in poor counties	321.46	18.68	6.23
All villages that have initiated the integrated village development work	455.51	23.72	7.91
All villages that have not initiated the integrated village development work	455.23	14.9	4.97
Villages in poor counties that have already initiated the integrated village development work	367.21	25.08	8.36
Villages in poor counties that have not initiated the integrated village development work	300.85	19.23	6.41

Source: Calculated based on data provided by the World Bank and the Rural Survey Group of the National Bureau of Statistics of China.

2 percent higher than the annual average income growth rate. In poor counties, the income growth rate of poor villages was 3.4 percent higher than for non-poor villages and 1.1 percent higher than the annual average income growth rate. The income growth rate of rural households in villages with integrated village development was visibly higher than that of ordinary poor villages, while villages in poor counties implementing the integrated village development strategy have registered the fastest income growth rate. Specifically, their annual average income growth rate reached 8.36 percent, 2 percent higher than for villages in poor counties that have not adopted the strategy, and 3.4 percent higher than for villages that haven't done so among all the samples. To sum up, both poor villages and those villages pursuing the integrated village development work have recorded a faster income growth rate, which demonstrates that the integrated village development and other poverty alleviation policies have played a role in enhancing the incomes of rural households in poor villages.

After controlling for other factors, quantitative analysis has also indicated that, from 2001 to 2004, the income growth rate of rural households in poor villages was about 2 percent higher than for rural households in non-poor villages within the same county. This result was statistically significant. In the same period, the income growth rate of rural households in villages with the integrated village development work was 8 to 9 percent higher than for rural households in villages without it. This result was not statistically significant, however, which indicates that there are large disparities in income growth among rural households in villages with the integrated village development work. Although on average, income growth in these villages was much greater than in those without the strategy, this may have come from only a portion of the rural households (background report, Wang Sangui 2006a). A further analysis of different types of rural households in villages with the strategy discovered that comparatively rich households grasped most benefits generated by poverty alleviation investments. Their income growth rate was 6.6 to 9.6 percent higher than for wealthy rural households in villages without the strategy. Their consumption growth rate was 8.8 to 11.4 percent higher. In contrast, no visible disparity in income and consumption growth exists between poor rural households in villages with the strategy and those in villages without it. The integrated village development work thus clearly benefits rural households that are relatively well off (Park and Wang 2006).

Why can't these projects equally benefit the poor population? This report's survey of poor regions revealed that many poor people are excluded because they lack the capacity to participate. Many projects targeting rural households request candidates to offer counterpart funds (whose amounts usually exceed 50 percent of total project costs). Those in absolute poverty simply cannot afford this. For a water cabinet project surveyed as an example, rural households had to pay 3.3 times the amount of the state's support fund; a biomass pool project required 3.6 times. In some cases, the poorest people do not benefit from public investment projects (such as the construction of roads and schools) because they cannot afford the service charges or do not use the facilities because of a poor match with their needs.

Similar problems have existed for production-related projects. For industrial development projects allowed interest-subsidized loans because they contribute to poverty alleviation, commercial banks have been formulating increasingly strict requirements in terms of project scale and profitability. Increased requirements for rural households applying for loans exclude numerous poor rural households. Industrial projects supported by financial allocations for poverty alleviation or funds conferred by forest or agriculture authorities are limited in their reach because they also require counterpart funds.

In short, the current project implementation practices have actually excluded people in absolute poverty and benefited wealthier people. It is necessary to stress, however, that the low average income level in poor villages means that a large portion of the population above the average still have very limited resources.

Training for labour transfers that help poor people tap the benefits of economic growth

Training to support labour force transfer is one of the three major poverty alleviation tasks under the 'Scheme of Rural Development for Poverty Alleviation' (Poverty Alleviation Leadership Group of the State Council 2001). In August 2004, the Poverty Alleviation Office of the State Council issued a 'Notice on Strengthening Training with Regard to the Transfer of the Labour Force in Poor Regions'. This symbolized the official start of this kind of training. Poverty alleviation organs in all provinces, cities and counties have subsequently used their local secondary technical schools and taken other measures to offer training, and to provide guidance on organizing and funding relocation.

In China, economic growth in urban areas is faster than in rural areas. Growth in economically better-developed eastern China is faster than in poverty-stricken regions of western China. Fast-growing cities and regions clearly offer many more job opportunities and higher wages. Integrated village development is intended to enhance productivity in poor regions through various poverty alleviation projects as a whole, in order to boost incomes and help poor rural households out of poverty. Training for labour force migration increases the qualifications and skills of the labour force in poor regions, and helps them obtain opportunities to work in industries and services other than agriculture, especially in urban areas and well-developed regions. This results in increased incomes and better living conditions for the transferred labour force and their household members.

The Asian Development Bank worked with the Poverty Alleviation Office of the State Council to conduct a pilot study on the mode of rural poverty alleviation in two villages within Guizhou Province since 1999. The aim was to determine the usefulness of infrastructure in alleviating poverty by providing small-scale facilities and technical support. The investments poured into these villages were four to five times the average amount made by the Government under integrated village development. The study found that although the two villages absorbed huge investments, received intensive support from outsourced experts, and saw an overwhelming percentage of their villagers take an active role in development projects, income growth over the five years of the initiative still largely resulted from labour exportation (Zhou Furong 2004). It follows that it is essential to use training to help rural households in poor regions find job opportunities outside their immediate locality. Training can also help poor regions adapt to current conditions in the labour market (see Box 4.4).

Box 4.4　A description of China's labour market

China's labour market has an equilibrium between supply and demand, except for certain structural contradictions (National Information Centre 2005). First, it remains hard for graduates from universities and colleges to find jobs. Second, some economically developed coastal regions have begun to suffer a shortage of rural labourers. The Report of the Survey of the Shortage of Rural Labourers, compiled by the Topical Research Group of the Ministry of Labour and Social Security, showed these shortages have arisen chiefly in regions with a high density of manufacturing factories, such as the Pearl River Delta in Guangdong Province, the southeastern part of Fujian Province, the southeastern part of Zhejiang Province, etc. The overall shortage is estimated to be about 10 percent of the total number of rural labourers that can be employed in these regions. The Pearl River Delta suffers the severest shortage, up to 2 million persons in the first quarter of 2005, according to the local labour security organization and expert estimates.

Third, the shortage of skilled workers hinders economic development. The Ministry of Labour and Social Security conducted a sample survey of skilled workers in 40 cities in April 2005. It indicated that labourers at all technical levels are hotly sought after, but the shortage of technicians and senior technicians is most severe. The ratios between the total numbers of senior technicians, technicians, senior workers, intermediate workers and junior workers demanded by enterprises and the actual numbers of personnel applying for these positions were 2.59:1, 1.84:1, 1.68:1, 1.54:1 and 1.5:1, respectively. Thus far, the ratio between the total number of skilled workers whom enterprises demand and the actual number of candidates applying for skilled worker positions has been higher than the ratio between the total number of required engineering technicians and actual job candidates. Labourers with certain skills enjoy rosy career prospects (background report, Li Wen 2006).

Since 2001, some provinces in central and western China have offered labour transfer training on a trial basis. By 2004, such training prevailed across the country. The Poverty Alleviation Office of the State Council established 'Pilot Centres for Training with Regard to the Transfer of the Labour Force in Poor Regions' in eleven provinces in 2004. By June 2005, the number of these centres had grown to thirty, covering most provinces. Poverty alleviation departments in all provinces, cities and counties have created additional offerings. Data from fourteen provinces and municipalities[15] in central and western China offered by the Poverty Alleviation Office of the State Council show that by 2005, 1,499 training centres existed to support labour transfer in fourteen provinces, with an average of 107 centres per province. The numbers of provincial, prefecture/city and county centres are 216, 278 and 1,005, respectively (background report, Li Wen 2006).

Training centres are generally vocational technical schools. Poverty alleviation departments and rural cadres are responsible for recruiting trainees. As the schools have already accumulated years of experience in vocational technical trainings and established stable employment channels, entrusting them to organize training not only brings down the training costs, but also makes it easier to meet market demands. Poverty alleviation departments request training schools to sign tentative employment agreements with employers before selecting appropriate majors and providing training. Based on statistical data on thirty exemplary training centres offered by the Poverty Alleviation Office of the State Council, on average, each school offers ten majors, in mostly household services, food and beverages, security control, hospitality, construction, manufacturing and electronics assemblage (these industries usually require a large number of labourers). The length of training time may vary from one month to six months according to the major. At graduation, trainees normally receive junior certificates of technical competence from local labour authorities.

Training funds come from the financial allocations for poverty alleviation offered by state and local governments, but these cannot be used for fixed assets. Trainees must pay for living expenses. As indicated by one representative survey, the total cost of skills training for three months (including living expenses) is over RMB 2,000 yuan. Each trainee normally bears more than half of such a cost. According to data on fourteen provinces in western and central China from 2001 to 2004, the total amount of funds invested in the training bases in different provinces, cities and counties reached RMB 610 million yuan; each province invested RMB 16.71 million yuan a year, on average. Of the total investment, 61 percent came from the financial allocations for poverty alleviation (background report, Li Wen 2006).

The data also indicated that during the same period, a total of 2.42 million rural labourers in poor regions were trained. Among them, 1.57 million persons were employed inside their original provinces, comprising 65 percent of the total. About 670,000 persons were employed in provinces other than their original ones, or 28 percent of the total. According to one representative survey, a majority of the trainees can find jobs, which is not surprising at all in today's labour market with its shortage of skilled workers. The monthly wage for a probation period is normally RMB 500 yuan to RMB 800 yuan. After the official employment contract is signed, the monthly wage will go up to a range between RMB 600 yuan and RMB 1,000 yuan. Each trained labourer is able to earn a 'transfer income' of at least RMB 3,000 yuan for his or her household within one or two years after such training. Assuming each rural household has an average headcount of four persons, the per capita net income of each household can be increased by RMB 750 yuan, thus helping it to emerge from poverty. Relative to the country's investment of RMB 600 yuan to RMB 1,000 yuan, such a rate of return and the consequent poverty alleviation effects are clearly satisfactory[16] (background report, Li Wen 2006).

Like the integrated village development work, current labour force training faces issues related to the selection of beneficiaries. Although it is stipulated that poor villages and households shall take precedence over others in receiving the training, in reality, trainees are those labourers in poor counties who are willing and able to take part. Many poorer people cannot participate because they are unable to pay the living expenses of more than RMB 1,000 yuan per person. Their chance of participating is much lower. One survey shows that when training projects begin, households with close relations with the organizers (especially cadres at village level) are more likely to take part ahead of others. It is necessary to carefully consider how training can reach more poor households.

Credit loans for poverty alleviation: conflicts between poverty alleviation goals and fund efficiency and security

Since the mid 1980s, credit loans for poverty alleviation have been important in rural areas. Among the three major types of poverty alleviation funds granted by the central Government, interest-subsidized loans constitute more than half the total. When the 'Interest-Subsidized Loan Plan' was implemented initially in 1986, the Government thought that the main roadblocks to income growth for poor peasants were poor funding and the inability to obtain proper credit resources. The Government also realized the importance of providing technical services. In beginning to issue loans, efforts were made to help rural households with crop farming, livestock breeding and the processing of agricultural products. According to an official survey conducted in 1987, in the first year after the plan was implemented, up to 92 percent of interest-subsidized loans were directly or indirectly issued to rural households (Zhou Binbin 1990).

In 1989, when the Government adopted the policy of helping the poor indirectly by encouraging the development of economic entities, loans to rural households largely ceased. Economic entities are enterprises, and ideally should help poor households by providing job opportunities. The new policy stipulated: 'Any economic entity that wishes to get a poverty alleviation loan must have more than half of its employees come from poor households.' Policy makers believed that most poor households were unable to effectively utilize poverty alleviation loans since they lack necessary production techniques and management capabilities, and have not reached a certain economic scale. The new policy mainly aimed to enhance the productivity and rate of recovery of loans. Some data have indicated that more than 70 percent of poverty alleviation loans were distributed to economic entities after 1989 (Wang Sangui *et al.* 1999).

A major undesired consequence, however, was the lack of a direct link between loans and the poor. Most loans have been issued to township or county enterprises that can help enhance the financial revenues of local governments, while not much benefiting poor rural households. Even worse, due to limited technical skills, managerial capabilities and market size, most of those projects failed, decreasing the rate of recovery of the loans. Data indicate that the rate of recovery in the 1980s was 65 percent (Zhou Binbin and Gao Hongbin 1993). From 1991 to 1997, the rate was only 44 percent to 62 percent (China Agricultural Development Bank 1998; State Science Commission 1995). At the Poverty Alleviation Work Conference in September 1996, the central Government decided to direct most interest-subsidized loans back to rural households' crop production and livestock breeding activities. Specific poverty alleviation loans were used to launch microcredit services on a trial basis. By 2001, these experiments had absorbed poverty alleviation funds totalling RMB 3.8 billion yuan.

After 2001, as the Agricultural Bank of China quickened its drive for commercialization and reduced its presence in rural areas, its capacity to issue loans to rural households declined. At the same time, the Poverty Alleviation Office under the State Council put forward agricultural industrialization as one of three major poverty alleviation measures in the new era, and also defined credit support as a main means for pursuing agricultural industrialization in poverty-stricken regions. The agricultural industrialization mode principally aims to plan out, in an integrated and far-seeing way, the production of agricultural products supported by numerous local resources and hotly demanded by the market. Similar to industrialization patterns, this helps to form characteristic industries with a regional leadership. The key point is to develop medium and large enterprises able to compete in the market, and then to mobilize these to offer pre-production, in-production and after-production services to poor rural households, helping improve the quality of their agricultural production, living conditions and income levels.

The Poverty Alleviation Office under the State Council specified the first batch of 260 enterprises, which have each played a pioneer role as the major receivers of interest-subsidized poverty alleviation loans. They also enjoy preferential treatment related to taxes, financial allocations, land use, etc. According to data on the sourcing of poverty alleviation funds for agricultural industrialization in eleven provinces provided by the Poverty

Alleviation Office of the State Council, in 2004, various preferential policies supported a total investment of RMB 1.7 billion yuan; 61.7 percent came from credit funds for poverty alleviation and 18.7 percent from financial allocations for poverty alleviation (Li Zhou and Cao Jianhua 2006). Statistics from the Agricultural Bank of China show that in 2005, the total amount of credit funds invested in agricultural industrialization projects for poverty alleviation was RMB 4.13 billion yuan; interest-subsidized loans totalled RMB 2.38 billion yuan, making up 57.6 percent of the total. Such funds were used to finance 1289 projects, each of which received RMB 3.21 million yuan on average. By the end of 2005, the balance of credit loans for poverty alleviation used in agricultural industrialization projects was RMB 13.62 billion yuan. The balance of interest-subsidized loans was RMB 5.46 billion yuan, 40 percent of the total.

Agricultural industrialization projects have now become the biggest absorber of interest-subsidized loans. According to statistics from the Agricultural Bank of China, among the mix of interest-subsidized loans in 2005, loans for agricultural industrialization made up 33.1 percent. In addition to agricultural industrialization projects, the Agricultural Bank of China has also issued interest-subsidized loans for infrastructure construction projects, industry and commerce, and projects other than loans to rural households. All interest-subsidized loans totalled RMB 7.18 billion yuan in 2005. Loans to rural households only made up 17.1 percent, while the remaining 82.9 percent went to enterprises and projects (see Figure 4.10).

Changes in the disbursement of loans for poverty alleviation (from rural households to economic entities and enterprises) reflect the conflict between the poverty alleviation goal, and the insistence by commercial banks on fund efficiency and security. To deepen the impact of poverty alleviation, however, loans must directly reach poor rural households to improve their production

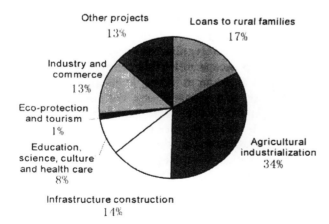

Figure 4.10 Usage of interest-subsidized loans in 2005.

Source: Calculated from data from the Agricultural Bank of China.

capacities. Due to a severe asymmetry in access to information and the lack of an effective incentive mechanism, the small-sum loans issued by commercial banks to rural households not only bear high costs, but also record a low rate of recovery, thus making it hard to keep such loans going in the long run. In order to cut down their operating costs, and also to satisfy local governments' pursuit of economic growth and financial revenues through business expansion, banks have naturally turned towards issuing more loans to enterprises and economic entities, especially when it has been difficult to recover loans issued to rural households. The targeting of loans to economic entities that emerged in the early 1990s, however, failed to improve the security of loans[17] at the price of sacrificing the poverty alleviation goal, which has inevitably sparked criticism.

In the late 1990s, poverty alleviation departments and the China Agricultural Development Bank once again started to issue more loans to rural households. But they failed to solve the issues related to information asymmetry and the lack of an incentive mechanism. Although microcredit came into being at that time, the operating mode of the China Agricultural Development Bank was not suitable for offering this service. Through its drive towards commercialization, the bank started to cancel and merge a large number of its sub-branches and service outlets at the grass-roots level, and eventually had to pass the duty of issuing and recovering small-sum loans to rural households to local governments. Local governments are not suitable for managing credit funds, however, since they take more account of short-term goals than the long-term security of funds. As a result, the quality of loans to rural households was further reduced. By the end of 2005, the accumulative balance of poverty alleviation loans issued to rural households recorded a bad loan ratio of up to 76 percent.

At the beginning of the new millennium, the China Agricultural Development Bank had no other option but to issue its poverty alleviation loans to relatively large-scale enterprises leading the drive towards agricultural industrialization, infrastructure construction projects, etc., although such a transformation deviated from the poverty alleviation goal. Because commercialization enabled the bank to escape restrictions exercised by local governments, thus gaining greater freedom in issuing loans, the re-targeting of loans has improved their quality to a certain degree. For instance, from 2000 to 2003, the bad loan ratio fell by 39 percent, despite some increases since, and is still lower than in 2000 by about 20 percent (see Figure 4.11)

Better loan quality mainly came from a relatively low bad loan ratio for loans issued for agricultural industrialization; infrastructure construction; education, science, culture and health care; the environment; tourism, etc. (see Figure 4.12). Interest-subsidized loans for poverty alleviation now exist in name only, however, and have a decreasing influence upon the poor population. Their bad loan ratio is still far beyond that of ordinary commercial loans.

China's experience in issuing loans for poverty alleviation affirms that

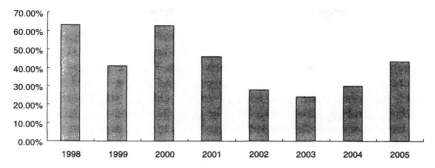

Figure 4.11 Bad loan ratio of interest-subsidized loans for poverty alleviation.
Source: Calculated from data from the Agricultural Bank of China.

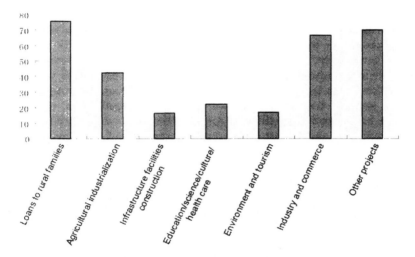

Figure 4.12 Bad loan ratios for different types of poverty alleviation loans in 2005 (%).
Source: Calculated from data from the Agricultural Bank of China.

operating through commercial banks can reduce links to the goal of poverty reduction. It is essential to reform the rural financial market and gradually foster financial institutions targeted to the poor.

Microcredit: struggling in an unfavourable financial market

As a financial service specifically for the poor, microcredit has spread in many developing and some developed countries since its inception in 1970. Mohammed Yunus, founder of the Grameen Bank, won the Nobel Peace Price in 2006 for establishing the very first bank for the poor, and providing millions of poor and low-income people with sustainable and effective financial services. His winning of the prize bolstered global enthusiasm for exploring the microcredit sector for poverty alleviation.

Influenced by other countries' successful practices, China began ushering in a microcredit service with the help of some international and non-governmental organizations in the early 1990s. Diverse projects have been launched, many with international support, and in line with the Grameen Bank's operating mode. They have covered a relatively small portion of the population and remained focused on the poor. Some non-governmental projects have achieved brilliant results, including a loan recovery rate of close to 100 percent.

At the beginning, poverty alleviation and financial organs doubted if the model would be applicable in China, but they found it could accomplish two goals beyond the reach of the Government's interest-subsidized loans: (1) the delivery of poverty alleviation funds directly to rural households, and (2) a high loan recovery rate. The Poverty Alleviation Office of the State Council and the China Agricultural Development Bank opted to use interest-subsidized loans to support microcredit services. The poverty alleviation departments of local governments have set up independent poverty alleviation societies, which usually employ governmental employees to assist in establishing loan terms, and issuing and recovering loans. Through governmental support and a huge sum of interest-subsidized loans, microcredit projects have expanded swiftly. By August 1998, they existed in 600 counties in 22 provinces, and almost dwarfed non-governmental microcredit services (Park *et al.* 2003).

Today, microcredit keeps evolving, but it has not been expanding as fast as it did at its inception, and faces a series of institutional and managerial problems. Since the late 1990s, the number of rural households participating in non-governmental projects has dropped. Some projects have failed; others have received only initial financial support from external donors, who then moved on to new initiatives (e.g., those projects launched by the UN Children's Fund, UN Population Fund, UNDP and World Bank). The Government's microcredit service has been shown to have serious institutional defects since its inception, such as a lack of long-term goal, a shortage of proper training, an inadequate incentive system and poor supervision. This has inevitably made it impossible to follow important principles for microcredit services. The loan recovery rate has dropped quickly, even as the government services expanded (Park and Ren 2001).

China's closed financial markets and the Government's monopoly over the financial industry remain root causes of ongoing problems with microcredit. Services operated by non-governmental and international institutions cannot enter the rural credit market in the mode usually adopted by financial institutions, so they can be operated only as poverty alleviation projects. Without the capacities of regular financial institutions, these groups cannot have long-term institutional development plans, attract outstanding talent dedicated to the microcredit cause, be brought under China's system of financial supervision, or expand their service and business scope by absorbing savings like some successful microcredit organizations abroad have done. They remain hobbled by dependence on external funds. When the funds run out, combined with other problems such as high operating costs, the lack of a long-term development goal, ineffective incentives and supervision, and managerial problems, many services have failed, even after having evolved for many years.

Even abroad, there has been no successful experience in providing microcredit services through a project implementation mode. The Government's microcredit service only used some standard microcredit operating techniques (such as group liability, and weekly or monthly repayment schemes), while neglecting innovations in the financial system needed for microcredit to flourish. The China Agricultural Development Bank, which has been ceaselessly pursuing urban markets, did not define microcredit services as one of its principal business modules, or revamp financial institutions in rural areas to supply rural households with efficient financial services, as the Bank Rakyat in Indonesia has done.[18] The bank deems microcredit as only a policy goal, while passing the responsibility to local governments. Such institutional arrangements are insufficient for developing sustainable microcredit organs.

In short, China's microcredit services for poverty alleviation have been struggling helplessly in a commercialized financial realm. Some experiences have been gained, but for further development, China must open financial markets to a wider range of services and enhance capabilities in financial supervision. The five-year period of protection for regular financial institutions, granted to China upon joining the World Trade Organization, ended in 2006. It seems inevitable that further opening up will take place. The Government has indicated that it will take steps towards the reform and adjustment of the rural finance system.

At the end of 2006, the China Banking Regulatory Commission released 'Certain Opinions with Regard to Adjustment and Loosening of the Policy Governing Financial Institutions' Access to the Financial Market in Rural Areas for the Sake of Conferring Stronger Support to the Construction of New Rural Areas with Socialist Characteristics'. The commission stated it had decided to adjust and loosen, to an appropriate extent as per the principle of sustainable commerce, the policy governing financial institutions' access to the financial market in rural areas, and make it easier for such institutions to enter this market; it also intends to intensify the restriction and supervision of this market. The objective is to confer greater support to rural areas for the sake of forming a banking and financial service system featuring a diversity of investments, a wide range of financial products, full coverage of the rural population, flexible governance and efficient service. The main policies and measures include: (1) to encourage various investors to establish new banking outlets at the village/town level to provide rural households with financial services; (2) to allow peasants and small-sized rural enterprises in rural areas to form, out of their own accord, community-level credit cooperatives and manage them in a democratic manner; (3) to encourage Chinese commercial and rural cooperative banks to set up proprietary subsidiaries specialized in providing loan services in rural areas; (4) to support various investors to share the stocks of, buy out, or reorganize banking institutions in rural areas, or transform credit cooperatives that have employed relatively standard management practices and recorded a relatively large business turnover in financial institutions; and (5) to help commercial and rural cooperative banks that have accumulated rich professional experience, recorded sound operating results and demonstrated solid internal management capabilities for setting up branch organs in rural areas, and to encourage rural cooperative financial organs to open more branches within their respective townships (towns) and administrative villages. The first batch of pilot initiatives has begun in six provinces (or autonomous regions) in central and western China: Sichuan, Qinghai, Gansu, Inner Mongolia, Jilin and Hubei (China Banking Regulatory Commission 2006). China's microcredit operators should seize this opportunity to graduate to a normal course of development.

Resettlement: a poverty alleviation path for regions with poor environments and limited resources

Before the Government started its rural poverty alleviation campaign on a large scale, resettlement to cope with poverty emerged as early as 1983 in the Dingxi and Hexi regions of Gansu Province, and the Xihaigu region of Ningxia Province. This has made a major contribution to reducing poverty in these three regions. By the end of 1999, Gansu Province had relocated 569,200 people from poor regions, while Ningxia Province had relocated 300,000 people. In the implementation period of the 'Eight-Seven Poverty Alleviation Plan', such provinces as Inner Mongolia, Guangdong, Fujian, Guangxi, Guizhou, Sichuan, Xinjiang, Qinghai, Hebei, Shanxi, Tibet, Hubei, Shaanxi, Yunnan, Liaoning, Chongqing and Anhui each launched a large-scale resettlement campaign for poverty alleviation. During that time, plans called for transferring 5 million rural residents. By 2000, the actual number had reached 2.58 million persons (Li Xiaoyun and Tang Lixia 2006).

Under the new 'Scheme for Rural Development for Poverty Alleviation' (Poverty Alleviation Leadership Group of the State Council 2001), resettlement has remained an important strategy. According to data from the Poverty Alleviation Office of the State Council, the total size of the poor population that China has to relocate amounts to 7 million persons. By 2003, 3.4 million persons had been relocated. Statistics from twelve provinces or autonomous regions show that, from 2001 to 2004, they relocated 1.16 million persons from 13,497 villages. Shaanxi, Shanxi, Ningxia, Jiangxi and Hunan provinces have each seen the total number of villages left by rural residents exceed 1,000. Overall, those places justifying a resettlement strategy have common traits: (1) poor natural conditions, mainly because they are in mountainous areas or face occasional geologic hazards, combined with a vulnerable environment; (2) poor infrastructure that would be extremely expensive to improve;

(3) arable lands in degraded conditions that cannot generate enough revenue for local residents' bare subsistence; and (4) a relatively low population density.

Resettlement for poverty alleviation is mainly organized by governmental departments; rural households participate out of their own choice. The departments contribute to determining where people come from, where they can go, their qualifications, the mode of resettlement, etc. The central Government has provided support on the policy-making and funding fronts. Most people have been relocated within their respective counties – according to some rough statistics, up to 93 percent. In Guangxi, Hebei, Henna, Jiangxi, Shanxi and Chongqing, almost 100 percent have remained within their counties. The benefits of this include lower costs, similar modes of production and ways of living, and easier administrative management. There have been two modes of replacement: the centralized mode and the scattered mode. Under the former, statistics suggest that approximately 63 percent of relocated people have gone to 3,368 centralized replacement locations equipped with water, power, roads and croplands, as well as cultural, educational, health care and other facilities. An overwhelming majority of relocated people remains engaged in agriculture. In better-developed regions, a small portion has moved into smaller towns to work in other industries.

Moving people out of places where they and their ancestors have been living for many years is an enormous task involving not only environmental and economic interests, but also such profound issues as production modes, ways of living, cultural customs, etc. China has seen both successes and failures in handling these intricate problems. Resettlement has improved the environment, bettered production and living conditions, increased access to public services, raised incomes and alleviated poverty (see Box 4.5). But it has also featured the following problems. First, the poorest people are often unlikely to be relocated, in large part due to inadequate funds. In addition to its investments in infrastructure construction, the Government can grant only small subsidies, which means relocated people may have to spend more than RMB 10,000 yuan in erecting their new houses and other living facilities. Second, the need for loans to erect new houses means many relocated people incur heavy debts. Local governments often request them to erect good-looking houses to make the new habitat look 'presentable', which increases financial hardships. Living conditions often deteriorate within a short period. Third, resettlement in some places has caused tensions between new arrivals and people already living there. Fourth, a considerable percentage of immigrants have moved back to their places of origin because of incomplete infrastructure, poor resources and conditions in the destination places, the inability to adapt to new production modes and ways of living, and incompatibility with prevalent cultural customs. For instance, in a relatively successful immigration project in Yunnan Province, nearly 20 percent of people who were relocated opted to move back to their place of origin (background report, Li Xiaoyun and Tang Lixia 2006). The local government failed to take account of all relevant factors when devising this project, having employed an overly simplistic methodology.

Box 4.5 The influence of resettlements in Suichuan County in Jiangxi Province

A portion of the poor population in Suichuan County in Jiangxi Province has lived in remote mountainous regions and areas prone to geological hazards. Owing to poor transport, a scattered population and high poverty alleviation costs, people there face difficulties in educating their children and obtaining medical care. The county relocated people into its town area and solved such problems satisfactorily.

For example, Dongxi Village is over 30 km from the town area and inaccessible by automobile. The only way to this village is a rather narrow footpath. It had only one elementary school, which was staffed with three teachers and ran only Grade 1 and Grade 2 classes. After that, students had to go to the school in the town area to continue their studies. That meant getting up at 5 a.m. every morning. Because boars and vipers can be found in the mountains, parents had to escort younger children to school, or children were kept out of school until they were older. After resettlement, children live in specific residential quarters only a 15-minute walk from their school.

The move has also meant easier access to medical services. As a person from Dongxi Village described vividly, 'If one man gets really sick, say, he will die in an hour, then he has to die, unless a helicopter comes to pick him up for a hospital elsewhere.' In the Xinyuan Residential Quarters erected specifically for relocated people, there are three doctors on duty. A general hospital is in the vicinity.

Source: background report, Li Xiaoyun and Tang Lixia 2006.

Usefulness of science and technology for the developmental mode of poverty alleviation

The main reason for low incomes among rural households in poor regions is low productivity, which is partly due to a shortage of material and human capital, and, in even larger part, due to the limited adoption of technological innovation and new production techniques. These are essential in helping the poor improve their lives. They can enhance production efficiency, save resources and bring down production costs, thus putting an end to the common problem of low revenues from rural activities.

For many years, the Government has attached importance to scientific and technological development work for rural poverty alleviation. The Poverty Alleviation Office of the Technology Development Centre for Rural Affairs at the Ministry of Science and Technology takes charge of this work. The Ministry of Science and Technology has accumulated ample experience in conducting pilot poverty alleviation work through scientific and technological development in the Dabie and Jinggang mountain areas, and in Shanbei in the northern part of Shaanxi Province. Its primary practices include disseminating advanced and applicable techniques, fostering pillar industries suitable for local circumstances, spreading scientific knowledge, providing technical training, creating best practice examples that can be replicated elsewhere, and cultivating science and technology talent. According to the statistics of the Ministry of Science and Technology, in the first fifteen years of rural development for poverty alleviation, the ministry mobilized science and technology specialists to visit poor regions for a total of 290,000 person-times. As a result, more than 9,400 applied techniques were shared in poor regions. Various science and technology projects were implemented, helping many peasants grasp practical new techniques (Ministry of Science and Technology 2001).

There have been visible impacts. For instance, Yingshan County in the Dabie mountain area of Hubei Province has used new technology to reinvigorate its tea planting industry (see Box 4.6). As indicated by the findings of an empirical study based on provincial statistical data and a multi-formula dynamic model, among the Government's investments in rural areas, those for education and research on agricultural science and technology have generated the best and second best effects in poverty alleviation, respectively. They have been better investments than those in material capital or credit (Fan Shenggen *et al.* 2004).

Box 4.6 Science and technology helps develop the tea industry in Yingshan County of Hubei Province

The Government designated Yingshan County of Hubei Province as one of the key poor counties. For many years, the tea industry had been a pillar of the county's economy. But economic inefficiency had resulted from outdated technology. In the mid 1980s, average income from the 20,000 *mu* tea garden in the county was less than RMB 300 yuan per *mu*. To enhance tea production, Yingshan County began to initiate independent research, and bring in outside experts and enterprises to increase technological innovation.

First, it managed to work out a technique that makes it possible to grow in the first year, reap in the second year and embrace a huge output in the third year, thus increasing the acreage of high-yield tea gardens by nearly 10,000 *mu* on an annual basis. This raised average income per *mu* to 1,000 yuan. Second, it successfully developed a technique for processing high-grade tea leaves. This was shared with 100 principal tea factories, raising the average revenue from each *mu* of tea garden to

3,000 yuan from 1,000 yuan. Third, it developed another innovative technique for vegetative propagation of quality tea species that helps reduce the construction costs of tea gardens, expands the acreage of older tea gardens, and increases the average revenue from each *mu* of tea garden to RMB 4,000 yuan. Large-scale processing enterprises were introduced to process low-grade tea leaves, in an attempt to reap higher sales revenue and income.

By 2004, the total acreage of tea gardens in the county amounted to 140,000 *mu*. The total yield of tea leaves was 13.8 million km, for a total output value of RMB 317 million yuan. There were 85,000 tea-growing households, comprising 85 percent of all households in the county. Thirty percent of county revenues and 47 percent of peasants' incomes are derived from the tea industry (China Rural Technology Development Centre of the Ministry of Science and Technology 2005).

In terms of poverty alleviation, the problems posed by science and technology include some of the following. First, poor regions have inadequate capabilities in technological innovation and few technical specialists. Second, there is an imbalance in the knowledge of technical specialists. The number engaged in crop production and animal husbandry at the county level and their counterparts at the township level together constitute 36 percent of all specialists officially registered with the competent national authority. But the number of technical specialists engaged in agricultural machinery and business administration comprises only 11 percent and 13 percent, respectively. Those engaged in aquaculture, cash crops and gardening make up less than 4 percent (China Rural Technology Development Centre of the Ministry of Science and Technology 2005). Third, the technical service system has not been fully implemented and faces a grave shortage of funds. Most poor regions cannot afford to maintain basic technology diffusion and technical service teams at the township level, much less other activities. Finally, poor rural households have not been the major beneficiaries of events to share exemplary rural technologies, which are often conducted in a project implementation mode.

Societal poverty alleviation: a potent complement to the developmental mode

In China, societal poverty alleviation refers to all activities other than those carried out under the Government's poverty alleviation plan. This primarily includes departmental efforts launched by individual government departments and their affiliates, joint eastern and western China poverty alleviation activities, international and bilateral development projects, and interventions by non-governmental organizations (see Box 4.7).

Box 4.7 Societal poverty alleviation activities in China

Departmental poverty alleviation activities refer to work by Communist Party and political organizations, public institutions and social groups. They apply their resources to support certain state-specified poor counties. Prior to the State Council's institutional restructuring in 1998, 122 party and administrative organizations directly under the central Government, enterprises, public institutions and social groups were involved in assisting 369 poor counties. After the institutional restructuring, some adjustment had been made. In 1999, 138 organizations assisted 350 state-specified poor counties. By early 2002, the number of organizations had increased to 272. In normal circumstances, assisted poor counties are in only one or two regions. A prominent aspect of this work is that its content and mode both closely correlate with the activities of the implementing department. For example, the Ministry of Agriculture focused its poverty alleviation endeavours in the Wuling mountainous area on agricultural development; the Ministry of Health assisted Sichuan Province on controlling endemic diseases and erecting grass-roots medical services. Another aspect is the importance attached to such social service sectors as education, training and health care, since quite a few of the organizations involved cannot adapt their activities to more general socioeconomic development. Even those departments that primarily focus on poverty alleviation also tend to use their funds in the social service sectors. Broadly speaking, basic education, the training of peasants and basic health care facilities require relatively small investments. These projects are easier to manage and supervise (such as the construction of school buildings and health care facilities, and provision of subsidies for pupils who have discontinued their studying due to financial hardship), and are thus relatively suitable for absorbing small-scale investments. In poor regions, the social service sectors are also in dire need of investments in whatever amount.

Joint eastern and western China poverty alleviation was a new measure emerging from the National Conference on Poverty Alleviation in 1996. It was intended to mobilize the economically better-developed provinces in eastern China to support the development of poverty-stricken regions. According to arrangements made by the Leading Group for Poverty Alleviation and Development of the State Council, 15 economically better-developed provinces and municipalities in eastern China assist 11 poor provinces and autonomous regions in western China (Beijing supports Inner Mongolia; Tianjin supports Gansu; Shanghai supports Yunnan; Guangdong supports Guangxi; Jiangsu supports Shaanxi; Zhejiang supports Sichuan; Shandong supports Xinjiang; Liaoning supports Qinghai; Fujian supports Ningxia, Shenzhen and Qingdao;

Dalian and Ningbo jointly support Guizhou; and Xiamen and Zhuhai jointly support Chongqing). The main modes of support include: (1) donation of funds to finance the construction of education, health care and other infrastructure; (2) donation of production materials and daily necessities needed for agricultural production and everyday life; (3) launch of economic and technological cooperation by utilizing the technical, managerial and marketing advantages of developed regions to boost the development of enterprises and industries in poor regions; and (4) a two-way flow of personnel under which developed provinces and municipalities send technicians and young volunteers to offer services in poor provinces and autonomous regions, and poor provinces and autonomous regions dispatch cadres in charge of administrative and technological affairs to receive training in developed provinces and municipalities – this includes the transfer of labourers to work in developed regions.

Poverty alleviation by international organizations involves a few organizations that launched poverty alleviation activities shortly after China put into force her policy of reform and opening up. In the 1990s, more international organizations established themselves in China and gradually organized a growing variety of poverty alleviation activities. These have included microcredit projects, small infrastructure construction, community development initiatives, environmental protection activities, technical assistance, capacity development and comprehensive development projects in rural areas. The World Bank has played a pioneer role through its generous sponsorship of the last category. Besides the World Bank, the Asian Development Bank and UNDP have helped the Chinese Government enhance its capabilities and efficiency in poverty alleviation by providing technical assistance in a number of forms. International non-governmental organizations have also launched poverty alleviation projects, some of which focus upon a fusion between poverty alleviation and environmental protection. Others stress community development and the cultivation of local capabilities.

Poverty alleviation by non-governmental organizations takes place with the support of both the central and local governments. Domestic non-governmental organizations and mass groups, which are represented by the China Poverty Alleviation Foundation, have established a number of intensive poverty alleviation activities, mostly in education and health care, along with microcredit services. In the political and legal environment of today's China, all legitimate non-governmental organs have a governmental background and engage in poverty alleviation work under the direct management of competent governmental departments. Compared to large-scale poverty alleviation work conducted by the Government, these activities are on a relatively small scale in some selected poor regions. They are mostly structured for a long period, and focus on certain trades and professions that non-governmental organizations are well acquainted with. For example, Project Hope mainly supports elementary education in poor regions; Project Happiness primarily provides women with microcredit services.

Societal poverty alleviation chiefly manifests its usefulness in four ways. First, it mobilizes all walks of life to participate in poverty alleviation activities and heightens the entire society's awareness of poverty alleviation. To a certain degree, it also cultivates the development of non-governmental organizations. Second, it helps reform governmental poverty alleviation through innovation, even though some innovative practices have not turned out successfully. For example, the Government's poverty alleviation projects were initially managed in a mode that originated in the times of the planned economy. All project plans were formulated from the top down (i.e., by governments at all levels) and implemented by local administrative departments. Due to the proven managerial experience accumulated by international and non-governmental organizations, the Chinese Government has now raised funds for poverty alleviation projects from many more sources, and has been able to manage these in new ways, such as by selecting projects based on village-level plans, gradually transferring powers for project examination and approval to local governments, and choosing project contractors for more and more projects by public bidding. As for the distribution and control of funds, the factor-method-based mode has been adopted not only by the Ministry of Finance of the central Government, but also by an increasing number of departments under local governments. On top of that, such internationally acknowledged practices as the management of poverty alleviation funds in specific accounts, the use of account-rendering systems and the provision of public information have been applied more and more frequently.

Third, societal poverty alleviation helps to mitigate the Government's lack of poverty alleviation funds, to a certain degree. As estimated by pertinent research, during the 'Eight-Seven Poverty Alleviation Plan' and the 'Tenth Five-Year-Long National Development Program (2000–2005)', funds raised through societal poverty alleviation efforts totalled RMB 113.7 billion yuan, comprising 28 percent of all poverty alleviation investments (Li Zhou and Cao Jianhua 2006). Fourth, societal poverty alleviation has partly mitigated the inadequacy of governmental investments in social and human capital development for poverty alleviation. In fact, all three modes described in Box 4.7 have stressed the improvement of public social services for education, medical care and training. For instance, the China Youth Development Foundation launched and successfully implemented Project Hope, which has played quite an important role in boosting the development of compulsory education in poor regions.

Societal poverty alleviation also has some problems. First of all, although poverty alleviation by pertinent departments has used a huge amount of resources, such a process has involved inequality. Some departments have used their influence and power to request funds for purposes other than poverty alleviation for certain counties and villages. Other departments, with less power, do not have enough resources for their designated targets. Governmental resources (including poverty alleviation funds) should have been distributed among poor counties and villages in a more equitable way. As it stands, the distribution of such funds has become complicated and unfair due to interference by different departments. Second, interventions by international and non-governmental organizations, when conditions are not ripe, can yield results contrary to expectations. For example, even if the Government broadens the provisions of microcredit services under the influence of non-governmental organizations and international institutions, China's inappropriate financial system and policies will hinder the goal of providing the poor with sustainable financial services.

Overall assessment of the effects of developmental poverty alleviation policies

In general, the developmental poverty alleviation measures adopted by China have increased economic development in poor regions. This is clear in several respects. First, infrastructure, production and living conditions in poor regions have visibly improved, laying a sound foundation for rural households to launch more profitable activities. Second, infrastructure, scientific and technological services, and the pursuit of industrialization have evolved, while credit support has helped enhance the average income level of rural households in poor regions. Third, gaps in incomes and living standards between poorer and wealthier regions have been restrained to a certain degree, especially through the facilitation of quicker development in poor regions. Without developmental poverty alleviation policies targeted to certain regions, the gaps would be much wider. Fourth, the environment has improved in some poor regions through resettlement and development.

The first problem that developmental poverty alleviation measures have encountered is that poverty-stricken populations in poor regions have not benefited equally from development work for poverty alleviation, as medium-income or even high-income rural households enjoy more benefits. This problem has been pervasive in integrated village development work, training for labour force transfers, access to credit, voluntary resettlements, and scientific and technological development, mainly because of the failure to employ a more effective poverty-targeting mechanism in implementing these projects. A second problem has been that some poverty alleviation projects have not been sustainable. In particular, credit funds for poverty alleviation have recorded a low recovery rate due to severe institutional defects. The return of people to their place of origin has hindered some resettlement projects.

Evolution of the social security system for rural areas

A limited social security system has existed in rural areas of China, although with much stricter restrictions on beneficiaries than the security system for urban areas. It is intended to support a few particular groups, namely by providing: (1) maintenance for rural households entitled to the 'five guarantees;' (2) assistance to households in absolute poverty; (3) assistance to special groups of people; and (4) minimum security for bare subsistence. The system has varied largely from one region to another.

Households entitled to the 'five guarantees'

The system for maintaining rural households entitled to the 'five guarantees' has been the best-known welfare project in rural areas. It was devised to provide minimum security to people who are elderly, physically vulnerable, living alone, widowed or disabled. Applicants for maintenance must pass a strict qualification examination. So far, the system has covered only those people who fit into the 'Three-NOs' description (elderly people, disabled people and minors). Before China's reform era began, the people's communes were liable for providing maintenance to qualified households; the system became a collective benefit project. By nature, it was categorized as part of the community welfare domain.

Even after reforms began, the system persisted as the most basic form of social welfare in rural areas, despite the disintegration of the people's commune system. From 1978 to 2001, the Government, by formulating policies, enacting laws and regulations, and providing certain financial support, requested rural communities (or villages) to provide cash and non-cash maintenance service to those entitled to the 'five guarantees'[19] Funds for maintenance mostly originated from the so-called 'money withdrawn by villages', which encompassed the public accumulation fund and public welfare fund withdrawn according to the per capita income of peasants, and outlays for village-level autonomous organizations. Township governments conferred a small portion of funds. Maintenance service was largely conducted by pertinent organizations at the township and village levels. Under some special circumstances, township governments would offer temporary allowances for maintenance work, generally to construct homes for the elderly and other infrastructure.

The tax reform initiated in rural areas since early 2000, however, has cancelled the 'money withdrawn by villages' and the funds planned by township governments, thus jeopardizing the fundraising foundation of the maintenance system. Transfer payments from governments at higher levels now constitute the major source of funds for community public welfare at the village level. This means that public welfare for rural households entitled to the 'five guarantees' will become a national welfare undertaking, and the central Government will play a more active role in developing it.

Although the size of the population entitled to the 'five guarantees' has been rising, the maintenance system has still failed to cover all qualified candidates. Figure 4.13 sets forth the number of people covered from 1985 to 2002, and their percentages of the total rural population. The number of those people accessing the maintenance system dropped in the late 1980s and began to rebound in 1993, before stabilizing for a number of years. There was a sharp increase in 2002, probably related to changes in the sourcing of funds. Transfer payments from higher levels of government have allowed wider coverage, but according to the statistics of the Ministry of Civil Affairs in 2002, 23.1 percent of people who should have been covered have not had access. Coverage ratios in different regions are not closely related to the degree of economic development. The accuracy of such data may be suspect, however, for they are collected from reports by authorities at lower levels (background report, Gu Xin 2006). According to the *National In-depth Survey into Special Groups of Rural People in Financial Hardships*, which was conducted by the Ministry of Civil Affairs in 2003, at that time 5.7 million people were entitled to the maintenance system, but only half were benefiting from it (Ministry of Civil Affairs 2004).

On average, the per capita amount of maintenance funds for rural households entitled to the 'five guarantees' is about 40 percent of the per capita annual net income of Chinese peasants, and reaches to the relative poverty line. The country's average figure masks huge disparities among different regions, however. For instance, the per capita amount of maintenance in Sichuan in 2002 was only RMB 664 yuan per year or 31.5 percent of the per capita income of peasants in Sichuan Province, although the sum was above the absolute poverty line.

Due to some long-standing defects in the maintenance system and incompatibilities between new and old approaches to it, problems have arisen in

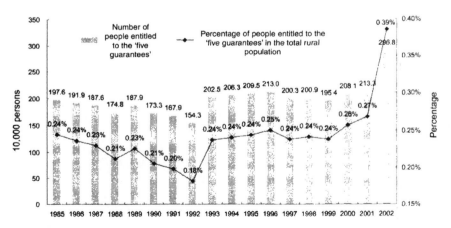

Figure 4.13 People entitled to the 'five guarantees' from 1985 to 2002.

Source: *China's Yearbook of Civil Administration Statistics* and *China Statistical Yearbook* for each of these years.

many places, especially in central and western China, except for places where local governments have powerful financing abilities. These problems include: low amounts of maintenance, a slow pace in offering centralized maintenance services (such as the erection of homes for the aged), hardship in providing maintenance support, and arrears in funds (background report, Gu Xin 2006).

Since 2003, a number of civil administration departments have brought households entitled to the 'five guarantees' into the minimum security system for bare subsistence, which assists people in absolute poverty. This has helped the coverage rate increase at a steadfast pace. By the end of 2006, the total number of people entitled to the 'five guarantees' had reached 4.85 million persons, with a coverage ratio of 85 percent (Ministry of Civil Affairs of the People's Republic of China 2007b).

Minimum security system for bare subsistence for people in absolute poverty

Since the mid 1990s, some local governments have gradually managed to put in place a minimum living standard system, and integrated into it the maintenance of rural households entitled to the 'five guarantees'. The earliest implementer was not a local government in an economically well-developed region, but the Civil Affairs Bureau in Yangquan City of Shanxi Province. In 1996, the Ministry of Civil Affairs formulated the 'Guiding Proposal for the Establishment of the Social Security System for Rural Areas', in an effort to share the successful experience in Yangquan City with the rest of the country. By the end of 2006, 2,133 counties and regions in 18 provinces (Beijing, Tianjin, Shanghai, Zhejiang, Jiangsu, Guangdong, Fujian, Liaoning, Hainan, Jilin, Shaanxi, Sichuan, Hebei, Inner Mongolia, Shanxi, Henan, Jiangxi and Heilongjiang) had established the minimum living standard system for rural areas, thus enabling 15.1 million rural residents (in 7.4 million households) to access it (He Ping 2006; Ministry of Civil Affairs of the People's Republic of China 2007c).

Varying from the maintenance system for rural households entitled to the 'five guarantees', the minimum living standard system is based on a comparatively objective factor – household income, instead of a more subjective judgement on the loss of the capacity to work. Household income determines the level of subsidies granted to an applicant. Pursuant to the latest data made public by the Ministry of Civil Affairs (2006), in the four quarters of 2006, the per capita amount of the minimum security subsidy for rural people was RMB 844 yuan per year, but again, subsidies vary by region. The standard for rural areas near some big cities equals that for urban areas. But in some parts of western China, the rural standard remains less than one third of that for urban areas. In regions where the minimum security service is available, funds are often raised in a three-tiered way (city, county and township) or a four-tiered way (city, county, township and village). In 2005, the country invested a total of RMB 2.51 billion yuan in minimum security funds for rural areas; in 2006, this figure rose to RMB 4.16 billion yuan, up 66 percent from the previous year. On average, every qualified candidate receives a subsidy of RMB 33.2 yuan per month (Ministry of Civil Affairs 2005a and 2006a).

In order to respond to appeals for larger coverage by the minimum security system for rural areas, the Ministry of Civil Affairs issued the 'Notice with Regard to Intensifying the Efforts in Succor of Rural Households Stuck in Absolute Poverty' on 22 May 2003 (in the form of an official document referred to as [2003] No. 6), which stipulated that, 'those regions where it is not feasible to set up minimum security for rural areas shall establish a welfare system for those rural households stuck in absolute poverty as soon as possible pursuant to the spirit advocated by the State Council'. After that, the Ministry of Civil Affairs organized more than one working conference and issued multiple guidance documents for the sake of helping establish the welfare system for rural households in absolute poverty. As required by the Ministry of Civil Affairs, local governments have conducted research and later laid down, on their own initiatives, livelihood support systems for rural households in absolute poverty based on circumstances in their respective territories. A majority of those regions that have not established a minimum security system for rural areas have at least established policies and systems for people in absolute poverty. To a large extent, these initiatives have benefited households in absolute poverty not entitled to the 'five guarantees'.

The welfare system for rural households in absolute poverty and the minimum security system for rural areas have similarities and disparities. Both have been devised to offer minimum income support (i.e., a fixed amount for people in absolute poverty, according to the local standard). A difference between the two is that with the welfare system, a poverty line has not been set, and funds are not considered in terms of complementing income. Instead, subsidies are granted to each candidate in absolute poverty according to the total funds raised and the total number of candidates. The per capita amount of a subsidy is usually between RMB 10 yuan and RMB 20 yuan per month, with the minimum as little as RMB 5 yuan per person per month. The welfare system for rural households in absolute poverty can be said to be a simplified version of the minimum security system (background report, Gu Xin 2006).

Figure 4.14 displays the size of the rural population subject to welfare assistance in China from 2003 to 2006. Both the minimum security system and the welfare system for rural households in absolute poverty expanded their coverage. The percentage of the rural population accessing rural social security grew from 1.5 percent in 2003 to 3.6 percent in 2006.

One issue for both systems is how to accurately identify qualified candidates. At present, most regions do this through village nominations or by publicizing candidates' names for public review. These methods appear to be feasible. Since the rural minimum security system is based on income, it faces the more difficult task of checking and verifying the income level of a candidate

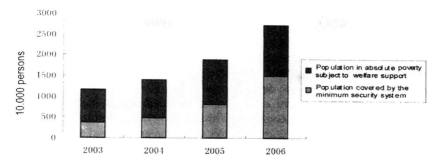

Figure 4.14 The size of the rural population covered by welfare support from 2002 to 2006.

Source: Ministry of Civil Affairs, *Statistical Development Gazette of Civil Administration Clause (2003–2005),* and data from the statistical bulletin of the civil administration in 2006.

household. Funding shortages in the system mean that the incomes of candidate households are often overestimated. As a consequence, some eligible people fail to qualify. Another significant problem has been that the financial inequalities among different regions have resulted in huge disparities in the provision of social security services.

Overall assessment of the effects of rural social security policies

Rural social security policies, including the welfare and minimum security systems, have played an important role in assisting some people in absolute poverty who lack the capability to secure enough food and clothing. Without the rural social security system, China's rural poverty would become more severe and widespread. The next task is to expand the system's coverage, enhance its security standard and eliminate the huge disparities among regions. Many poor people without the capability of working have not yet been reached, along with many who remain below the absolute poverty line. The main direction of reform should be the expansion of services to cover everyone in rural areas who is below the absolute poverty line. Due to sampling errors by the National Bureau of Statistics of China, the actual size of this population will turn out to be far beyond the figures that have been made available.

Influence of other preferential policies on poor populations in rural areas

In recent years, China has launched a number of important policies to promote economic and social development as well as environmental protection in rural areas. As discussed below, those policies have generated positive or negative impacts on rural poor population.

Influence of basic education reform upon poor regions and the poor

China has made stunning accomplishments in its basic education sector. Before China adopted the policy of reform and opening up, the total schooling rate recorded by elementary schools in rural areas reached 86.4 percent in 1978, due to community-level collective fundraising endeavours and despite the low degree of economic development at that time (Zhang Deyuan 2004). The degree of development of elementary education was higher than that registered by many other countries with much better developed economies. After 1978, due to reform and economic development, as well as the promulgation of the Compulsory Education Law, rural education developed further. In the early 1990s, the country adopted a policy on school building and management at multiple tiers, and passed the responsibility for raising educational funds and managing rural educational institutions to governments at the township and village levels. This produced financial hardship, particularly in poor regions, and triggered a series of problems such as a high schooling discontinuity rate, arrears in teachers' wages, dilapidated school buildings, and a widening gap between urban and rural schools. Nevertheless, despite all these hindrances, education continued to steadily improve, with the schooling rate of Chinese children reaching 99.2 percent in 2005 (National Bureau of Statistics of China 2006).

Since the late 1990s, in order to improve basic education in western China, the Government has worked out a series of policies and implemented many compulsory education projects, including the national 'Compulsory Education in Poor Regions' project. This includes the rebuilding of dilapidated school buildings and construction of boarding schools in rural areas. To alleviate financial burdens on peasants, the Government also implemented the 'One Fee System' reform and the 'Two Exemptions and One Subsidy' policy. To save resources, it put into force the 'Redeployment of Elementary and Middle Schools' proposal. The 'Modern Distance Education in Elementary and Middle Schools in Rural Areas' project helps improve the quality of education in rural areas and upholds the right of children in poor rural areas to have equal access to compulsory education. The following section uses data from a basic education survey conducted in Gansu Province between 2001 and 2004[20] to assess the influence of these policies.

National 'Compulsory Education for Poor Regions' project

The main purpose of the 'Compulsory Education for Poor Regions' project is to improve education conditions in poor rural regions, including by reconstructing dilapidated elementary and middle schools; erecting new school buildings; offering teaching devices, books, documents, desks and chairs; training teachers and schoolmasters, etc. Progress can be judged by looking at some of the indicators from Gansu Province in Table 4.3. From 2000 to 2004, indicators for elementary and junior high schools varied. The percentage of

Table 4.3 Material prerequisites in elementary and junior high schools in sampled counties of Gansu Province from 2000 to 2004

	Elementary schools		Junior high schools	
	2000	2004	2000	2004
Percentage of dilapidated schoolhouses	0.2	0.19	0.22	0.16
Percentage of rainwater-proofed classrooms	0.77	0.79	0.64	0.84
Percentage of classrooms with a sponge glass blackboard	0.07	0.11	0.15	0.38
Percentage of classrooms with a cement blackboard	0.77	0.46	0.87	0.49
Percentage of classrooms with a magnetic blackboard	0.05	0.06	0.01	0.13
Percentage of students not supplied with desks/chairs	27.50	0	15	0
Percentage of schools with a science laboratory	25	28.57	81.25	83.16
Percentage of schools with a library	71.21	76.43	87.50	96.84
Average number of books collected	2,585.10	3,666.11	5,460.57	11,526.15

Source: Jin Lian 2006.

dilapidated schoolhouses improved slightly, the number of books collected increased, and the percentage of students without desks or chairs dropped to zero. The percentage of classrooms with a cement blackboard declined. Analysis shows that improvements in material prerequisites in state-specified poor counties have been greater than in other counties.

From 2000 to 2004, the percentage of trained teachers increased by 25.65 percent in elementary schools and 27.97 percent in junior high schools in Gansu. The ratio between the number of students and teachers dropped, but to a small extent. The overall level of academic degrees for teachers has improved, particularly through an increase in teachers with at least a secondary technical school degree.

The compulsory education project has played a role in improving educational conditions in poor regions, despite hindrances in some respects. Government investments in educational infrastructure have helped mitigate the financial burdens on local governments and poor households. According to the findings of one study, the improvement of various school facilities has enhanced the schooling rate and had a positive influence on academic scores (background report, Jin Lian 2006).

'One Fee System' reform

In order to prevent schools from levying exorbitant charges, to further stand-ardize and intensify the school fee collection and management system, and to alleviate financial burdens particularly for poor rural households, the Minis-try of Education, the State Development Planning Commission and the Min-istry of Finance in 2001 jointly issued the 'Notice with Regard to Putting an Out-and-Out End to Exorbitant Charges Levied by Elementary and Middle Schools in Rural Areas'. This stipulated that, 'starting from 2001, each prov-ince, autonomous region and municipality has to take into account the actual circumstances in elementary and middle schools within its territory, and put into force the "One Fee System" fee collection method in poor regions'. The 'One Fee System' means determining a total amount of school fees, including tuition and incidental fees, textbook costs and homework book costs. The sums are stringently checked and verified in the compulsory education course, and then one fee is levied upon students (see Box 4.8 for a description of this reform).

The implementation effects of the 'One Fee System' can be assessed by look-ing at the experience in Gansu Province. The single fee is meant to cover all necessary and optional fees. The former include tuition, incidentals, text-books, heating fees, class activity fees, etc. The latter comprise extracurricular counselling fees, accommodation costs, sponsorship fees, health insurance premiums, accidental injury insurance premiums and other insurance pre-miums paid directly by students' households. In 2004, among all sampled schools, 73 elementary schools had implemented the 'One Fee System' along with 44 middle schools. The total fees levied by those schools with the 'One Fee System' were lower than those levied by schools that have not. This also applied to a breakdown of necessary and optional fees. Among the total tuition fees levied by these two types of schools (either elementary or middle schools), the amount of necessary fees paid by all students in each grade in non-one fee schools is higher than that paid by all students in each grade in one fee schools. In 2004, the total per capita tuition fee per annum of elem-entary schools that have implemented the 'One Fee System' was RMB 160 yuan, while it was RMB 247 yuan in schools without the system. The per capita amount of necessary fees was down by RMB 56 yuan, and the per capita amount of optional fees by RMB 30 yuan. The total per capita tuition fee of junior high schools with the 'One Fee System' was RMB 312 yuan, but it was RMB 492 yuan in junior high schools without the system. Differences in the amounts of per capita necessary and optional fees were RMB 156 yuan and RMB 25 yuan less, respectively (background report, Jin Lian 2006).

Schools with the 'One Fee System' have seen the amount of necessary and optional fees for students decline at each grade, to varying degrees, and there are fewer disparities in fees across different grades. In schools without the system, fees for different grades have varied largely. The amounts of

---

Box 4.8 'One Fee System' reform for compulsory education

In 2001, the 'One Fee System' was implemented on a trial basis in three elementary and junior high schools in rural areas within state-specified major counties subject to poverty alleviation. From 2002 onwards, the system was implemented in all the state-specified poor counties. By the end of 2003, twenty-two provinces (autonomous regions and municipalities) had adopted the system on a trial basis. In March 2004, the Ministry of Education, the National Development and Reform Commission, and the Ministry of Finance jointly formulated the 'Opinion with Regard to the Implementation of the "One Fee System . . ." Fee Collection Method in Schools across China in the Compulsory Education Stage', which requested: 'From the autumn semester of 2004 onwards, it is necessary to put into force the "One Fee System" in all schools in China in the compulsory education stage.' This meant the introduction of the system in urban areas.

The ceiling amount of the fee under the 'One Fee System' is jointly determined by the Ministry of Education, the National Development and Reform Commission, and the Ministry of Finance. After checking and verifying the rates of incidental charges; taking full account of the need to standardize textbook costs, long-distance education and English language education in elementary and middle schools, and considering the actual circumstances in poor regions, the ceiling amount in 2001 was determined as RMB 120 yuan per student in each academic year in rural elementary schools, and RMB 230 yuan per student in each academic year in rural junior high schools (later adjusted to RMB 160 yuan and RMB 260 yuan, respectively). Each province is allowed to increase or decrease the ceiling amount in line with its circumstances, but not in excess of 20 percent.

---

necessary and optional fees paid by students at higher grades have all been substantially greater than those for low grades (see Figure 4.15).

The 'One Fee System' reform has helped stem the overly speedy growth of educational fees and alleviated financial burdens on peasants. As indicated by the findings of Jin Lian (2006) in a background report, the system in Gansu Province has enhanced, to a certain degree, the schooling rate of children. Since this reform has not been consistent with other policies, however, schools have found it hard to run themselves normally after cutting down their fees. Some have even incurred heavier debts, which have resulted in deteriorating teaching and learning conditions for teachers and students. So while the 'One Fee System' has alleviated financial burdens on peasants, there has been a sacrifice in the quality of education. Particular problems exist in the intersection of this reform with others related to the financial and educational fundraising systems.

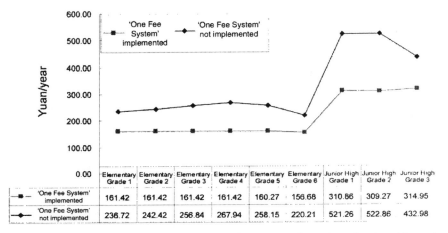

	Elementary Grade 1	Elementary Grade 2	Elementary Grade 3	Elementary Grade 4	Elementary Grade 5	Elementary Grade 6	Junior High Grade 1	Junior High Grade 2	Junior High Grade 3
'One Fee System' implemented	161.42	161.42	161.42	161.42	160.27	156.68	310.86	309.27	314.95
'One Fee System' not implemented	236.72	242.42	256.84	267.94	258.15	220.21	521.26	522.86	432.98

Figure 4.15 Variations in tuition fees levied upon students in schools with and without the 'One Fee System' in 2004.

Source: 2006 background report by Jin Lian.

Redeployment of elementary schools and high schools

In 2001, the State Council reached its 'Decision upon Reform into and Development of Basic Education', which announced a rearrangement of the schools offering compulsory education in rural areas, and stressed the necessity of conducting this in accordance with the actual circumstances in rural areas. Specifically, the decision required children to go to the nearest elementary and middle schools. It called for optimizing the distribution of educational resources, and consolidating some elementary and middle schools. The main intention was to reduce educational costs and enhance the quality of education. In 2004, the country closed 31,700 elementary schools and 973 junior high schools. Over 40,000 elementary and high schools were closed by 2004 (Ministry of Education 2005).

Overall, this step improved the distribution of educational resources, and the efficiency and quality of education in rural schools. Limited resources are now used in a centralized way to improve teaching conditions, update teaching facilities and enhance the utilization ratio of educational resources. Schools that remained open have employed outstanding teachers, who have precedence over less skilled or incompetent teachers, some of whom have been dismissed. Peasants no longer have to raise funds to buy new teaching devices or provide labour to construct infrastructure.

Some regions have encountered many unexpected problems, however. First, since some schools do not provide accommodation, or even if they do students cannot afford the costs, pupils in some rural elementary and high schools have to walk 10 or 20 *li* (one *li* = 500 m) a day along rugged narrow paths to attend schools in the nearest towns. In Guizhou, Ningxia and Gansu, nearly one third of the students have to travel more than 3 km every day and nearly one-eighth of the students have to travel 5 km–10 km each day. Many elementary and middle-school students have to sleep less (by up to two hours a day) and get up very early in order to get to school on time, before going home in the dark (Zeng Yiyu 2005). Owing to such long daily trips and a number of hidden hazards en route, some kids have not started to seek schooling until a higher-than-normal age. Others have given up going to school.

Second, the closure of elementary and middle schools has increased educational costs for peasants, although it has reduced public expenditures on each student. Worse still, the educational costs for poor rural households in mountainous areas have become heavier. These costs come from additional tuition fees (better schools charge more) and for expenses to support students living away from home because of the distance to their school. Third, some role-model elementary schools have been crammed with a suddenly increasing number of students, even though the intent was to improve educational services through school merging. They have suffered a greater pressure in terms of accommodation, funding and staffing, which has affected their functioning (Li Yaqin 2004). The influence of these changes on academic scores is best proven by the findings of the basic education survey in Gansu referred to earlier. According to this survey, provided other conditions are identical, the further the distance between a school and a child's home, the more probable it is that the child will discontinue his or her studying, and the worse his or her academic scores will be (background report, Jin Lian 2006). The Ministry of Education has become aware of all these problems and stressed the necessity of maintaining teaching outlets in remote regions in its latest policy statement documents.

National 'Two Targets' plan for western China

The national 'Two Targets' plan for western China (2004–2007) aimed to expand the reach of the nine years of compulsory education in that area and eliminate illiteracy among young adults. The plan had seven major measures: (1) to launch a plan to construct boarding schools in rural areas; (2) to implement the 'Two Exemptions and One Subsidy' policy to help students with financial hardships; (3) to carry out the 'Modern Distance Education for Elementary and High School Students in Rural Areas' project; (4) to make greater endeavours in training teachers for rural areas; (5) to advance educational reform and enhance the quality of educational services; (6) to intensify educational exchanges among different regions; and (7) to clarify the responsibilities of governments at all levels for accomplishing the 'Two Targets' plan.

The Government has planned to invest RMB 10 billion yuan over the four years of the scheme to build new boarding schools, and reconstruct or expand existing ones (most of which are junior high schools). By 2006, the

Government had provided RMB 9 billion yuan and erected 7,651 boarding schools. The total building area of new and reconstructed schools amounts to 13.81 million sq m.

The 'Two Exemptions and One Subsidy' policy was adopted to mitigate the difficulties of children from poor households in backward regions in accessing education, as required by China's 'Law of Compulsory Education'. The central Government is mainly liable for providing textbooks free of cost, while local governments at all levels are liable for exempting poor students from their incidental fees and providing them with a subsidy to cover boarding expenses. Targets of this policy are students at the stage of compulsory education who live in rural areas (including townships, towns and counties) but are unable to afford textbook costs, incidental fees and boarding expenses due to familial financial hardship (inclusive of those students in certain counties subject to special education). In 2004, the Government spent up to RMB 1.17 billion yuan in implementing this policy, which has generated staggering social benefits. In 2004 alone, 32 percent of the total number of students from poor households in central and western China were provided with free textbooks. In 2005, the total number provided with free textbooks was about 30 million. From 2005 to 2007, the Government planned to invest RMB 1.3 billion yuan, with local governments adding another RMB 2.81 billion yuan, to provide about 14 million elementary and middle-school students from poor households in the 592 state-specified major counties subject to poverty alleviation with free textbooks. They have also been exempted from incidental fees, and boarding students have been granted living subsidies. The Government decided to spread this policy to all rural areas between 2006 and 2007, enabling many more children from poor households to access educational opportunities.

The 'Modern Distance Education in Elementary and Middle Schools in Rural Areas' project aims to facilitate the sharing of quality educational resources between urban and rural areas, and enhance the quality and efficiency of rural education. On the basis of pilots conducted in 2003, the project has worked to furnish rural junior high schools with computer classrooms, and elementary schools with a satellite-assisted teaching device, a compact disc player and a full set of teaching compact discs. From 2002 to 2004, the technical level of modern teaching devices in rural areas of China grew significantly, and the gap between urban schools and rural ones diminished. The number of computers for every 100 students in rural junior high schools increased from two to three, a growth rate of nearly 60 percent. The percentage of rural schools with internet access rose from 6.3 percent to 13.1 percent.

On the whole, the policies and measures adopted by the Government since the mid 1990s have greatly improved the teaching conditions and quality of education in poor regions. But there are some mixed results. Reforms such as the 'One Fee System' and the 'Two Exemptions and One Subsidy' plan have clearly assisted poverty-stricken households. Other measures, such as the consolidation of schools and the launch of the boarding system, have had some negative impacts. To achieve more consistent results, such measures have to be better coordinated with each another. Overly speedy implementation of some measures and the failure to adopt necessary forms of support have caused problems. The competent education authority in China has become aware of these problems, and is thus working on more integrated measures to boost basic education in poverty-stricken regions and benefit poor populations at large.

Market-orientation in basic medical services stretches the means of impoverished people

The health care sector in rural areas has suffered the strongest impact from China's economic reform. Although the country's economy keeps growing at a stunning speed and the overall living standard of the Chinese people is increasing, the quality of medical services for rural populations (especially those who are poor) has been decreasing for a long time.

The rural cooperative medical system in China was formed in the 1960s. It played a significant role in extending basic medical services to rural areas, drawing much attention from the international community. Medical personnel in villages (alternatively called 'barefoot doctors') withdrew their wages, which were calculated on a point-accumulation basis, from their respective production teams. Villagers could purchase drugs at cost, and most had access to low-grade but affordable medical services. Health indicators such as the death rate of infants and per capita life expectancy in rural areas dramatically improved (Zhu Ling 2000). China was regarded by the global community as a role model for social development, despite its low-income level (Drèze and Sen 1989). By 1975, the free medical services system and the labour protection medical care system, which were funded by the Government and state-owned enterprises, and the cooperative medical care system, which was funded by rural communities, jointly covered nearly 90 percent of the total Chinese population, including almost all the urban population and 85 percent of the rural population (background report, Han Jun 2006).

After China embarked on reform and opening up, the institutional foundation for the cooperative medical care system eroded. This was accompanied by financial sustainability problems and growing inequalities in income distribution (Gu Xin and Fang Liming 2004; Zhu Ling 2000). By 1998, the percentage of people in the entire population who were not covered by any medical care system had grown to 76.42 percent. In rural areas, the figure has been as high as 94.78 percent. China was ranked last but three among the 191 member nations of the World Health Organization in terms of fairness in health care funding. What is more, China has failed to enhance medical services efficiency, even despite the sacrifice in fairness. With no public financing, a majority of Chinese peasants have had to rely on themselves and their household members to manage health care. Even medical services in rural areas have gradually embraced a market-orientation, which requires them to survive by constantly increasing the prices of both their medical services and drugs. The problems existing in the country's overall medical care management system, including the abuse of power for personal gain, have given a further stimulus to the excessive growth in prices of services and drugs.

Market-oriented reform in rural medical care and poor management practices has caused problems such as the following. First, a wide gap has grown between urban and rural areas in primary medical coverage. In 2004, the neonatal mortality rate, infant mortality rate, mortality rate of children under five years and the maternal mortality rate in rural areas were 2.1 times, 2.4 times, 2.4 times and 2.4 times those recorded in urban areas, respectively.

Second, the incidence rate of disease in rural areas remains relatively high, with epidemic diseases still noticeable in some regions. In normal circumstances, with socioeconomic development, health care conditions will improve and disease incidence will decline. But in China since the 1990s, the two-week morbidity rate of Chinese residents rose from 128.2 per thousand to 139.5 per thousand. Worsening control and prevention of epidemic diseases mean incidence and death rates in rural areas have continued to increase.

Third, a wide gap exists between urban and rural areas in the availability of medical services. Availability is even worse for low-income rural populations and those in remote areas. The third national medical service survey found in 2003 that 61.1 percent of rural residents were less than 1 km from their nearest medical service outlet, a figure 20.7 percent less than for urban residents. Another 4.8 percent of the surveyed households were more than 5 km from their nearest medical service outlet, while 34.1 percent were 1 km–5 km away. The availability of medical services in low-income rural areas (defined in the survey as having a per capita annual income of RMB 1187 yuan) is even worse. Only 37.9 percent of the surveyed households were less than 1 km from their nearest medical services outlet; 18 percent were more than 5 km away (Statistical Information Centre of the Ministry of Health 2004). From 1985 to 2002, the percentage of administrative villages with a village-level medical services outlet in the total number of administrative villages dropped from 87.4 percent to 74.1 percent.

Fourth, the medical expenditure burdens borne by peasants have swiftly grown heavier. Health care has become the third largest expenditure for many households, after only food and educational expenses. From 1980 to 2003, the per capita net income of rural residents rose from RMB 191.33 yuan to RMB 2622.24 yuan, a growth rate of 1371 percent. Per capita personal consumption expenditure grew from RMB 162.21 yuan to RMB 1943.3 yuan, a growth rate of 1,198 percent. Per capita medical and health care expenditures climbed from RMB 3.42 yuan to RMB 115.75 yuan, far outstripping income gains with a growth rate of 3,385 percent (Rural Survey Group of the National Bureau of Statistics of China 2004). Given that a considerable portion of rural residents' income and consumption is in kind, and medical expenses are all incurred in cash, the drain on cash reserves for their medical expenses will be particularly great. In 2003, the per capita personal consumption expenditure in cash of rural residents was RMB 1,576.64 yuan; medical expenditures comprised 7.34 percent of this.

Fifth, peasants have a low-level medical security system. As indicated by the third national medical service survey, only 21 percent of rural residents have access to medical security, compared to 55.25 percent of urban residents. In rural areas, the cooperative medical system is the most prevalent mode of medical security. It has started to evolve quickly and in a positive way. By the end of 2005, this system covered 179 million peasants, or 19 percent of all rural residents.

The impact of a lack of basic medical security varies from one group of people to another, but it is clear that those most in need are people too poor to afford necessary medical services. They are exposed to greater disease risks, including tuberculosis and sexually transmitted diseases. The incidence rate of epidemic diseases among the poorest quarter of the rural population is three times that of the richest quarter. The death rate of infants among the poorest quarter is twice that of the richest quarter (World Bank 1993, 1997).

A lack of basic medical security for poor and low-income populations also means that not only will medical expenditures consume already limited personal consumption expenditures, but also that people below the poverty line will fall into deeper poverty, and low-income people may fall below the poverty line.

The influence of diseases on poverty can be seen from changes in the incidence rate of poverty after the introduction of out-of-pocket health payments. Provided per capita household consumption expenditure and per capita income are used as household welfare indicators, and the absolute poverty line and the low-income line of the National Bureau of Statistics of China are the yardsticks for identifying poor households, the medical expenses paid annually by a household can be divided by the headcount of this household to work out per capita payments. This allows the calculation of changes in the incidence rate of household poverty after the introduction of out-of-pocket payments, which indicate the influence of health care costs on poverty. As shown in Table 4.4, after medical expenses are incurred, the percentage of those households below the poverty and low-income lines varies largely. When medical expenses in cash are not deducted, the percentage of households with a household per capita consumption expenditure below the poverty line is 4 percent; after medical expenses in cash are deducted, the incidence rate of absolute poverty goes to 8.4 percent, rising by 110 percent. Likewise, after the occurrence of medical expenses, the percentage of those households with household per capita consumption expenditure below the low-income line grows from 11.7 percent to 21.2 percent, up by 81.2 percent. This implies that the staggering medical expenses of low-income rural households can almost double the size of the poor population in rural areas.

Another consequence of a lack of medical care is that a large number of poor people don't seek services after getting sick. This results in physical

Table 4.4 Influence of out-of-pocket payments on poverty

Item	Consumption below RMB 637 yuan (%)	Consumption below RMB 991 yuan (%)	Income below RMB 637 yuan (%)	Income below RMB 991 yuan (%)
Incidence rate of poverty prior to out-of-pocket payments (%)	4	11.7	12.2	20.8
Incidence rate of poverty after out-of-pocket payments (%)	8.4	21.2	22.9	32.7
Extent of the change in terms of the incidence rate of poverty (%)	4.4	9.5	10.7	11.9
Degree of influence of out-of-pocket payments upon poverty[a] (%)	110	81.2	87.7	57.2

Source: Survey data from the Department of Rural Economy Research under the Development Research Centre of the State Council.

Note:

a The degree of influence refers to changes in the incidence rate of poverty after the introduction of out-of-pocket payments (i.e., to divide the incidence rate of poverty after out-of-pocket payments by the incidence rate of poverty before out-of-pocket payments).

deterioration or chronic diseases. Some eventually lose a part or all of their capability to work, or they even die. The decrease in the number of labourers in a household will depress income, thus starting a vicious circle. A survey of thirty poor counties found one third of low-income households do not use medical services at all; in comparison, only 16 percent of high-income households do not do so. The per capita number of visits to outpatient services for the lowest quarter of the surveyed households is only 60 percent of that of the highest-income quarter (World Bank 1998).

As indicated by data in the second national medical services survey, among various other factors resulting in poverty, sickness is the second most important, next only to lack of labourers. In reality, the lack of labourers is often caused by sickness or disability. In rural areas, sickness could be considered the most important reason for poverty (background report, Han Jun 2006). A survey conducted by the Development Research Centre of the State Council found that about 41 percent of poor households have been trapped in poverty by major diseases. In eastern China, many cases of poverty have been incurred by disease: up to 50 percent among rural households. In central and western China, poverty is caused by more reasons, but about 38 percent of rural households in poverty have ended up poor through suffering diseases.[21]

Excessive adherence to the market orientation principle in the rural medical services sector has triggered problems that have caught the attention of the

Government. Since 2003, it has started to develop the cooperative medical care system and plans to implement a new type of rural cooperative medical structure in all rural areas by 2008. According to data from the Ministry of Health, at the end of 2005, 678 counties have set up the new rural cooperative medical system. They comprise 23.7 percent of the total number of counties in China. About 236.3 million rural residents are covered by this system. The total number of rural residents taking part amounts to 178.8 million persons, or 75.7 percent of the total rural population in these counties. In central and western China, 343 counties have implemented the new system on a trial basis, comprising 15.8 percent of the total number of counties in these regions, and covering 105.2 million rural residents. About 74.5 million rural residents are covered, constituting 70.83 percent of the total rural population. In 2005, the country devoted RMB 9.283 billion yuan to this new system, including RMB 3.693 billion yuan in subsidies granted by local governments at all levels and RMB 542 million yuan in subsidies from the central Government.

The rural cooperative medical system is already helping to mitigate medical expenses for rural residents to a certain degree. In 2005, the total spending of the national medical fund for the rural cooperative system was RMB 6.175 billion yuan; it financed a total hospitalization volume of 5.8 million person-times. In addition, physical checkups totalled 21.2 million person-times. Strong fundraising capabilities in better-developed regions make these effects more visible there.

The rural cooperative medical system has also encountered problems, such as inadequate support to implementation, lack of funds due to fiscal decentralization, high management costs and excessive adherence to the market orientation principle. These problems have limited the sustainability of the new system and reduced its impact (Gu Xin and Fang Liming 2004; Zhu Ling 2000; Zhou Haojie 2005; Jia Kang and Zhang Licheng 2005). The most severe problem is the lack of equal access to services. The system has set a bottom line and a ceiling amount for each application for reimbursement of medical expenses. Because hospitalization is expensive, almost every inpatient has to pay a few thousand or even tens of thousands of yuan. Reimbursement, restricted by the ceiling amount, may not be enough to cover these costs. Patients may have to pay for some items and services, even if others are reimbursed. For those rural households with a relatively high income, such expenses are manageable. Households with a low income or in poverty are either unable to take part in the system due to their financial hardship, or cannot fully enjoy its benefits because they cannot afford to pay for even a portion of medical expenses (background report, Han Jun 2006).

The Government implemented the rural medical rescue system in 2002. It is mainly targeted to those rural households entitled to the 'five guarantees' or living in absolute poverty, as well as other groups of poverty-stricken people. The system can either provide medical subsidies for people with major diseases or help them access their local cooperative medical systems. The central Government invests RMB 300 million yuan each year in this initiative. In

2004, local governments provided counterpart funding of RMB 800 million yuan. Thus far, 31 provinces have developed proposals for medical rescue systems in rural areas. In regions with rural cooperative medical systems, most rural medical rescue subsidies are used for people in absolute poverty to pay the fee for taking part in the new rural cooperative medical system.

In 2005, the medical rescue system benefited 3.04 million rural residents with financial hardships. The main problem with the system has been its rather limited coverage. In regions where poor households are financed through the medical rescue system to take part in the rural cooperative medical system, there are questions about whether or not the poor have equal access to medical services.

To what degree has agricultural policy reform benefited the poor?

In order to boost the development of agriculture, facilitate environmental protection and increase the income level of peasants, the Government in recent years has adopted various policies with regard to taxation reform, the conversion of croplands into forests and the provision of agricultural subsidies. These adjustments have eased the burdens of peasants and stimulated the growth of direct income earned by rural households. This in turn helps reverse the decrease in agricultural efficiency spurred by the fall of the market prices of agricultural products since the late 1990s. This section will look at the degree to which these policies have helped people in poverty.

Reform of agricultural taxes

The reform of agricultural taxes primarily features four cancellations, two adjustments and one reform – namely, to cancel fees collected by township governments, fundraising for education in rural areas, the butchery tax and the *yiwugong* (labour tax). This has involved adjusting the agricultural tax policy and the agricultural specialty tax policy, and reforming the method for monetary withdrawals by villages. In 2000, an intensive package of work was done on a trial basis for the sake of this reform. In 2004, eight provinces exempted peasants from agricultural taxes. Eleven principal grain-producing provinces and autonomous regions brought down their agricultural tax rates by 3 percentage points, and eleven provinces reduced their agricultural tax rates by 1 percent. In 2004, this policy reduced the tax burdens on peasants by about RMB 28 billion yuan, and decreased the per capita tax burden on peasants by RMB 30 yuan, a decline of 44.3 percent. In 2005, twenty-eight provinces exempted peasants from agricultural taxes; three provinces (Hebei, Shandong and Yunnan) also, as requested by the Government, adjusted their agricultural tax rates to be as low as less than 2 percent. State-specified poor counties exempted peasants from agricultural taxes and cancelled their animal husbandry taxes as a whole.

Since 2006, agricultural taxes have been cancelled nationwide. According to the Ministry of Finance, the reform of agricultural taxes has alleviated the financial burdens upon peasants by approximately RMB 125 billion yuan each year. The Government will arrange a transfer payment fund of RMB 78.2 billion yuan to facilitate such reform of agricultural taxes on an annual basis. Local governments have made counterpart funding arrangements as well (see www.people.com.cn 2006b).

Agricultural tax reductions and exemptions constitute a policy that benefits all rural residents. At first, the central Government focused on agricultural and animal husbandry taxes in all the nationally designated key poor counties, which accords with the country's principle of providing poor regions and poverty-stricken populations with benefits ahead of all others. As China's agricultural taxes are land-based, for many years, these taxes were regressive (in other words, the percentage of income going into taxes is higher for poor households more dependent on agriculture than for better-off households). Data from the National Bureau of Statistics of China's survey of rural households in 592 state-specified poor counties show that for rural households, the percentage of income taken up by taxes decreases with income levels. For rural households with a per capita net income below RMB 100 yuan, the percentage of per capita tax in their per capita net income has been up to 101 percent – their incomes in a full year are not enough to cover the taxes due. As for those rural households with a per capita net income between RMB 100 yuan and RMB 300 yuan, the percent of per capita tax in their per capita net income was 24.65 percent. In the highest income group, with a per capita net income above RMB 3,000 yuan, the per capita tax was only 2.32 percent of per capita net income. Both the percentages and the absolute amounts of taxes have been regressive. For instance, rural households in the lowest-income group paid RMB 59.2 yuan per person, higher than that of the following three higher income groups (see Figure 4.16). Tax reductions and

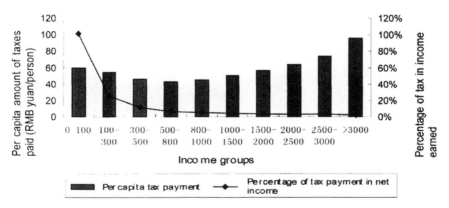

Figure 4.16 Taxes paid by rural households in different income groups in major counties subject to poverty alleviation in 2002.

Source: Rural Survey Group of the National Bureau of Statistics of China 2003.

exemptions will naturally benefit poor households to a greater extent, and should be considered a policy with a potent impact on poverty alleviation. In fact, the decrease in the size of the poor population in 2004 and 2005 is closely correlated with the reform of agricultural taxes.

The state-specified poor counties carried out agricultural tax reductions and exemptions in 2005. The influence of this on poor and low-income households can be deduced by comparing changes in the absolute and relative amounts of tax reduction conferred on rural households in different income groups. Using data from a poverty surveillance survey made public by the Rural Survey Group of the National Bureau of Statistics of China, this report divided rural households surveyed from 2002 to 2005 into five comparable income groups,[22] before calculating the amount and degree of tax reduction for each group in 2005 compared to 2002. The results are set out in Figure 4.17. It shows that an overwhelming majority of taxes on rural households in poor counties have been reduced or cancelled, and that the degree of tax reduction is bigger in the lower-income groups. For instance, the amount of taxes upon poor and low-income households with a per capita net income falling between RMB 0 yuan and RMB 800 yuan was reduced by 92.6 percent. Taxes on rural households with a per capita net income above RMB 3,000 yuan declined by 87.95 percent. The degree of tax reduction for the low-income group is 4.65 percent more than for the high-income group.

As tax reduction is tantamount to net income growth, it is possible to estimate the contribution made by tax reduction to income growth for rural households in different income groups between 2002 and 2005. The result proves that tax reduction contributed conspicuously to the income growth of rural households in the poor and low-income groups. In 2005, tax reduction comprised 7.26 percent of per capita net income for people with a per capita

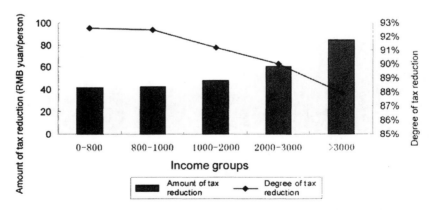

Figure 4.17 Degrees of agricultural tax exemptions and reductions for rural households in different income groups, 2002–2005.

Source: Rural Survey Group of the National Bureau of Statistics of China 2003 and the Department of Rural Affairs of the National Bureau of Statistics of China 2006.

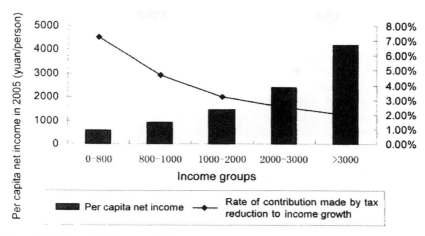

Figure 4.18 Contributions made by tax reduction to income growth among rural households in different income groups from 2002 to 2005.

net income between RMB 0 yuan and RBM 800 yuan, the lowest income groups. This percentage decreases with the increase in income. For the high-income group with a per capita income above RMB 3,000 yuan, tax reduction contributed to 2.01 percent of income, which was 5.25 percent lower than for the poorer group (see Figure 4.18).

Various subsidization policies

Starting in the late 1990s, the Government promulgated a series of policies to boost agricultural development and facilitate environmental protection. It granted various monetary subsidies to rural households nationwide and those involved in certain projects (see Box 4.9).

Box 4.9 Primary agricultural subsidization and environmental protection policies

Subsidies for grain, fine breeds and agricultural machinery in primary grain-producing areas: Since 2003, the Government has started to implement fine-breed subsidization projects aiming at households that adopt high-yield varieties, and provided a total subsidy of RMB 300 million yuan for the production of soybeans and wheat in nine major grain-producing provinces (Inner Mongolia, Liaoning, Jilin, Heilongjiang, Hebei, Henan, Shandong, Jiangsu and Anhui). In 2004, the fine-breed subsidy was expanded to cover the production of paddy rice, wheat, corn and soybeans, totalling over RMB 1 billion yuan and covering four more provinces (Hunan, Hubei, Jiangxi and Sichuan). In

2005, the Government extended the project to some minor grain-producing areas. After trials in 2003, it began granting subsidies directly to peasants in the main grain-producing counties in thirteen major and sixteen minor grain-producing provinces. These subsidies totalled RMB 11.6 billion yuan and benefited 600 million peasants. In 2005, the total amount increased to RMB 13.2 billion yuan. A subsidy specifically for purchasing agricultural machinery was offered in 500 counties in thirty-four provinces, autonomous regions and municipalities, expanding a 2004 programme for 66 counties in sixteen provinces.

The 'Conversion of Croplands to Forests' project: In 1999, this project was initially implemented in Shaanxi, Gansu and Sichuan provinces. In 2002, it expanded to cover 1,897 counties in twenty-five provinces (autonomous regions and municipalities). As of 2005, a total forest acreage of 17.342 million ha (about 260 million *mu*) had been planted. About 7.83 million ha were converted from croplands to forests; an additional 9.5 million ha of barren hills and lands had been planted with trees. The cost was RMB 63.7 billion yuan, of which RMB 58.3 billion yuan was provided by the central Government. An important policy under this project is to provide food and cash subsidies for up to eight years to rural households that have relinquished their croplands for the sake of conversion to forests – the amounts of subsidies are determined based on acreage (State Forestry Administration 2004).

'Conversion of Pasture into Grasslands' project: The Government began this project in 2003. It was intended to regenerate grassland areas in eastern and western Inner Mongolia, Gansu and Ningxia provinces, the Jiangheyuan area of the Qinghai-Tibet Plateau and the north of Xinjiang. The project has involved 116 counties in eight provinces and autonomous regions (Inner Mongolia, Sichuan, Yunnan, Tibet, Qinghai, Gansu, Ningxia and Xinjiang), as well as the Xinjiang Production and Construction Corps. The targeted areas are all affected by poverty. In 2005, the total acreage of pasture converted into grasslands was 190 million *mu*. The total acreage of grasslands where grazing is prohibited, suspended or allowed only on a rotating basis has exceeded 1.2 billion *mu*. The total acreage of grasslands already contracted out to local residents for a balanced use and protection has amounted to 3.54 billion *mu*, or more than 70 percent of total usable grasslands in the country. The Government has also conferred food and forage subsidies to herders who have relinquished their pastures for grasslands.

Compensation for ecological benefits from forests: The Government's compensation fund for ecological benefits from forests reimburses forest planting, fostering, protection and management expenses incurred by people taking care of major public forests that benefit public welfare. The compensation standard is RMB 5 yuan per *mu* per year on average. RMB 4.5 yuan goes towards the above expenses, while the other RMB 0.5 yuan covers fire control expenditures and other public control expenses (Agricultural and Animal Husbandry Department of Inner Mongolia Autonomous Region 2004). In 2001, 658 counties and 24 state-level natural reserves in eleven provinces and autonomous regions adopted this compensation system. On 10 December 2004, the system was officially launched across the country. Since 2004, the Government has been investing RMB 2 billion yuan on an annual basis in the country's major public forests, whose total acreage reaches 400 million *mu*.

Due to a lack of reliable data, it is not possible to analyse the impact of each policy on the poor population. One small survey indicates that the 'Conversion of Croplands into Forest' project has stepped up income growth for poor households. It surveyed 143 rural households that converted their croplands into forests and 66 rural households that have not done so in the southern mountainous areas of Ningxia Province. In 1999, before the conversion took place, the per capita net income of those rural households that would later convert their croplands was RMB 856 yuan and their per capita direct personal consumption expenditure was RMB 299 yuan. These figures were 19 percent and 29 percent, respectively, lower than for rural households that did not convert. In comparative terms, rural households that have converted their croplands into forests are extremely poor; large cash subsidies under the conversion project provided substantial benefits. From 1999 to 2003, the growth rates of per capita net income and consumption expenditure for rural households that converted their croplands were both higher than those for rural households that have not done so – per capita net income growth was 3.2 percent greater while the gap in per capita consumption expenditure shrank to 24 percent (Topical Research Group of Nanjing Agricultural University 2006; see Figure 4.19).

Overall assessment of the poverty alleviation effects of other policies beneficial to peasants

Compared to the developmental poverty alleviation and rural social security policies, the reform of policies beneficial to peasants is targeted to the entire rural population. The poverty alleviation effects of these policies largely depend on the degree of participation by poor households. Those more willing to participate are more likely to draw benefits.

In general, the reform of policies for peasants has visibly helped poor households and helped fuel the momentum behind the decline in the size of the rural poor population. For the poor, the most radical reform measures have been agricultural tax reductions and exemptions, and the conversion of croplands into forests. These two policies have generated relatively marked poverty alleviation effects, partly because they are, *per se*, more beneficial to the poor. For example, the 'Conversion of Croplands into Forests' project

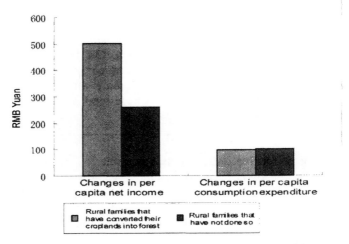

Figure 4.19 Changes in income and expenditure for rural households converting or not converting their croplands into forests in Ningxia Province from 1999 to 2003.

Source: Topical Research Team of Nanjing Agricultural University 2006.

focuses on arable lands in mountainous regions where most people earn a lower income. Tax reform has solved the problem of higher taxation burdens on the poor.

Poor people do not have to pay for such policies, therefore it is impossible for them to be excluded, as they have been at times under the developmental mode of poverty alleviation. Some people, for example, cannot afford the new cooperative medical system because of the portion of medical expenses that they have to pay on their own. In education, on the whole, reform has been positive for poor households. The 'One Fee Reform' and the 'Two Exemptions and One Subsidy' policy have reduced educational expenses for poor households. But some other policies, such as the consolidation of schools and the introduction of the boarding school system, have increased educational costs because they did not fully account for the needs of poverty-stricken households. In some cases, this has reduced educational opportunities for children from poor households.

THE POVERTY ALLEVIATION EFFECTS OF ANTI-POVERTY POLICIES IN URBAN AREAS

The minimum living standard system in urban areas and other social security policies

The minimum living standard system for urban areas is a pillar of China's anti-poverty campaign, and the largest national social welfare project in

China (Duoji Cairang 2001). It entitles any person, no matter whether he or she has the capacity to work and has a source of income, to receive the minimum living standard subsidy provided by the Government and other welfare subsidies, as long as the income of his or her household is below the minimum living standard line set by the local government. The following section reviews the implementation of this system, examines how it has targeted the low-income population in urban areas, and assesses its record in achieving its goal of covering each and every eligible person.

The overall coverage ratio of the minimum living standard system can be looked at through the variations in the size of the population that benefits. When cities first implemented the system on a trial basis, on their own initiatives, the population covered was low. As the system spread across the country, the size of the population involved began growing rapidly, especially since 1998. By 2003, 22.47 million persons were using the system (constituting 4.3 percent of the total urban population). Through the gradual institutionalization of the system, the population covered has remained stable since 2002, with the coverage ratio slightly above 4 percent (see Figure 4.20). The coverage ratio varies largely from one province to another. In 2004, the highest ratio was recorded in Jilin Province, at 11.25 percent; the lowest ratio was in Zhejiang Province, at 0.72 percent (see Table 4.5).

A significant feature of the minimum living standard system is to provide income allowances to all households with incomes below their local security line for bare subsistence, so incomes can be brought up to this level. An important yardstick for assessing the system is to see if it has achieved its coverage goal. Using data from a comprehensive 2004 survey of urban areas conducted

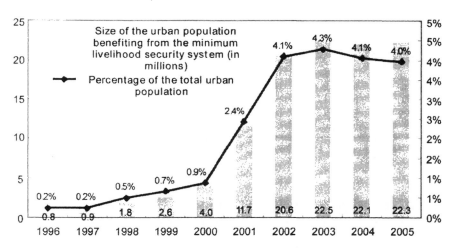

Figure 4.20 The size of the urban population using the minimum living standard system and coverage ratios from 1996 to 2005.

Source: Ministry of Civil Affairs 2006c and *China Statistics Yearbook of Civil Administration 2006.*

Table 4.5 Sizes of urban populations covered by the minimum living standard system and coverage ratios in different provinces in 2004

Region	Number of urban residents covered by the minimum living standard system (persons)	Total number of urban residents (10,000 persons)	Coverage ratio of the minimum livelihood security system (%)
Beijing	160,774	854.7	1.88
Tianjin	205,118	556.17	3.69
Hebei	811,250	1,809	4.48
Shanxi	848,643	1,321.7	6.42
Inner Mongolia	717,128	911.8	7.86
Liaoning	1,373,887	1,996.5	6.88
Jilin	1,352,550	1,202.4	11.25
Heilongjiang	1,570,046	2,014.5	7.79
Shanghai	403,580	1,097.6	3.68
Jiangsu	382,390	3,580.98	1.07
Zhejiang	88,461	1,224.1	0.72
Anhui	990,415	1,342	7.38
Fujian	201,772	1,086.3	1.86
Jiangxi	1,005,048	1,119.3	8.98
Shandong	654,942	2,951	2.22
Henan	1,348,304	2,103	6.41
Hubei	1,578,315	2,627.8	6.01
Hunan	1,358,225	2,377.7	5.71
Guangdong	378,446	3,797.9	1
Guangxi	566,210	902	6.28
Hainan	134,472	304.5	4.42
Chongqing	699,189	785.8	8.9
Sichuan	1,514,778	1,914.3	7.91
Guizhou	474,805	1,025.9	4.63
Yunnan	658,451	724.1	9.09
Tibet	43,418	40.1	10.84
Shaanxi	779,516	922	8.45
Gansu	610,036	749.2	8.14
Qinghai	200,777	207.5	9.68
Ningxia	199,685	207.8	9.61
Xinjiang	739,574	690.1	10.72
Nationwide	22,050,205	54,283	4.06

Source: Ministry of Civil Affairs 2005c and China Statistical Yearbook of Civil Administration 2005.

by the National Bureau of Statistics of China in 2004 and the urban security lines for bare subsistence in 35 medium and large cities, a calculation shows that 8.13 percent of residents in these cities should be covered. The average gap between the income of these people and the security line for bare subsistence is RMB 892.8 yuan. The data shows the actual coverage ratio of the system is 3.91 percent, close to the national ratio. The per capita minimum living standard subsidy, calculated on an annual basis, is RMB 850 yuan. The calculation reveals that at least 50 percent of people whose incomes fall short of the security line for bare subsistence are not covered by the minimum living standard system. For those who are covered, however, the average amount of the minimum living standard subsidy can largely offset poverty (Wang Youjuan 2006).

Further analysis demonstrates that among people who should be covered by the system, 32.6 percent have received the minimum living standard subsidies and 67.4 percent have not. Among people who should not be covered because their incomes are above the security line for bare subsistence, 1.4 percent have received the subsidies. They comprise 32.2 percent of the total number of people with subsidies. In 2004, the minimum living standard security system actually covered only one third of those people who should be covered; among those people receiving subsidies, only 67.8 percent have been accurately identified (see Figure 4.21).[23]

An effective social security measure should distribute more relief funds to the poorest populations. All those households surveyed in 2004 by per capita household income (after deducting the security fund received) can be ranked from low to high and divided into 10 groups, with the first group re-divided into two sub-groups. The distribution of people receiving the relief fund and the distribution of relief funds in these groups will then be apparent. As illustrated in Figure 4.22, the 5 percent lowest income group has 53.17 percent of the population covered by the minimum living standard system and has obtained 60.13 percent of all subsidies. The 10 percent lowest income group has 73.2 percent of people covered by the system and has garnered 77.46 percent of subsidies. Obviously, a household with a higher income should receive a lower subsidy. These figures provide evidence of the satisfactorily accurate targeting of the minimum living standard system.[24]

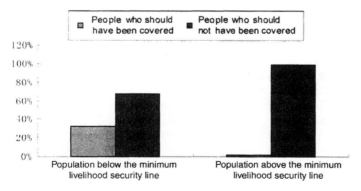

Figure 4.21 Coverage ratios of the minimum living standard system for people who should and should not be covered by this system.

Source: Wang Youjuan 2006.

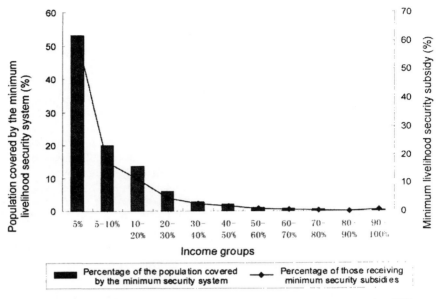

Figure 4.22 Coverage ratios of the minimum living standard system for different income groups.

Source: Wang Youjuan 2006.

Overall, the minimum living standard policy has generated a relatively apparent effect on poverty alleviation. A large majority of households receiving subsidies have seen their income levels exceed the security line for bare subsistence, and the system has now become a primary component of urban poverty alleviation. After the 'Rules upon the Minimum Living Standard for Urban Residents' were promulgated, and as the system has been standardized and institutionalized, funds have increased and the number of covered urban residents has kept growing. Up to 68 percent of people receiving subsidies has been accurately identified. Those at lower income levels are more likely to receive a higher amount of subsidies. At present, the main problem for the minimum living standard system is the failure to reach every eligible person. About two-thirds of people who should be covered are not.

Besides the minimum living standard system, China has also set up endowment, medical, unemployment, industrial injury and childbirth insurance systems for urban residents (see Box 4.10). These systems have greatly reduced the risks of most urban residents, who are employed by formal sectors, in terms of ending up in poverty due to senility, sickness, unemployment and injury at work. This has helped cities maintain a relatively low incidence rate of poverty. Childbirth insurance has played an important role in ensuring the health and living standards of women of childbearing age.

Box 4.10 Different forms of insurance for urban residents

Basic endowment insurance is mainly targeted to employees of enterprises. Such insurance funds have stemmed from endowment insurance premiums paid by enterprises and their employees, and interest generated by endowment insurance funds. Social insurance organizations have set up basic endowment insurance accounts for each worker, based on 11 percent of his or her wage being subject to payment of such insurance premiums. Workers receive retirement pensions from the state-stipulated dates of their retirement to their death. Such retirement pensions are distributed monthly.[25] By the end of 2005, the number of urban residents in China with basic endowment insurance totalled 174.87 million persons, and the total number of retirees withdrawing pensions had reached 43.67 million persons. By the end of 2005, 17.48 million workers and 26.55 million retirees participated in the pension system. The accumulated balance of basic endowment insurance funds in 2005 reached RMB 40.41 billion yuan (Ministry of Civil Affairs 2005b).

Unemployment insurance is targeted to workers in all enterprises and public institutions in urban areas. In practice, urban enterprises and public institutions pay unemployment insurance premiums amounting to 2 percent of total wages and salaries payable to their employees. Workers contribute 1 percent. This entitles them to receive unemployment insurance funds on a monthly basis during unemployment, along with medical subsidies, funeral arrangement subsidies and compensation subsidies, the amounts of which are usually formulated by the provincial people's governments. By the end of 2005, 106.48 million persons had unemployment insurance; 3.62 million were withdrawing unemployment insurance funds. The accumulated balance of unemployment insurance funds had reached RMB 51.1 billion yuan. At that time, the registered unemployment rate in urban areas of China was 4.2 percent, and 3.65 million people could withdraw unemployment insurance funds (Ministry of Civil Affairs 2005b).

Basic medical insurance is for all employees in urban areas except those in township enterprises or who are self-employed. Funding for this system stems chiefly from nationally raised basic medical insurance funds, which comprise 70 percent of medical insurance premiums paid by employers. Individual accounts include medical insurance premiums paid by employees on their own, along with the 30 percent of medical insurance premiums paid by employers. Employers pay medical insurance premiums not in excess of 6 percent of the total wages and salaries payable to their employees. Employees pay 2 percent of their wages and salaries. Those insured can seek medical services from specified medical institutions on presentation of their insurance cards and buy drugs from specified pharmacies.[26] By the end of 2005, 137.83 million persons had this insurance, including 100.22 million workers and 37.61 million retirees. The accumulated balance of basic medical insurance funds was 127.8 billion yuan. The balance of nationally raised funds was 75 billion yuan, and the total balance in individuals' accounts had climbed to 52.8 billion yuan (Ministry of Civil Affairs 2005b).

Industrial injury insurance is designed for workers who fall victim to work-related accidents or occupational diseases. Enterprises pay a certain percentage of the total amounts of wages and salaries into insurance funds. After suffering any industrial injury, workers have part or all of their medical expenses reimbursed; those who are injured or disabled, or their household dependants or relatives, are entitled to compensation money and subsidies of different amounts. By the end of 2005, 84.78 million persons were covered, and about 650,000 persons were using this insurance each year. The accumulated balance of funds in 2005 amounted to RMB 16.4 billion yuan (Ministry of Civil Affairs 2005b).

Childbirth insurance is meant for working women and comes mostly from employers. Insured women are entitled to maternity leave, a childbirth allowance, and medical service during the pregnancy, childbirth and infant-nursing periods. By the end of 2005, 54.08 million persons were covered by this insurance. Insurance was conferred 620,000 person-times. The accumulated balance of funds amounted to RMB 7.2 billion yuan (Ministry of Civil Affairs 2005b).

Re-employment project

From 1998 to 2004, 27 million workers were laid off in China, 21.6 million of whom lost jobs with state-owned enterprises. In the latter category, 19.4 million people were re-employed, constituting 89.8 percent of laid-off workers. According to labour force survey data from the Chinese Academy of Social Sciences, among those people successfully re-employed within the twelve months' period prior to the survey, the ratio of re-employment of males was higher than that of females. For both males and females, the highest ratio of re-employment was in the age group 16–29 years; the ratio declined with age. The ratio of re-employment also rose with the degree of education (Cai Fang *et al.* 2005).

According to data from the *Employment and Social Security Survey in Urban Areas of China* in 2004, among those labourers aged 16 to 60 years who answered 'ever laid off or unemployed', 47 percent of them were 'being employed for the time being'. More specifically, 53 percent of males and 42 percent of females were 'being employed for the time being'. This confirms that the ratio of re-employment of males is higher than that of females. Thirty-three percent of people with an educational degree from an elementary school or below were 'being employed for the time being', compared to 43 percent of those with a junior high school degree, 49 percent of those with a degree from a senior high school or secondary technical school, and up to 66 percent of those with an educational degree from a college or above (see Figure 4.23).

Both policies and individual efforts have helped laid-off workers find new work. The Government, community and society have all attached importance to the re-employment issue, and provided financial and material resources and manpower (all deemed as indispensable) to help address it. In the final analysis, however, re-employment success also depends on the personal qualifications and endeavours of people who have lost their jobs.

Labour survey data in five cities shows that among sampled people who have lost their jobs but not of their own accord, people who are eligible for early retirement wait longest for re-employment. People who have used minimum livelihood subsidies as laid-off employees or have registered for receiving unemployment insurance funds spend a much longer time in unemployment than people who do not use any form of public security. The pace of re-employment by people with no security is apparently faster than that of the first two groups. This affirms the notion that welfare level is inversely proportional to attempts to secure new work.

The usefulness of re-employment in helping laid-off and unemployed people emerge from poverty is clear from data from the *Employment and Social Security Survey in Chinese Cities in 2004*. Among all households with

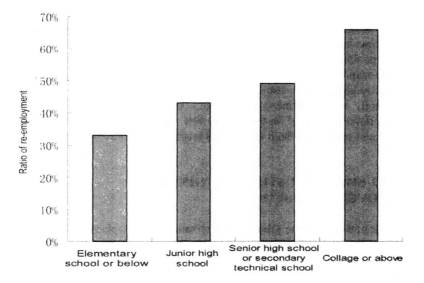

Figure 4.23 Ratios of re-employment recorded by unemployed or laid-off labourers with different educational degrees.

Source: 2006 background report by Cai Fang and Wang Meiyan.

labourers who were ever laid-off or unemployed, only 12.4 percent of those with labourers who have become re-employed were in poverty, compared to up to 28.1 percent of those with labourers who have not been re-employed.

Re-employment training to enhance the capabilities of laid-off and unemployed people has not generated a satisfactory effect. One survey suggests it has not had broad enough coverage. The survey, conducted in five cities, found an overwhelming majority of laid-off people have not received re-employment training. While 12 percent said their re-employment training was compulsory, an even smaller number of people have actually participated in training. The World Bank carried out a study of the effect of re-employment training for laid-off workers in two cities, Wuhan and Shenyang, which have a relatively large number of people laid off by state-owned enterprises. The study found that re-employment projects implemented by the Government have helped laid-off workers in Wuhan but generated some negative fallout in Shenyang (World Bank 2002a). This suggests that even well-intentioned policies for the labour market need to take into account a variety of factors.

Overall evaluation of the effects of poverty alleviation policies for urban areas

The implementation of urban poverty alleviation policies, which are centered on the minimum living standard system, has played a critical role in reducing urban poverty and strengthening social stability. The minimum living standard policy for urban areas has been satisfactory in selecting target groups and providing income subsidies. A large majority of people who use this system are impoverished. Their minimum living standard subsidies can help their household income levels rise to the security line for bare subsistence. At present, the primary problem of the minimum living standard system is its failure to cover everyone who is eligible. Nearly two-thirds of households with incomes below the security line for bare subsistence have not been covered.

Although re-employment endeavours have assisted poor households, impacts remain limited because too few people have taken part in re-employment training, which also varies largely from one region to another.

CONCLUSIVE EVALUATION OF CHINA'S ANTI-POVERTY POLICIES

Since the mid 1980s, the Chinese Government has implemented a series of customized poverty alleviation and sectoral policies that have contributed to increased socioeconomic development in poverty-stricken regions and helped poor populations escape poverty. These policies can be roughly divided into three types: (1) developmental policies for poverty alleviation, which are primarily targeted to poor regions within rural areas; (2) social security policies, which are chiefly targeted to poor and vulnerable groups in urban areas, and are also implemented in some rural areas; and (3) other types of policies beneficial to peasants that also affect the poor population, most of which are implemented in rural areas.

Various policies have played important roles in alleviating urban and rural poverty. They have had diverse influences in different regions and at different times. The developmental policies for poverty alleviation, which aim to reduce poverty through development, have given a marked boost to economic development in poor regions. But since these policies are targeted to certain regions, instead of being targeted to the poor population, their poverty alleviation effect has been reduced with the declining size of the population in poverty. During the middle and late 1980s and the early 1990s, when a large poor population existed, developmental poverty alleviation was more likely to benefit a greater number of poor people. Since the late 1990s, although this strategy shifted to targeting poor villages instead of poor counties, the population in absolute poverty has been increasingly less likely to benefit due to its shrinking size and some problems arising in the implementation of poverty alleviation projects. At present, developmental policies for poverty alleviation are more useful in slowing the widening income gap between poor and wealthier regions. In the future, better-customized developmental policies for poverty alleviation should focus on the development of human capital, enabling the population in poverty to reap more benefits.

The implementation of social security policies has played a decisive role in curbing urban poverty. The minimum living standard system along with endowment, unemployment, medical and other forms of insurance have helped the vast majority of urban residents to avoid poverty. The main problems that urban social security policies now face involve workers in informal sectors and migrants who cannot access social security on an equal basis, and the fact that the minimum living standard system has failed to cover everyone entitled to it. The latter issue is often due to the limited financing powers of local governments. Future adjustments should broaden coverage and enhance equilibrium among cities in terms of the degree of their coverage.

In rural areas, social security will have an increasingly important influence on poverty alleviation. It will be targeted mainly to those rural poor households without development potential, and poor populations suffering disease or other disasters. Rural poverty alleviation policies should be adjusted to feature a fusion between more customized developmental poverty alleviation and a package of appropriate social security systems.

Although some policies beneficial to peasants are not entirely targeted to the poor population, these policies generally produce either more advantages or heavier damages for the poor. The agricultural tax reductions and exemptions, the conversion of croplands to forests, and the 'Two Exemptions and One Subsidy' approach to basic education have yielded clear benefits for the poor, making major contributions to recent declines in the numbers of people in rural poverty. In contrast, the general adoption of a market-orientation principle in medical services and the consolidation of schools have penalized the poor. When adjusting policies, it is essential to consider the possible influence on populations in poverty, adopt as many policies beneficial to the poor as possible, and restrict policies not beneficial to them. If policies generate adverse influences on poor populations, it is necessary to work out forms of compensation.

Notes

1 As indicated by the World Bank's recent analysis of data on sampled rural households offered by the National Bureau of Statistics of China, only 0.4 percent of impoverished rural households have no labour capacity (Park and Wang 2006).

2 In addition to the interest-subsidized loans for poverty alleviation managed by the Agricultural Bank of China, other small-sum loan programmes target poverty-stricken regions. These include loans for revolutionary base areas, regions populated by people of national minorities and remote regions offered by the People's Bank of China in 1984, the common loan for poverty alleviation with a normal interest rate initiated by the Agricultural Bank of China in 1984, loans specific to pastoral areas offered by the Agricultural Bank of China in 1988, and loans for county enterprises provided by the People's Bank of China and the Industrial and Commercial Bank of China in 1988 to state-specified poor counties. Poverty alleviation loans released by other banks persisted for only a few years. The common loan for poverty alleviation offered by the Agricultural Bank of China was not categorized by the Poverty Alleviation Office under the State Council as part of poverty alleviation funds because of the difficulties in identifying its claimed usage (poverty alleviation) and also due to its lack of interest subsidy.

3 As the amount of interest-subsidized loans dropped dramatically in 2005, the growth rate of the amount of such loans from 1986 to 2005 was only 3.5 percent.

4 The 563 poor townships in Jiangxi Province were determined by a yardstick of the per capita net income of peasants from 1997 to 1999 being lower than RMB 1300 yuan. When determining the first batch of poor villages, the Poverty Alleviation Office of Jiangxi Province stipulated that 20 percent of those villages in poor townships within poor counties can be determined as poor villages, and 14 percent of those villages in poor townships within non-poor counties can be determined as poor villages.

5 As the determination of poor counties and villages involves a series of economic, social and political factors, it is not easy to judge if they have been determined accurately. Considering the fact that the National Bureau of Statistics of China has measured rural poverty chiefly by per capita income, and the foremost goal of rural development for the sake of poverty alleviation is to enhance the income level in poor regions and among the poor population, income is used here to judge if a country or village shall be determined as poor.

6 Owing to an insufficient set of data on county-related income, the total number of poor counties grouped by income level in 1993 was 509, taking up 86 percent of the total number of poor counties.

7 Please see Riskin 1994 for the controversy over the percentage of the poor population in poor counties out of the total national population in rural poverty.

8 The author of this article assessed whether living in a state-specified poor county would have a bearing on the growth of household expenditures, holding other factors that may influence income growth constant, and discovered that there might have been an overestimation of the poverty alleviation effects. Some public expenditure funds received by these projects may not have been brought into statistics, as they were directly consumed without being invested. Community

variables may have neglected certain factors that are conducive for poor counties to realize income growth.

9 The author of this article utilized the county-level data from the Ministry of Agriculture to estimate the impact wielded by poverty alleviation investments upon the average income growth in poor counties. Due to the unavailability of accurate statistical data with regard to poverty alleviation investments from other sources, only the investments from the central Government were considered when calculating the rate of return on investments.

10 The author of this article used data on poverty alleviation investments in 43 poor counties in Shaanxi Province from 1986 to 1991 and has not taken into account work relief funds, which may affect the assessment of the effects of infrastructure.

11 Integrated village development work forms village project plans in a participatory way and integrates all poverty alleviation resources. The plans are targeted to administrative villages, and determined according to the requirements for local socioeconomic development and the joint demands of village collectives. According to surveys for this report in Henan, Shaanxi, Guizhou, Guangxi and Hunan, the basic steps for formulating village-level plans are as follows. First, the villagers' team puts forward a project proposal that is discussed in the villagers' meetings (comprising the villagers' representatives, representatives of party members and cadres at the village level). Some villages determine their projects directly at the meetings. Second, experts, such as cadres from the county's poverty alleviation office and the provincial government, are invited to the village to discuss and assess the projects and help devise the funding plans. Third, projects are sent to the competent authority for examination and approval. Finally, the village submits the approved projects and funding plan to the township authority, before sending them to the county authority to be included in a poverty alleviation development project repository. The projects are then made public. Communications with ordinary rural residents suggest they are not clearly aware of what village-level poverty alleviation plans are, which indicates that they have not participated in their formulation.

12 These 21 provinces (municipalities or autonomous regions) include: Hebei, Shanxi, Inner Mongolia, Jilin, Heilongjiang, Jiangxi, Anhui, Henan, Hubei, Hunan, Guangxi, Hainan, Chongqing, Guizhou, Sichuan, Yunnan, Shaanxi, Gansu, Qinghai, Ningxia and Xinjiang.

13 These 16 provinces (autonomous regions) include: Hebei, Jilin, Heilongjiang, Jiangxi, Anhui, Henan, Hubei, Hunan, Guangxi, Hainan, Sichuan, Yunnan, Shaanxi, Qinghai, Ningxia and Xinjiang.

14 We have categorized all those poor villages having launched poverty alleviation investments according to village-level poverty alleviation plans as villages that have initiated the integrated village development work, and categorized other villages as those that have not initiated the integrated village development work.

15 These 14 provinces are: Hebei, Jianggxi, Hainan, Henan, Heilongjiang, Hunan, Hubei, Inner Mongolia, Qinghai, Shaanxi, Sichuan, Xinjiang, Yunnan and Chongqing.

16 Because trained labourers can find jobs with a slightly lower wage rate even if they do not receive such training, accrediting all the work remuneration to the training will exaggerate its results.

17 The failure of those loans issued to enterprises in the early 1990s was, in large part, a result of the direct interference of local governments. Many projects were doomed to collapse as soon as they were launched; others went unfinished.

18 Bank Rakyat in Indonesia is also known as a state-owned commercial bank serving rural areas. Its reform since 1984 has successfully transformed it from a state-owned bank with a severe deficit into a high-performing joint-stock commercial bank. It has provided a vast low-income rural population with effective financial services.

19 The 'Working Regulations on Maintenance of Rural Households Entitled to the Five Guarantees' and the 'Provisional Measures for Management of Homes for the Aged in Rural Areas' were enacted in 1994 and 1997, respectively.

20 The basic education project in Gansu Province is a vertical, multi-layered study on the welfare level of Chinese children in rural areas, touching upon their education, health care and socio-psychological development. This project has involved two surveys in up to twenty counties, covering 2000 rural households and those schools where they are studying.

21 The survey conducted by the Development Research Centre under the State Council was not based on random sampling: 402 households affected by major diseases were selected, comprising 34.3 percent of the total sample. The percentage of rural households trapped in poverty due to diseases estimated by such data is apparently higher than the actual figure.

22 According to data from the National Bureau of Statistics of China, the division of income groups in 2002 is slightly different from that in 2005. This report used five comparable income groups, after weighting population size for each group.

23 The survey data may have included an underestimation of residents' income levels, as similar surveys have done, which is bound to produce an overestimation of incomplete coverage.

24 Compared with Argentina's Trabajar project, China's minimum living standard policy has delivered a markedly better targeting performance. In Argentina's project, the 5 percent lowest income group has 40.2 percent of the households involved, and 38.8 percent of those people involved in this project, a figure more than 10 percent below that achieved by China's minimum living standard project (Wang Youjuan 2006).

25 'Decision of the State Council with Regard to the Establishment of a Uniform System of Basic Endowment Insurance for Workers and Staff Members in Enterprises' (file reference: [1997] No. 26).

26 'Decision of the State Council with Regard to Establishment of a Basic Medical Insurance System for Workers and Staff Members in Urban Areas.'

5 Governance and poverty alleviation

Governance has a direct bearing on the overall effect of anti-poverty efforts. The key factors include a reasonable organizational structure, a rational division of duties, coordination between governmental and societal poverty alleviation efforts, and effective incentives and supervision mechanisms. This chapter discusses issues related to the public administration of poverty alleviation initiatives, and delves into an analysis of certain problems. This is meant as a step towards establishing more effective poverty alleviation mechanisms and enhancing the overall quality of anti-poverty work.

The success of the Chinese Government in implementing poverty alleviation is rooted in its unswerving political determination and powerful organizing abilities. These have allowed poverty reduction programmes to be broadly implemented, within a short time, and sustained over the long term in both rural and urban areas. By drawing in large part on the existing administrative system of the Government, poverty alleviation has not caused administrative management costs to spike, despite its large scale. In this regard, China's institutional practices have dovetailed with prevailing capacities and resources.

The main problems include limited efficiency because of government predominance, poor targeting accuracy, and limits on the coverage of many anti-poverty investments and projects. These problems have been worse at times because of a lack of coordination and cooperation among multiple governmental departments.

THE ORGANIZATION OF CHINA'S POVERTY ALLEVIATION FORCES AND THEIR FUNCTIONS

The organization of poverty alleviation tasks in rural areas and division of responsibilities

The organization of public administration for rural poverty alleviation work is totally different from that for urban poverty alleviation work. Both the central and local governments have set up interdepartmental leading groups for poverty alleviation and development to coordinate departments working on rural poverty alleviation. Under these groups, a number of development offices have been created (see Figure 5.1).

Departments in charge of poverty alleviation work

China's highest-ranking rural poverty alleviation organization is the State Council's Leading Group for Poverty Alleviation and Development, which was founded in 1986. The head of this group is the vice premier of the State Council in charge of agricultural affairs or a councillor of the State Council (who plays this role concurrently). The group's main duties are to formulate poverty alleviation policies, determine primary poverty alleviation investment plans and the scale of poverty alleviation investments, decide on the targets to be supported (such as poverty-stricken counties), and coordinate relations with all central government departments in relation to poverty alleviation work. The Leading Group for Poverty Alleviation and Development is not a standing organization. The Poverty Alleviation Office of the State Council is a standing organ responsible for handling routine affairs related to poverty alleviation. Its main duties are to: (1) survey and study changes in rural poverty, and the implementation and effects of governmental policies, and render suggestions for adjustments to the Leading Group; (2) work with other poverty alleviation fund management departments to put forward plans and proposals for poverty alleviation funds to the Leading Group; (3) cooperate with the National Bureau of Statistics of China to collect basic statistical data on the distribution, spending and recovery of poverty alleviation funds in provinces and poverty-stricken counties; (4) expose cadres responsible for poverty alleviation in poverty-stricken regions to training to better their managerial skills and working abilities; and (5) directly take part in the management of related rural poverty alleviation projects funded by the World Bank and other bilateral and multilateral development organizations. In China's entire structure for rural poverty alleviation, the Leading Group for Poverty Alleviation and Development, under the State Council and its Office, play an irreplaceable role in formulating rural poverty alleviation policies and are regarded as major forces behind rural poverty alleviation work.

The administrative structure for poverty alleviation in local governments (primarily at the provincial and county levels[1]) mimics the model set by the central Government by comprising an interdepartmental leading group for poverty alleviation and development and a poverty alleviation office. At the provincial level, these enact the central Government's rural poverty alleviation policies, lay down poverty alleviation plans that fit local circumstances in accordance with central policies, and designate poor villages. They also determine the scales of poverty alleviation investments for local governments and proposals for the distribution of poverty alleviation funds based on local financial conditions. In 1996, the central Government clarified its guiding principle governing rural poverty alleviation work: 'Each province is held

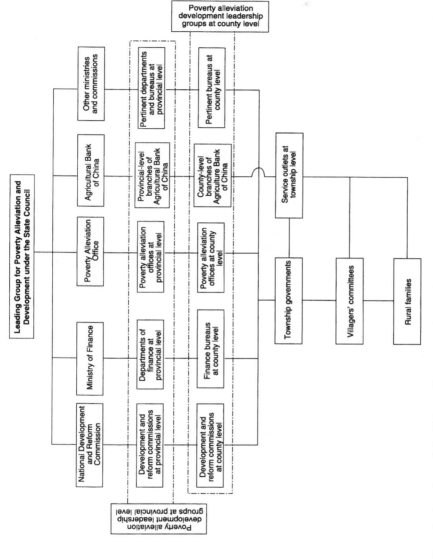

Figure 5.1 Organization chart of the Chinese Government for rural poverty alleviation work.

generally responsible for poverty alleviation work upon its territory.' It set four requirements: 'Each province is required to allocate funds, exercise powers, perform tasks and shoulder responsibilities, all in regard to poverty alleviation work on its own.' The provincial leading groups for poverty alleviation and their poverty alleviation offices constitute a core link in the implementation of rural poverty alleviation policies and plans.

Counties are the basic units of rural poverty alleviation work in China and occupy an all-important position in the administrative hierarchy. Their most critical task is the selection and targeting of poverty-stricken communities and populations. The accuracy of such targeting has a direct bearing on the effects of all poverty alleviation policies and investments. A majority of China's poverty alleviation funds are eventually passed to counties through a variety of channels, and organized and managed by county leading groups for poverty alleviation and development and their associated offices. Whether poverty alleviation funds and projects can achieve their desired impacts depends to a great extent on county decisions.

Development and reform commissions

Development and reform commissions have likewise occupied a significant position in China's rural poverty alleviation work. They manage an important poverty alleviation component – the food-for-work plan. This emerged initially in 1984, and mainly aimed to construct infrastructure (roads, water conservancy facilities, croplands, drinkable water systems for animals and humans, etc.), conduct re-forestation and the regeneration of land parcels in poor regions, and provide job opportunities and income sources to poverty-stricken rural families. The plan was meant to elevate short-term income levels and also long-term development capabilities (Department of Agricultural Economics, State Planning Commission 1997).

The National Development and Reform Commission has set up a poverty alleviation division under its Regional Development Department. The division renders preliminary proposals for the distribution of food-for-work funds, determines the major sectors for allocating such funds, and formulates regulations for the management of funds and related projects. The division needs to work with the Poverty Alleviation Office to jointly present fund distribution proposals to the Leading Group for Poverty Alleviation and Development of the State Council for examination and approval. Prior to 1997, the poverty alleviation division of the State Planning Commission was still responsible for examining and approving food-for-work projects directly. With the implementation of the four requirements for each province described above, the power to examine and approve food-for-work projects has been given to development and reform commissions at the provincial level.

Unlike the central Government, which created a poverty alleviation division under the National Development and Reform Commission only to manage food-for-work funds, most local governments have set up their own interdepartmental leading groups for food for work, which are at the same level as the leading groups for poverty alleviation. They are often headed by vice governors (deputy heads of counties) in charge of planning work. The deputy heads and members of the groups are usually deputy directors of development and reform commissions, finance bureaus, poverty alleviation organs and other public departments. The main duties of the leading groups for food for work are to coordinate relations among departments taking part in food-for-work projects. Food-for-work offices have been set up under the development and reform commissions at the county and provincial level to coordinate the activities of all departments involved in food-for-work projects. The establishment of these independent groups and offices is conducive to strengthening the management of food-for-work projects, but has also made it difficult to coordinate between leading groups for food for work and their offices and leading groups for poverty alleviation and their offices.

Finance departments

Half of the rural poverty alleviation development funds of the central Government come from the Ministry of Finance. It arranges for poverty alleviation funds in its financial budget, including food-for-work and budgetary development funds. The Ministry of Finance also directly manages financial development funds, which are mainly used to finance construction projects, small infrastructure, basic education, health care services, cultural activities, the dissemination of science and technology, training and industrial development in poverty-stricken regions. In addition, the ministry provides interest subsidies for loans for poverty alleviation (Ministry of Finance and World Bank 2003).

The Ministry of Finance has established a poverty alleviation division under its department of agriculture. This division is responsible for formulating preliminary proposals for the distribution of budgetary development funds, laying down fund management regulations, maintaining an information system, granting interest subsidies for loans for poverty alleviation and studying relevant policies. The division works with the Poverty Alleviation Office under the State Council to prepare the annual proposal for the distribution of funds that is sent to the Leading Group for Poverty Alleviation and Development of the State Council for final examination and approval. The proposal is circulated to the department of finance in every province after being approved by the National People's Congress. Unlike the National Development and Reform Commission, which manages food and work projects, the Ministry of Finance does not directly examine and approve poverty alleviation projects supported by budgetary development funds. This power remains with provincial and county governments.

The division of agriculture under the department of finance in each province manages the budgetary development funds, subject to administration by the provincial leading group for poverty alleviation and development. There is no poverty alleviation division or development fund office or independent leading group like that established specifically for food-for-work projects. Such institutional arrangements are conducive to coordination among poverty alleviation departments.

Development fund projects are managed differently across provinces. In some provinces, the department of finance examines and approves projects; in others, the poverty alleviation offices do so. Some provinces have even shifted a portion of their budgetary development funds onto poverty-stricken counties, and enabled county departments of finance and poverty alleviation offices to examine and approve such projects. As required by the central Government, provincial departments of finance provide counterpart funds of a certain percentage for food-for-work and budgetary development funds.

Regardless of whether the projects are examined and approved by departments at the provincial or county level, most budgetary development funds are distributed to bureaus of finance in poverty-stricken counties according to the fund distribution proposal worked out by provincial leading groups for poverty alleviation and development. The disparities among varied modes of project examination and approval in procedural terms are as follows. When a provincial government takes the responsibility for project approval, the concerned county bases projects on the fund quota set by the province; projects are first examined and approved by the provincial department of finance or poverty alleviation office, and then approved by the leading group for poverty alleviation and development, before funds are allocated to the county bureau of finance. When provincial governments give the power of project approval to county governments, funds are directly allocated to bureaus of finance in poverty-stricken counties in accordance with provincial fund distribution proposals; then county departments of finance and poverty alleviation offices determine the projects and submit them to county leading groups for poverty alleviation and development for approval. After the projects are determined, the county bureaus of finance are responsible for managing and distributing funds, and organizing governmental departments (traffic, water and power, education, health care, etc.) to implement and manage the projects. Just like the provincial departments of finance, the county departments of finance need to provide counterpart resources to food-for-work and budgetary development funds. Many find it difficult to do this, however.

China Agricultural Development Bank

Loans are a major component of poverty alleviation funds, constituting more than half of all financing. Poverty alleviation loans mainly aim to supply poverty-stricken regions and families with direct credit support to assist productive activities and economic development. They are largely used to help develop crop production, labour-intensive enterprises, agricultural processing enterprises, trading enterprises and infrastructure construction projects that can help poverty-stricken populations earn more income.

Although the China Agricultural Development Bank is a state-owned commercial bank, it has been performing such policy-mandated duties as issuing, managing and recovering loans for poverty alleviation for many years. After the Leading Group for Poverty Alleviation and Development of the State Council determines the annual proposal for the distribution of poverty alleviation credit funds, the People's Bank of China distributes the funds through the network of the China Agricultural Development Bank, which has branches in every province. In conformity with the fund distribution proposals of provincial leading groups for poverty alleviation and development, the provincial branches of the bank then allocate the funds to bank sub-branches at the regional and county levels. In the 1980s and 1990s, the county sub-branches and poverty alleviation offices were jointly liable for managing interest-subsidized loans at the county level. At that time, a project had to be first approved by the county poverty alleviation office, and then ratified by the bank sub-branch before loans for poverty alleviation could be disbursed. In the network of the China Agricultural Development Bank, the sub-branches played a decisive role in the distribution and use of such funds. If a sub-branch deemed any project as too inefficient or risky, it could refuse to fund it (Wang Sangui, Li Wen and Li Yun 2004).

In recent years, as the China Agricultural Development Bank has reformed in line with greater market orientation and gradually withdraws from the rural market, most interest-subsidized loans have been issued to pioneer enterprises and medium or large infrastructure projects, instead of to rural families and smaller enterprises. Local poverty alleviation offices and sub-branches of the bank have lost their influence over the distribution and use of interest-subsidized loans.

Other governmental departments

As members of leading groups for poverty alleviation and development at varied levels, governmental departments are involved in a variety of rural poverty alleviation activities. Transportation, water conservancy, agriculture, forestry, education and health care departments not only are responsible for developing their sector in poverty-stricken regions, but also take part in the implementation of relevant poverty alleviation projects (such as infrastructure projects supported by food-for-work funds). Relatively large and technical projects are mostly conducted by the relevant departments under county governments. Smaller, more labour-intensive projects are mostly carried out by villagers organized by township governments and villagers' committees. Under the current administration system in China, except for those projects directly reaching villages and rural families, most government-supported poverty alleviation projects are carried out by governmental departments. Certain departments manage projects specifically targeted to poverty-stricken regions – for example, education departments implement compulsory education projects in poverty-stricken regions.

Although the developmental mode of poverty alleviation has prevailed in rural areas, it is still the responsibility of governments at all levels to guarantee the bare subsistence of those people who have lost their capabilities to work, have no other sources of income and have no legal carer (people with the 'three-NOs'). According to the government division of duties, departments of civil affairs are responsible for offering basic social security services in rural areas. Most rural social security funds come from the financial revenues of local governments and transfer payments of higher-up governments. In recent years, the rural minimum livelihood security system and the welfare system for people in absolute poverty have gradually been established in some provinces (background report, Gu Xin 2006).

The organization of poverty alleviation tasks in urban areas and the division of responsibilities

Urban poverty alleviation work has been chiefly conducted by departments of civil affairs of governments at all levels and funded by finance departments of governments at all levels (see Figure 5.2). As the central Government has given local governments the responsibility of setting up a minimum livelihood security system for urban residents, local departments of civil affairs and finance have played a significant role in urban poverty alleviation work. Central government departments have primarily played a 'motivator' role by formulating pertinent laws, regulations and policies with national coverage. Most minimum livelihood security subsidies come from district or county finance departments. District or county civil affairs departments are directly responsible for managing the population covered by the minimum livelihood security system, putting them at the core of urban poverty alleviation work. Normally, civil affairs bureaus have sub-district offices to handle managerial affairs, including the identification of candidates for the minimum livelihood security system, the issuance of qualification certificates, the release of subsidies, etc.

Owing to the limited human and financial resources in these sub-district offices, local governments have mobilized neighbourhood committees, which are autonomous organs created by urban residents, and encouraged them to take an active part in the minimum livelihood security work in urban areas. In some regions, neighbourhood committees conduct household surveys and verify the family details of people applying for subsidies, as commissioned by sub-district offices, while not being responsible for management work. In other regions, neighbourhood committees shoulder more responsibilities and have taken over management of the minimum livelihood security work. They are responsible for not only conducting household surveys, but also identifying eligible people and recommending appropriate applicants (Tang Jun *et al.* 2003). In fact, mobilizing urban residents to participate extensively in minimum livelihood security work has become a major characteristic of China's urban poverty alleviation campaign. This builds on the advantage of neighbourhood committees in terms of the possession of information about their communities, and helps cut down management costs. Of course, once neighbourhood committees are overly involved in the management of minimum livelihood security work, some problems will also come into being, mainly those related to the influence wielded by social connections.

The Ministry of Labour and Social Security also takes part in urban poverty alleviation work. It is mainly liable for implementing re-employment projects for employees laid off by state-owned enterprises and issuing basic subsistence funds to laid-off workers. It establishes re-employment service centres; pays endowment, medical and unemployment insurance premiums; and organizes vocational guidance and re-employment training (development report, Cai Fang and Wang Meiyan 2006). Unlike the minimum livelihood security system, re-employment projects mainly benefit former workers at state-owned enterprises, instead of all unemployed people in urban areas.

THE CHINESE GOVERNMENT'S PRIMARY EXPERIENCES IN POVERTY ALLEVIATION

China's significant accomplishments in reducing poverty stem not only from speedy economic growth and multiple poverty alleviation policies, but also from unique approaches to organizing and governing poverty alleviation endeavours. These can be summarized as the participation of the entire society under the Government's leadership, the Government's unswerving and persistent determination to tackle poverty, and occasional adjustments to anti-poverty tactics in response to changing circumstances.

Governmental leadership

The Chinese Government's prominent role in alleviating both rural and urban poverty is evident on several fronts. First, the Government has led the formulation of poverty alleviation tactics and policies. Second, it has been the primary organizer and mobilizer of poverty alleviation resources. Central and local governments have allocated a huge sum of funds for rural development and the establishment of a social security system in urban areas, and have mobilized social forces by multiple means (including some compulsory measures) to take part in poverty reduction. Third, the government uses its well-structured administrative hierarchy to distribute poverty alleviation funds and implement projects, ensuring that policies and investments have national reach in a short amount of time. The Government's predomination in rural and urban poverty alleviation work has been considered an inevitable choice, since non-governmental and other types of social organs have not been developed fully. Of course, this also produces some problems that will be discussed later in this chapter.

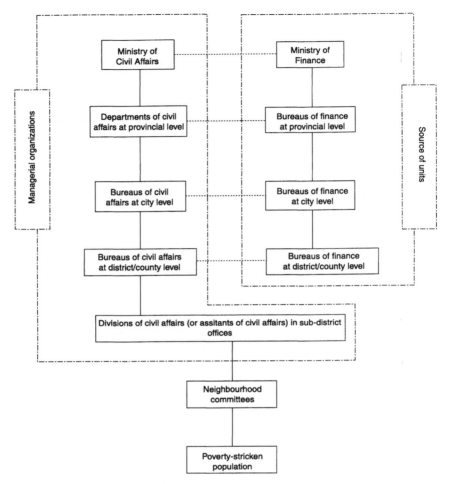

Figure 5.2 Organization chart of the Chinese Government for urban poverty alleviation work.

A combination of multiple public departments and other organizations

China's poverty alleviation work brings together multiple public departments
and other organizations. Rural poverty alleviation work has the most complicated organizational structure and the largest number of participating
public departments. As shown in the division of departmental responsibilities, some departments are principally responsible for formulating policies
and monitoring poverty; some manage funds allocated by the central and local
governments; others are chiefly responsible for implementing projects. Such
institutional arrangements have been made to: (1) adapt the developmental

mode of poverty alleviation to rural areas in an integrated way; (2) mobilize all governmental functional departments to contribute their specific expertise; and (3) reduce administrative costs by avoiding the establishment of giant departments dedicated to poverty alleviation work. Multiple departments help guarantee the implementation of various rural investment projects for poverty alleviation on a broad scale, although this has also led to coordination issues that are discussed below.

Mobilization of the general public

During the past twenty-odd years of poverty alleviation efforts, the central Government has continuously mobilized various types of governmental departments, social groups, state-owned enterprises and public institutions to take part in poverty reduction in selected regions. It has called upon local governments in developed regions to help their counterparts in underdeveloped regions, and invited non-governmental and international organizations to contribute as well. Following this example, governments of provinces, autonomous regions, municipalities and counties have mobilized their affiliated organizations, and the enterprises, public institutions and social groups located in their territories. It is fair to say that poverty alleviation has become the most intensively participatory social task in the country. Extensive mobilization has brought forth a vast sum of funds and provided a constant supply of experiences to guide the ongoing evolution of poverty alleviation practices.

Unswerving political determination

China's stable political environment has supported consistent economic development and a constant decline in poverty, and allowed the Government to make poverty alleviation a central task. Substantial progress has not reduced the determination to reach the now much smaller population in poverty. Instead, the theory of building a well-off, harmonious society that includes everyone was put forward. Poverty alleviation today has not only spread from rural to urban areas, but has started to feature a more comprehensive range of poverty alleviation practices, in addition to the developmental mode in rural areas and social security in urban areas. Local governments at all levels have been investing increasing resources in reducing poverty.

Constant learning and reform

The Chinese Government's poverty alleviation practices have involved constant exploration and learning from experiences, paired with regular attempts to improve management and increase efficiency. To facilitate the sharing of experiences, public departments working on poverty alleviation convene annual conferences to summarize their activities and learn from each other. High-ranking governmental officials attend regular meetings to discuss problems arising in the implementation of policies, and also review new policies on the basis of past experiences and lessons. Local officials are regularly trained and organized to conduct field surveys in support of necessary policy adjustments. For example, both the Leading Group for Poverty Alleviation and Development of the State Council and the parallel groups for local governments have organized a number of training programmes and field surveys to advance implementation of the plan for village-level participatory development.

Many changes have taken place in the modes of management for poverty alleviation funds and projects. The earliest projects fell under the former planned economy system, and featured an approach where governments at all levels laid down their respective project plans, and local administrative departments carried them out. With the gradual establishment of a market-oriented economy and a new emphasis on the participation of poor people in shaping poverty plans, changes have taken place in project management. Projects are selected per village-level plans, and villages have been playing an increasingly important role in selecting, examining and approving projects. An increasing number of engineering projects have been put out for public bidding.

In terms of the distribution and management of funds, the factor-method-based distribution mode has been adopted not only by the Ministry of Finance of the central Government, but also by an expanding number of local government departments. Some proven practices in international projects, such as the management of poverty alleviation funds in specific accounts, the account-rendering system and the system for publicizing account information have been employed by a growing number of domestic fund and project management departments. The experiences of foreign-funded projects have encouraged the participatory mode of poverty alleviation, with initial trials having already garnered positive results (Wang Sangui and Li Wen 2005).

THE MAIN PROBLEMS WITH THE CHINESE GOVERNMENT'S ADMINISTRATIVE PRACTICES FOR POVERTY ALLEVIATION

Although the Chinese government has achieved unprecedented results in alleviating rural poverty and demonstrated many successful approaches to the issue, a few critical problems still plague its poverty alleviation mechanisms and governance structure, thus affecting the efficiency of its work overall.

Managerial problems

Governmental departments dominate the distribution and use of poverty alleviation resources

Compared with other developing countries, China has a powerful and well-organized government, and a substantial capacity for resource mobilization. With the fast growth of the country's economy, the Government has successfully mobilized an immense amount of funds and other resources, and applied them to rural development for the sake of poverty alleviation on a scale that has not been achieved in any other developing country. A vast governmental structure, however, has hindered the development of non-governmental organizations and autonomous organizations of peasants. As a consequence, many poverty alleviation resources can be managed by only governmental organizations, which have become used to organizing, controlling, approving and managing these on their own. Governments at all levels have multiple objectives, and those at different levels may have conflicts of interest that cause deviations from their initial goals. Numerous poverty alleviation resources have failed to reach their targets due to these conflicts of interest.

In consideration of social equity and political stability, the central Government has expressed a strong political commitment to eliminate rural poverty. In mobilizing enormous funds and other resources, the Government intends local governments at all levels, as it has requested, to use all poverty alleviation funds for that purpose. But local governments, especially those in poverty-stricken counties and townships, are faced with pressures and financial conditions that vary widely from those of the central Government. Compared to many other important objectives (to maintain the normal operations of local governments, ensure teachers receive wages on time, uphold social stability, boost public revenue growth and stimulate the local economy), poverty alleviation is not the most significant objective in the eyes of many counties, even those defined as impoverished. Higher-up governments' assessments of the working performance of local governments and the promotion of local officials are more related to the accomplishment of objectives other than poverty alleviation. What is more, there is no reliable method to collect statistics on variations in the population in poverty at the county level or below, as local governments are likely to make false declarations to evade sanctions.

Under this institutional scenario, local governments have a compelling motivation to transfer poverty alleviation funds to applications they deem more important. Since poverty alleviation resources, even if they pass through governments at various levels, eventually end up controlled by governments at the county and township levels, it is possible for them to divert the funds, channel them into local economic growth, or improve the indicators used to measure their performance – all without generating good results in poverty alleviation.

The poverty alleviation authority under the central Government is aware that non-governmental organizations can make important contributions to poverty alleviation in rural areas. It has reached agreements with eleven domestic non-governmental organizations to allow them to directly take part in the implementation of governmental projects, a move designed to enhance the efficiency of poverty alleviation work. In the future, non-governmental organizations will play an increasingly prominent role in this area.

Problems in the financial system

Since China's financial reform in the early 1980s, governments in poverty-stricken counties and townships have encountered severe, long-lasting difficulties in balancing their revenues and expenditures. As a result of the reform, China gave up highly centralized financial arrangements. Under the former system, poverty-stricken regions received various allowances to cover their expenditures. But under the new system of sharing tax revenues between central and local governments, the latter need to seek financial revenues on their own to cover a majority of their expenditures (including the most fundamental costs for education and access to medical services). As poverty-stricken regions are economically underdeveloped (particularly in terms of industry and services) and have limited sources of income, they cannot obtain an adequate amount of financial revenues to satisfy their expenditures for the wages of government officials, teachers, medical workers and personnel of other social services organizations. Such expenditures constitute more than half their budgets.

Fiscal and taxation reform from 1993 to 1994 chiefly aimed to levy value-added taxes and share tax revenues between central and local governments. This reform had an adverse impact on governments in poverty-stricken counties, however, as sharing revenues meant a drop in their financial resources. The central Government originally planned to make up such a disparity through a fiscal transfer from wealthy regions to poverty-stricken regions, but this has not fully taken place (World Bank 2001).

The most severe consequence of the financial deficits faced by local governments in poverty-stricken regions is their reduced ability to invest in social welfare and public services. Compared with urban residents and populations in better-developed regions, people in poverty-stricken regions have to pay huge charges for basic social services such as education and health care. These financial difficulties have played a major role in the tendency to divert poverty alleviation funds from the central Government, and even from international or bilateral development organizations at times, into other expenditures (mostly wages). Even if poverty alleviation funds are used to finance production and construction work, governments in poverty-stricken counties are more prone to investing them in the industrial sector, township and village enterprises, and those areas with a higher rate of return, instead of in the agricultural sector and areas with the worst poverty.

Excessive demands for counterpart funds for poverty alleviation have also generated an adverse influence. As all poverty-stricken counties have suffered severe financial deficits, they are unable to render counterpart funds required under the poverty alleviation projects of higher-up governments and international development organizations. When it is necessary to do so, they have two countermeasures: (1) to exaggerate the scale of projects or reduce the scale of actual investments in order to evade their provision of counterpart funds; and (2) to call on rural families to provide volunteer workers, or to pay part of the costs in order to participate in poverty alleviation projects. The consequences include heavier financial burdens for rural families and the exclusion of those unable to provide their own funds (background report, Wang Sangui 2006b). Poverty-stricken rural families are also more likely to be excluded because of a heavy emphasis on pursuing quickly visible results instead of better performance in poverty alleviation.[2]

Similar problems have existed in urban poverty alleviation initiatives, because the funds raised for the minimum livelihood security system in urban areas have mostly come from governments at the district and county levels, whose financial abilities are the weakest. There are also huge gaps between county and city governments in different regions in terms of their financial revenues, which produce wide variations in minimum livelihood security lines. In some regions, many people who should be covered by the minimum livelihood security system are not (background report, Gu Xin 2006).

In recent years, inequalities in the public finance system have caught the attention of the central Government, which has been making larger transfer payments to alleviate the financial hardships suffered by poverty-stricken regions. But to date, the roots of these inequalities have not been cut.

Conflicts of interest related to policy-based poverty alleviation loans issued by commercial banks

Since the Agricultural Bank of China has quickened its drive towards commercialization, there have been increasing conflicts between the bank's commercial profit orientation and its role in managing interest-subsidized loans for poverty alleviation. The bank has issued most interest-subsidized loans to medium and large infrastructure projects of higher efficiency and lower risk, innovative village enterprises operating at a satisfactory efficiency level, and wealthy rural families. In some regions, interest-subsidized loans are even used to offset the bad loans issued to rural families. Only a small portion of interest-subsidized loans arrive in the pockets of poverty-stricken rural families. As shown by a survey conducted by the Ministry of Finance, among interest-subsidized loans totalling RMB 750 million yuan in Jiangxi in 2002, only RMB 150 million yuan went to rural families (who were not necessarily impoverished). In Pingjiang County of Hunan Province, and Suichuan County and Le'an County of Jiangxi Province, no rural families have received loans in recent years (Wen Qiuliang 2003).

More loans have been issued to enterprises and wealthy rural families due to the following factors. First, poorer people have smaller demands for loans and incur higher transaction costs. Second, many have been unable to negotiate the complicated formalities for applying for loans. Third, the Agricultural Bank of China requests applicants to render a guarantee in kind, in order to make sure they will repay the loans. But most poor people are unable to furnish this. Fourth, the conflict between the bank's responsibility for undertaking the loan repayment risks and its role as a commercial bank has forced it to issue more loans to commercial enterprises and wealthy rural families (World Bank 2001). Fifth, a majority of the bank's sub-branches at the township level have been closed or merged. Finally, for the sake of local economic development, local governments have tacitly consented to the Agricultural Bank of China's investing poverty alleviation funds in medium and large infrastructure projects and enterprises, and even facilitated interest subsidies from the Ministry of Finance. These are all serious problems that need to be redressed.

Problems in poverty alleviation funding and project management

Distribution and management of poverty alleviation funds

At present, most of the funds passed by provincial governments to county governments are still distributed by the 'base number' method and chiefly obtained through the declaration of projects. The 'base number' method is easy and convenient to apply, but it cannot make timely adjustments to the distribution of funds based on the size of the population in poverty and the degree of poverty in each county. Even if funds are passed from the central Government to provincial governments and a portion is then sent to county governments based on certain parameters, the definition of these will not be complete enough to prevent local departments from making their own adjustments. For instance, among the nine parameters of the 'Measures for Management over Financial Funds for Poverty Alleviation Purpose', two items – 'national guiding policy of poverty alleviation' and 'miscellaneous' – have been defined in a vague way. Fund distribution departments could easily come up with multiple interpretations. The flexibility in fund distribution means there is greater local control, but also an enhanced possibility of abusing powers for personal gains without unambiguous restrictions imposed by relevant policies and systems. Fund distribution departments will not, on their own initiative, give up such a flexibility. They will in fact try varied means to maintain it. This is the main explanation of why different departments are constantly scrambling to control fund distribution.

Another common problem in fund distribution and management is the issuance by officials of private slips to secure advantages through their personal influence. This has edged out some projects by governments at lower levels. To cope with this, departments in some provinces and municipalities have to reserve a certain percent of poverty alleviation funds for those projects specified by officials.

The direct consequence of the examination and approval of projects from one level to another is that county and township governments spend a considerable portion of their energy in asking for special support from provincial and municipal departments for certain projects (including those waiting for approval and specified by officials). Some applicants have even dispatched specialists or set up specific offices to ask for such support, and spent large sums to cover travelling and business entertainment expenditures, instead of investing fully in the projects themselves. In the final analysis, higher-up departments should be held responsible for allowing lower governments to spend resources on requesting financing support. Without a stringent fund management system, however, people who receive prioritized financing support can count on departmental or personal gains, which encourages them to continue in this direction. The result has been the centralization of powers and interests in higher-up departments, which again explains why many departments hope to grasp the powers to determine projects and distribute funds (Ministry of Finance and World Bank 2003).

Both the private slips issued by officials and the attempts to secure prioritized financing support interfere with normal project management practices and diffuse the focus on poverty alleviation. They also foster corruption and the abuse of power for personal gains.

Managerial problems with poverty alleviation projects

The current procedures for the declaration, examination and approval of poverty alleviation projects are largely the same as those employed under the planned economy system. They thus bear some inherent defects dating back to that era. All practices take place within administrative organs in a sealed and non-transparent way. People in poverty have little say in which projects are approved or not. Cadres are never held responsible for whether or not a project is accomplished or conducted effectively.

Poverty-stricken people do not participate in managing poverty alleviation projects and funds owing partly to the old-fashioned attitudes of project and fund managers, and to certain contradictions in the existing mechanisms and mix of interests. Under the planned economy system, the government predominated in the planning and management of projects at all times, and was prone to doubting the abilities of rural families (those in poverty in particular) in taking part in project management work. More importantly, rural families' participation would mean a certain curtailment of the powers of managerial authorities. Authorities would have to acquire the consent of rural families for decisions they are used to making on their own – rural families might even have a stronger say. A participatory mode would also mean that authorities and personnel would need much more patience and have to spend more energy in dealing with rural families in an equitable manner. Without specific institutional restrictions or external supervision (such as external supervision over international projects), it is hard to imagine that local government departments will launch participatory project management modes on their own initiative, much less be enthusiastic about doing so.

Propelled largely by poverty alleviation departments, the implementation of the participatory village-level planning mode has provided a new and effective means for rural families to engage in the planning and management of poverty alleviation projects. But a series of problems are bound to arise when it comes to conducting this work on a large scale. First, few people have had experience of participatory planning. Cadres in county or township governments in most regions are responsible for organizing village-level planning, but most have only been exposed to training that lasts a day or two. In many regions, rural families have not participated in the formulation of village-level plans, and the contents fail to address their demands. Second, due to limited funds, village-level plans can be implemented only within different poverty-stricken villages in batches. In those provinces and autonomous regions that have accomplished village-level planning work at one go, some villages have not been able to implement their projects until a couple of years after they were planned. As the country's economy keeps evolving in a positive way and with the changes arising from the market climate, some planned projects will no longer be feasible and must undergo adjustments. For instance, Datong County in Qinghai Province has 100 poverty-stricken villages. It will take eight years for this county to finish the implementation of plans if it can carry out projects in thirteen villages a year; in this case, a number of villages will not be able to have their plans implemented until seven or eight years later.

Third, an important purpose of participatory village-level planning work is to integrate the multiple kinds of poverty alleviation resources, which used to be scattered across government departments, and then to carry out projects related to infrastructure, social development, production, the development of capabilities, and so on. Since the management of poverty alleviation funds by different departments persists, however, it is still a tricky issue to have all resources integrated in an effective way. What is more, in the course of conducting participatory village-level planning work, major departments – such as the poverty alleviation offices, departments of finance, development and reform commissions, the Agricultural Bank of China etc. – that have been managing poverty alleviation projects and funds have not closely coordinated their activities with one another. So far, most project funds under the participatory poverty alleviation plans have been budgetary development funds and (partly) food-for-work funds; planned projects can hardly be accomplished as scheduled due to lack of funds (background report, Wang Sangui 2006b).

Lack of coordination among poverty alleviation departments

Under the current system, multiple public departments participate in the management of poverty alleviation projects and funds. These come from all different sectors, have been administered by different authorities, and have been headed by administrative officers at different levels and in charge of different regions. There is no acceptable mechanism for cooperation based on a division of labour. Therefore, each department has to spend a lot of time and energy to coordinate its relations and interests with other departments, and is often faced with numerous contradictions. At the provincial level, the project and fund management practices have varied largely, and have mainly depended on the relations between different departments and their respective cadres or administrative officers, the power and influence of individual departments, and the attitudes of leading cadres. Some provinces are able to pool poverty alleviation funds and use them for implementation of their village-level plans; in other provinces, varied departments have their respective project plans and do not identify at all with the village-level plans. In some provinces, poverty alleviation offices are responsible for the management of development funds and newly added financial funds for poverty alleviation; in others, the departments of finance are responsible for doing so. In some provinces, development and reform commissions are solely responsible for managing food-for-work projects; in others, food-for-work funds are managed by varied departments according to a categorization of their usages. The management of projects and funds by multiple departments prevents a reasonable division of labour, mainly because different departments are lobbying for fund distribution powers for the sake of their own interests. In fact, the amount of benefits yielded by such power to departments and individuals directly correlates with whether funds have been distributed in a rational and standard way. Once the fund distribution procedure and standard are clarified and endeavours made to restrict the flexibility of departments in terms of fund distribution, they will be largely discouraged from seeking fund distribution powers and able to focus their main energy on project management and supervision.

Muddled management and the unclear division of work have resulted in high costs for coordination, especially when it is required for the joint use of funds for the sake of implementing village-level plans. The pooling of funds means the curtailment of the departments' powers and liberty. But in the same poverty-stricken region, when multiple departments are formulating, examining and approving poverty alleviation projects and distributing funds, the outcome is the scattering of human, material and financial resources. It becomes difficult to channel limited funds into the regions and projects that need them most. In this way, the utilization efficiency of poverty alleviation resources declines. Poverty-stricken counties end up investing much more money and energy than necessary to obtain financing support, which increases the costs of projects, because all the expenses incurred will eventually be covered by project funds.

Lack of effective supervision, evaluation and accountability

In the case of conflicts of interest between the central and local governments that cause the local government to deviate from its poverty alleviation objective, the central Government may adopt two countermeasures: (1) to align the principal working objectives of the local governments in poverty-stricken regions with the poverty alleviation objectives of the central Government; and (2) to intensify the supervision and management of funds and projects, and make it difficult for local governments to put funds into other uses, or guarantee that local governments are aware that once they put funds into other uses, such doings will be easily discovered and punished. The purpose of the first measure is to foster local governments' own initiatives, under the precondition that all the assessment indicators will concentrate on the impacts on poverty alleviation.

The purpose of the second measure is to ensure that poverty alleviation funds from the central Government are actually used for poverty alleviation work. Although the central Government defined the responsibilities of key local officials with respect to poverty alleviation work as early as 1996, none have been punished for poor performance. Furthermore, there have been no accurate statistics on people in poverty from administrative units below the provincial level. The data from counties and townships have all been put forward by local governments, and cannot be used to assess poverty alleviation efforts.

Supervision, management and sanction by the central Government could better guide the behaviour of local governments. In recent years, the Ministry of Finance has been gradually experimenting with systems on a trial basis, such as the management of funds in specific accounts, the account-rendering system, the system for publicizing projects and public bidding for engineering projects to reduce the leakage of poverty alleviation funds. Such endeavours have, to a certain degree, prevented the diversion of funds for poverty alleviation. These systems are not yet well structured, however, and are incomplete in many respects, including the following.

1   Coordination in fund and project management has been poor. At present, departments of finance are intensifying their fund supervision and management initiatives. In regions using the new systems introduced by the Ministry of Finance, local governments will be less likely to channel poverty alleviation funds into salaries or routine office expenses. The supervision and management of funds can only ensure these funds will be used in projects, however. This will not guarantee all the projects serve the purpose of poverty alleviation and are helpful to the poor. In fact, local governments are still allowed to select those projects that help boost economic growth and enhance financial revenues without generating a satisfactory poverty alleviation effect.

2   Projects have to be examined and approved by too many authorities.

Since governments may direct funds into projects unrelated to poverty alleviation, most provinces have given the power of project examination and approval to poverty alleviation and project management departments at the provincial level. But this practice has resulted in many other problems. Located far from the project sites and having received tens of thousands of applications, provincial poverty alleviation and project management departments have limited information to assess the projects. In most circumstances, the examination and approval of projects are conducted in a rather superficial way, and have failed to exclude those projects not intended for poverty alleviation at all. Moreover, this approach also involves protracted time for examination and approval, delays in the provision of funds, and the need for local governments to expend enormous energy and costs in seeking financing support.

3   An institutionalized evaluation and accountability system is not in place. There is no standard, scientific mechanism for fund and project supervision and evaluation. Current practices are not effective, and mainly target financial details and funds. No hard efforts have been made to scrutinize project examination and approval practices, and few attempts have been made to assess these practices in terms of the effects on poverty alleviation. All of these factors reduce the supervisory usefulness of existing examinations.

Notes

1 Leading groups for poverty alleviation and development and poverty alleviation offices at the prefecture level have also been established. Since governments at the prefecture level are mainly the detached offices of provincial governments and are not independent governments, however, they are mostly responsible for communicating on poverty alleviation between higher-up and subordinate governments. For instance, poverty alleviation funds are distributed from provinces directly to counties – governments at the prefecture level are responsible for only passing such funds along. Poverty alleviation projects are also passed directly to poverty alleviation departments at the county level after being examined and approved by poverty alleviation departments at the provincial level; governments at the prefecture level usually do not have the right to examine and approve such projects. Normally, governments at the township level do not take part in managing poverty alleviation funds and projects either. They mainly participate in implementation by referring projects to the competent authorities.
2 In normal circumstances, provincial governments have specific requirements for projects carried out by governments in poverty-stricken counties, and county governments have similar requirements for poverty-stricken villages (e.g., how many biomass pools should be built). When invested funds are inadequate and grass-roots organizations are required to offer counterpart funds, the only way out is to give those rural families who are able to offer counterpart funds precedence over those who cannot. This can ensure the completion of the project, without contributing to poverty alleviation.

6 Suggestions for poverty alleviation policies

China's anti-poverty campaign is now undergoing an important stage of strategic adjustment. This follows three decades of unprecedented accomplishments that have enabled the vast majority of the Chinese population to secure basic capacities to obtain enough food and clothing. As the tasks specified under the 'Scheme for Rural Development for Poverty Alleviation (2001–2010)' will be finished in the next few years, and as China considers its overall development strategy, it is necessary to fine-tune the targeting of future poverty alleviation efforts and define key priorities. When the minimum livelihood security system for rural areas reaches the entire population in need, what should be the next target? When the 'Construction of New Rural Areas' project has been launched across China, what features of developmental poverty alleviation should be most prominent? When China has become a middle-income country instead of a low-income one, how should the country design poverty alleviation practices to ensure the remaining poor and needy have enough food and clothing? All these questions have to be answered by the Chinese Government and the parties involved in poverty alleviation.

This report has put forward new thinking on the elimination of poverty through development. It argues that poverty alleviation work should benefit not only the population in subsistence poverty, which still lacks enough food and clothing. There is also an urgent need to reach the population in a state of developmental poverty. This means that poverty alleviation as a whole should encompass developmental strategies to improve production and living conditions, and other modes that enhance people's abilities to embrace development through education, training, medical care, cultural activities and social security. In this, poverty alleviation work should focus on the existing poor as well as their offspring to prevent poverty spreading from one generation to the other.

While the Government should exercise the primary leadership role in poverty alleviation, it is also necessary to mobilize the vast number of other social resources, including non-governmental organizations, on a wider scale. Successful poverty alleviation work should enable poor people to have more opportunities to participate in economic activities and allow them to enjoy the results of economic growth.

The following suggestions, grouped under nine crucial areas of public policy, are formulated for the consideration of policy makers.

ESTABLISH A DEVELOPMENTAL POVERTY LINE AND ADJUST LONG-TERM POVERTY ALLEVIATION OBJECTIVES

Poverty standards will vary with the level of economic development, so the poverty line used to measure the size of the population in poverty should rise with socioeconomic advancement. In the mid 1980s, the Chinese Government drew a rural poverty line (i.e., the subsistence poverty line) that fitted China's economic development at that time. It is still in use today, even though China's per capita gross domestic product (GDP) has increased several times. In remaining at a relatively low level, and since it was set without considering the need for developing the capabilities of people in poverty, it no longer suits China's level of development.

Poverty alleviation policies designed today based on this standard will not be able to completely address current issues. For the poor to emerge from poverty over the long term, they must have the opportunity to develop their capabilities, not just enough food and clothing. Poor children need equal access to education, for example. Labourers need more chances to receive training. All people in poverty should have access to basic medical insurance, social security and a wholesome cultural life. This means it is necessary to raise the poverty line, and in the course of formulating poverty alleviation policies, to pay attention to both the population in subsistence poverty and the population in developmental poverty. The long-term poverty alleviation task of governments at all levels should be to solve developmental poverty.

This report proposes that a developmental poverty line should replace the current poverty line. At the moment, the issue of developmental poverty as a whole is still under discussion. Before using this as the basis for policy formulation, a lot of work must be done, starting with the determination of a rational developmental poverty line. Competent public departments should form a poverty standard research group for in-depth study and strive for including a new yardstick in the next 'Plan for Poverty Alleviation Work (2011–2020)'. In the meantime, a new round of research into poverty alleviation strategies should begin as soon as possible and lay down a foundation for working out the next ten-year plan.

ESTABLISH A REASONABLE CREDIT MECHANISM FOR POVERTY ALLEVIATION AND DEFINE THE FINANCIAL SECTOR'S PARTICIPATION

In many developing countries, the provision of financial services has proven one of the most effective modes of poverty alleviation. Small-sum credit has been particularly successful in serving people in poverty. The following suggestions could help improve financial services for poverty alleviation in China.

Scope of financial market: to enable small-sum credit services to genuinely support development, the first step needs to be a broadening of the scope of China's financial market, including by allowing various types of small-sum credit organs to enter the market and establish a legitimate capacity. Pilot practices in six provinces involving the setting up of village and township banks, aid societies and small-sum loan companies have created new ways for non-governmental funds to flow into the rural financial sector. It is necessary to spread such practices to other provinces and municipalities as quickly as possible.

Classification: small-sum credit organs should be managed by classification, with more favourable policies for small companies that issue loans only from their own capital funds. Consideration should be given to cancelling the restrictions against commercial banks holding 100 percent stock equities in small-sum loan companies and to loosening the requirement that commercial banks must hold more than 20 percent of stock equities in village and township banks.

Interest rates: restrictions on the interest rates of small-sum credit organs should be eased and a ceiling interest rate established that is no more than four times the base interest rate. Small-sum credit organs should decide on their interest rates on their own in accordance with market conditions and their respective operating costs, after the liberalization of interest rates in the entire financial market.

Competition: it is essential to encourage competition, and use the resulting pressure to ensure that small-sum credit organs reduce their costs and improve the quality of their services by means of constant innovation, thus supplying the poverty-stricken population with sustainable financial services. Other financial institutions may proffer loans to village and township banks, aid societies and small-sum loan companies.

Non-profit and charity organisations: experience in other countries shows that purely commercial small-sum credit organs will not issue larger loans in areas where poverty is severe. Non-profit or charity agencies have played a better role in satisfying needs in this situation. It would be appropriate to consider loosening the restrictions on non-profit or charity small-sum credit groups entering the financial sector. They should be allowed to set up small-sum loan firms and issue loans with their own funds. Until such organizations are mature, however, regular banks should issue loans to them.

The Government can also provide special preferential taxation policies to support these groups.

Legislation: a rural community investment law should be passed at an opportune time. In such developing countries as Thailand and India, it has been stipulated that financial institutions should issue about 20 percent of their loans to rural areas. The United States has also a law stating that a certain percentage of loans should be issued to local communities. China can use such successful experiences for reference in devising a statute that fits current circumstances and helps utilize peasants' deposits to meet their financial needs.

ESTABLISH AND COMPLETELY IMPLEMENT THE SOCIAL SECURITY SYSTEM FOR RURAL AND URBAN AREAS

In the future, with the continued development of China's economy, the transfer of the labour force and increasing progress in poverty alleviation, many more people will emerge from poverty. A growing percentage of those who remain poor will be elderly, physically weak, sick, disabled or without the capability to work. In rural areas, it will be necessary to reconsider the reasons resulting in poverty and adjust poverty alleviation policies accordingly. The developmental mode, which focuses on production work, will not be able to solve these problems, while temporary aid measures cannot ensure continued assistance. To meet people's need for subsistence in an ongoing and effective way, the social security system and public service system for rural areas should be established and full implemented. A series of systems – including the minimum livelihood security system, the new rural cooperative medical care system, the rural medical rescue system and the rural community medical service system – need to be set up and supported by relevant polices.

In the past couple of years, marked progress has been made in setting up the minimum livelihood security system for rural areas. The latest statistics of the Ministry of Civil Affairs, as of the end of June 2007, show that thirty-one provinces, municipalities and autonomous regions in China have established fledgling minimum livelihood security systems, which cover 20.68 million rural residents affected by poverty. These efforts need to be continued, as well as those to enhance the accuracy of targeting, reduce omissions, and ensure that rural residents with sickness or disability have access to necessary medical services. In establishing a robust social security system for rural and urban areas, this report proposes the following steps.

First, accurately identifying urban families entitled to the minimum livelihood security system is the foundation of poverty alleviation work in urban areas. It is necessary to improve the method for estimating family income, and establish a national uniform urban poverty line that also reflects the disparities among different regions. A priority should be to avoid inadequate coverage arising from an overestimation of the family income.

Second, the social security system needs to cover all unemployed people in urban areas, people employed by organizations other than regular departments and migrants from rural areas. In the trial implementation of the basic medical insurance system for urban residents, extra heed should be paid to the affordability of insurance premiums and medical expenses for families entitled to the minimum livelihood security system and other low-income families.

Third, when it comes to implementing the minimum livelihood security system in rural areas, it is essential to accurately identify the population in poverty and manage the minimum livelihood security funds properly. But it is impossible to define with complete accuracy the per capita net income of rural residents across China. A workable substitute method is to distribute the indicators in a proper way and apply them to villages per the demographic distribution of impoverished people and also in view of the administrative division, and establish an open, transparent villagers' appraisal system at the village level. Given the discrepancies among different regions in terms of income level, there should be an allowance for adjustments in the living expenses indicator to enhance the security standard in high-income regions and lower it where living expenses are small. This will help prevent the coverage of the minimum livelihood security system from becoming too limited or extensive, while managing the discrepancies in living costs among different regions.

Fourth, it is necessary to institutionalize, standardize and make transparent the minimum livelihood security system for rural areas, so as to enhance social safety nets and the efficient utilization of funds. A strictly managed, society-supervised fund management system and a village-level democratic assessment system will be key to the success of the system, and also of great significance in bolstering rural social management mechanisms.

Fifth, poverty among disabled and elderly people should draw concerted attention. Gradual steps should be taken to establish an endowment insurance system for everyone and an annuity system for the elderly. In urban areas, rest homes should be expanded, and in rural areas, some rest homes should be built on a trial basis. The Government may consider granting appropriate subsidies to impoverished elderly people in rest homes. As for disabled people in poverty, the primary task is to provide them with basic medical services and accomplish the goal of ensuring every disabled person has access to medical care by 2015. A priority task is to create a community medical service system across the country and enhance medical services abilities at the community level.

SUPPORT THE DRIVE FOR URBANIZATION, AND PROVIDE SOCIAL SECURITY AND PUBLIC SERVICES TO MIGRANTS FROM RURAL AREAS WORKING IN URBAN AREAS

Urbanization is an inevitable part of the journey to modernization and an important factor in reducing rural poverty. The progression of urbanization depends, in large part, on the speed of the flow of rural residents into urban areas. Such a transfer is influenced by urban welfare policies. It is critical to supply migrants from rural areas with necessary social security, so that a majority can become long-term urban residents.

At present, rural labourers enjoy the freedom of relocating to find work. Compared to a decade ago, their social status and protection under policies and laws have improved. After arriving in urban areas, however, they hardly benefit from the urban welfare system. This is not only because of the poor financial powers of many local governments, but also because of the supply–demand relationship in the labour market and the income level of rural labourers. It may be necessary to adopt some expedient measures, adapted to the needs of different regions, to integrate migrants in the urban social welfare system. In the current stage, the following policies and measures are advised.

First, new channels for employment and relocation should be created, in addition to support for finding housing in urban areas and gaining higher education certificates. Rural labourers who have worked for a certain number of years (for example, three to five years) and have paid their social insurance premiums should enjoy the same full range of welfare benefits as urban residents do, including basic medical insurance, children's education and the leasing of houses at low rates. Allowing urban and rural residents to have equal access to social welfare benefits would benefit economic development and enhance the urbanization ratio.

Second, a basic and compulsory social insurance system should cover all labourers in rural and urban areas, including rural labourers. There should be sanctions on employers who fail to perform their responsibility for providing social insurance for their employees. They should be urged to comply through social supervision and a non-performance reporting mechanism.

Third, more considerations should be given to the unstable employment and higher turnover rates that most rural labourers face. In some industries, such as construction, the flow of a substantial number of labourers in and out of jobs will likely continue for a long period. A relevant system should allow them to continue their insurance when changing their jobs or work sites.

Fourth, the urban social welfare system has to include some institutionalized measures that target the migrant population, enabling it to receive rescue services and temporary social aid in case of emergency or special difficulties.

Fifth, all Chinese cities should allow rural labourers' children to have the same access to schooling opportunities as urban residents' children. There should be no discriminatory policies towards rural labourers' children, and they should be able to take part in all nine years of compulsory education. Public education and finance departments should make arrangements for schooling prerequisites and educational funds, use the opportunity arising from a decrease in the number of school-age children in urban areas and some schools' failures in recruiting a sufficient number of students to reintegrate educational resources, and increase educational investments in rural labourers' children.

Sixth, small and medium-sized enterprises have posted a comparatively high labour/capital ratio, and their development can directly boost employment opportunities, particularly for poorer people. Their development should be supported. A governmental purchasing system could confer preferential treatment on these enterprises; set up a stock equity investment system targeting them; develop business expansion funds, venture capital funds, angel investments and industrial funds; issue bundled bonds; and quicken the pace in launching the growth enterprise stock market.

Finally, under the current circumstances of in-depth adjustments to the foreign trade system, increasingly high standards for environmental protection and energy saving, tightening standard safety control practices and the launch of more macroeconomic control measures, many enterprises have to restructure themselves or close. Many are small and medium-sized enterprises that have employed a number of rural labourers. In the course of their restructuring, extra heed should be paid to what becomes of these employees. Enterprises and local governments should not only make necessary subsistence arrangements for laid-off labourers, but also consider training them for other types of work and employing them in new jobs, so as to prevent them from falling back into poverty.

PROVIDE FAIRER EDUCATIONAL OPPORTUNITIES

In 2006, the Central Committee of the Communist Party of China and the State Council jointly decided to exempt children in western China from all tuition and incidental fees for the nine years of compulsory education, and also offer subsidies to poverty-stricken students for covering textbook and accommodation expenses. They proposed adopting this measure in all parts of China by 2007. The two authorities stated that it was essential to continually intensify efforts to make financial transfer payments and grant special subsidies to those areas that are economically backward, so that compulsory education in rural areas can be financed entirely by the public system. This means children from poor families in poverty-stricken regions will have steadily improving educational conditions, which will exert a visible influence in reducing rural poverty. Expenditure on basic education is a long-term investment in society that generates a gigantic return in the form of an economically developed, powerful, highly civilized nation.

Education level has a strong influence on employment and income, and a far-reaching education system not only helps alleviate poverty in the short term, but also prevents it from spreading across generations. In today's China, large disparities persist among urban and rural residents, and also among people at different income levels in terms of their children's access to educational opportunities. An essential component of the anti-poverty campaign should be to offer all children fairer educational opportunities, especially through more favourable policies for children from poverty-stricken families who are exposed to a poorer learning environment and whose parents cannot afford high educational costs. The following policies and measures are recommended.

First, it is necessary to continually improve the boarding conditions in elementary and high schools in those regions where children have to travel long distances following the recent consolidation of schools. The policy of granting accommodation and living expense subsidies to students from poverty-stricken families should be upheld, including through guaranteed coverage and accurate targeting. This would help eliminate discontinuities in schooling for these students.

Second, there should be concerted and continued efforts to improve educational conditions in elementary and high schools in impoverished rural regions, enhance the qualifications of teachers and teaching quality, and better the treatment of teachers so as to increase the attractiveness of their position.

Third, in supplying equal educational opportunities to children of rural labourers working in urban areas, special financial subsidies should be granted to elementary and high schools to encourage attendance. Education departments should help improve conditions and teaching quality in non-governmental schools set up for these children. They should not impose sanctions on reasonable initiatives to provide schooling.

Fourth, elementary and high schools in rural areas should provide necessary caring and psychological counselling services to children of rural labourers who suffer a lack of parental care, organize them to carry out beneficial extracurricular activities and help solve problems related to breaks in schooling.

Fifth, as children are in a state of physical development and growth, poverty will cause them to suffer malnutrition and stunted growth. In this sense, the impact of poverty on children is heavier than on adults. To address children's malnutrition, many countries have implemented children's nutritional subsidy programmes. China should launch something similar, first in poverty-stricken regions. In offering compulsory education in these regions, central and local governments should ensure the flow of regular funds to provide students with nutritional meals.

Finally, special policies should be worked out for cities that have not yet established the nine-year compulsory education system and for children from poverty-stricken rural families. Largely reducing or even cancelling the tuition fees of poor children studying at governmental universities, colleges and vocational schools should be considered. The central Government could offer certain subsidies, and also mobilize banks to issue loans to students to cover their living expenses.

PROVIDE MORE INTENSIVE TRAINING TO RURAL LABOURERS ON EMPLOYMENT, OCCUPATIONAL SKILLS AND LABOUR TRANSFERS

The provision of agricultural technology and occupational skills training to rural labourers, and assistance in organizing them to work elsewhere, help increase human capital in rural areas, enhance rural residents' incomes, mitigate rural poverty and facilitate the transfer of rural labourers. These initiatives have covered a relatively small number of people, however, especially in occupational skills training and labour transfer initiatives. Only 1 percent to 2 percent of surveyed rural families have benefited from such projects in the past half decade. In the future, it will be imperative to develop human capital in rural areas as the most important task under the developmental mode of poverty alleviation. Financial allocations originally planned for productive development projects for poverty alleviation could be channelled into the greater development of human capital. Some specific suggestions for policy makers are as follows.

First, it is essential to step up the dissemination of agricultural technologies, offer more intensive agricultural technology training for rural families, and allow poverty-stricken and low-income families to take precedence over others in free technical training to help them increase their agricultural production and their capabilities for generating an income.

Second, rural labourers require more intensive occupational skills training and support in working elsewhere. The emphasis should be on projects that fuse labour training and transfers. They should gradually be made available to all rural labourers who are competent and willing to relocate.

Third, training should increase in quality and better meet the needs of trainees. Quality should be supervised and safeguards put in place to protect the interests of all parties (trainers, trainees and employers). This would ensure sustainability, encourage non-governmental organizations to grow stronger, and curb fraudulent behaviours.

Fourth, occupational skills training should be tailored to migrant rural labourers and local unemployed people in view of the supply and demand of the labour market. Non-governmental investors could finance the training of rural labourers in urban areas and open occupational skills schools specifically for those who have worked in urban areas for some time. This would enable them to routinely improve their skills and incomes, and gain a sound footing as they become permanent residents.

IMPROVE RURAL MEDICAL SERVICES

Poverty resulting from excessive medical expenses remains a serious concern, particularly in rural areas. The new rural cooperative medical care system has begun to alleviate this problem, but not the roots of it. Beyond implementing this system, the following issues should be addressed.

First, the rural cooperative medical system has a relatively low ratio of medical expenses reimbursement. Most people still have to pay a large portion of their medical expenses on their own. Poverty-stricken and low-income rural people may not be able to afford these, or they may not receive benefits for some procedures, so they are effectively excluded from the system. So far, the system has mainly benefited medium- and high-income residents in rural areas. Special subsidies need to help poverty-stricken people cover their medical expenses so they have equal access to care. The minimum livelihood security system for rural areas should link with the rural cooperative medical system under certain criteria.

Second, it is essential to simplify the application for reimbursement of medical expenses under the new medical system, improve fund management practices and ensure funds are paid in. Competent public departments should reinforce their supervision of medical services, establish an information disclosure system and work out an effective system to allow migrant labourers to have their medical expenses reimbursed outside their places of origin.

Third, it is necessary to continually reform China's medical management system, separate dispensing drugs from prescribing them, straighten out the medical market, standardize drug prices, enhance the transparency of drug transactions, mobilize the general public to monitor the medical market, open up the medical market on a wider scale, break monopolies, and allow qualified non-governmental medical organizations and rural doctors to enter the medical service sector on an equal footing. Fostering fair competition would help in checking medical expenses and drug prices.

Fourth, to address some of the root causes of poverty stemming from sickness or disability, new initiatives need to improve the basic living environment in rural areas (such as the safety of drinking water); intensify public health, and epidemic control and prevention efforts; spread health care, and epidemic control and prevention knowledge; and reduce the incidence rates of sickness and disability. In those regions where the natural environment has been polluted by enterprises, thus damaging the health of local residents, it is necessary to adopt powerful means to force these enterprises to control their discharges, switch to other product lines or close down their operations. They should also be requested to clean up pollution they have caused.

ESTABLISH A REASONABLE PUBLIC FINANCE-ASSISTED POVERTY ALLEVIATION MECHANISM AND REINFORCE GOVERNMENTAL OVERSIGHT

In China, local governments largely provide public services (such as education, medical care and infrastructure). Since the transfer payments made by the central Government are not sufficient, services in poor regions are on a relatively low level and fall short of full coverage. Progress on poverty alleviation depends on a relatively strong institutional coordination capability and the integration of the resources of all government departments. Some multi-departmental coordination has taken place under the leadership of the Leading Group on Poverty Alleviation and Development under the State Council. Ongoing coordination has been effective mainly in mobilizing resources, but less so in fund and project management. The following suggestions could be considered.

First, the central Government should increase its financial transfer payments to poverty-stricken regions and reinforce the financing powers of local governments there. There should be an emphasis on using funds to establish social security systems for both rural and urban areas, and ensuring all people in poor regions can access public services related to education, health care and the dissemination of science and technology.

Second, agricultural subsidy policies should give preferential treatment to poverty-stricken rural families and complement poverty alleviation policies to support scientific and technological advancement. This would help these families achieve enhanced output and labour efficiency.

Third, in addition to continually ploughing financial allocations into infrastructure in poor regions, the development of human capital there should become a major priority. A reduction in direct productive investments could provide room for professional financial institutions to explore this realm, possibly with increased efficiency.

Fourth, to improve the effectiveness of poverty alleviation efforts, poverty alleviation resources scattered in different governmental departments could be integrated through uniform planning and utilization procedures. There is a need to reinforce the appraisal, supervision and investigation of the application of financial allocations for poverty alleviation.

EXPAND THE ROLE PLAYED BY NON-GOVERNMENTAL ORGANIZATIONS IN POVERTY ALLEVIATION

For China, the ideal mode of poverty alleviation involves the Government allocating funds for large infrastructure and public service projects, complemented by peasants' and professional non-governmental organizations devising and implementing smaller projects closely attuned to particular needs. This is a mode of poverty alleviation successfully adopted by many countries.

For its part, the Government has a strong capacity to organize and mobilize resources and to provide social security and basic social services that remain outside the scope of non-governmental organizations. But these organizations can also play an irreplaceable role in poverty alleviation. They have great flexibility and can concentrate on specific issues faced by people at the grass-roots, including those in poverty. These traits have enabled them to carry out some poverty alleviation activities with great effectiveness. The following recommendations are for expanding the role of these groups.

First, it is necessary to improve laws and clarify the roles, organizational principles and supervision of non-governmental organizations working on poverty alleviation. This would be a critical step towards granting them a greater right to take part in poverty alleviation work and facilitating multiple forms of participation.

Second, cooperation between the Government and non-governmental organizations should intensify. To boost the efficiency of public funds for poverty alleviation, the utilization of resources in competitive ways should be explored, including by allowing more non-governmental organizations to become operators of government-subsidized poverty alleviation projects. Poverty alleviation departments should, in view of the operating performance and business reputation of these operators, allocate resources to those that are the most efficient competitors, and supervise them in line with the principles of openness and transparency.

Third, non-governmental financial institutions can make unique contributions through small-sum credit services. They have access to places and people that commercial financial institutions are not willing to support. In addition to issuing loans, non-governmental financial institutions could provide their borrowers with training, technical support, and professional advice about marketing and community development, in an effort to enhance the poverty alleviation effects of small-sum loans.

Fourth, non-governmental organizations should constantly improve their organizational capacity to play an essential role in filling gaps that will not be filled by profit-oriented organizations and may have been overlooked by governmental departments. They should accept supervision and leadership by the Government and society, on their own initiative.

IN CONCLUSION

In brief, the suggestions put forward above and the opinions expressed throughout this report have all been founded on a basic understanding. With the constant, rapid growth of China's economy and increasing economic strengths, and as China enters the stage of being a well-off society with opportunities for people at all levels, it is better equipped than ever before to help impoverished people and regions emerge from poverty. Gradually, the poverty alleviation standard can be raised. A great deal remains to be done to improve economic structures, policy making and pragmatic interventions, even while recognizing that China is still a developing country (per capita GDP is only US $2000 dollars, thus defining China as a middle-income nation). It has to formulate the objectives and strategies for poverty alleviation based on current circumstances. Policies and measures that exceed productivity levels and the country's financial capacity will not proceed in a sustainable way.

It is hoped that this report can be of help for Chinese and foreign parties to comprehend the progression of China's anti-poverty efforts, and that it will contribute to China's continued strong pursuit of poverty alleviation.

Bibliography

Agricultural and Animal Husbandry Department of Inner Mongolia Autonomous Region. 2004. 'Public Welfare Forests in China to Enjoy Eco-efficiency Compensation Subsidies.' [www.nmagri.gov.cn/news/about.asp?id=38771, 13 December.]

Avenstrup, R., X. Liang and S. Nellemann. 2004. *Kenya, Lesotho, Malawi and Uganda: Universal primary education and poverty reduction: A case study on reducing poverty – what works, what doesn't and why.* Conference paper. Washington, DC: The World Bank.

Banerjee, Benabou and Mookherjee, eds. 2006. *Understanding Poverty.* Oxford University Press.

Benjamin, D., L. Brandt, J. Giles and Sangui Wang. 2006. 'Income Inequality During China's Economic Transition.' In L. Brandt and T. Rawsk, eds., *China's Economic Transition: Origins, Mechanisms, and Consequences,* Cambridge University Press.

Beresford, P. and M. Hoban. 2005. *Participation in Anti-poverty and Regeneration Work and Research: Overcoming Barriers and Creating Opportunities.* York: Joseph Rowntree Foundation.

Besley, T. 1995. 'Non-Market Institutions for Credit and Risk Sharing in Low-Income Countries.' *The Journal of Economic Perspectives*, 9(3).

Bourguignon, F. 2004. 'The Poverty-Growth-Inequality Triangle.' Mimeo. Washington, DC: The World Bank.

Bourguignon, F., and C. Morrisson. 2002. 'Inequality among World Citizens: 1890–1992.' *American Economic Review*, 92(4), pp. 727–744.

Bowles, D. and Hoff, eds. 2006. *Poverty Traps.* Princeton University Press.

Bowles, D. and Gintis. 2002. 'The Inheritance of Inequality.' *Journal of Economic Perspectives*, 16(3), pp. 3–30.

Cai Fang, Du Yang and Wang Meiyan. 2005. *Transformation and Development of China's Urban Labour Market.* Beijing: Commercial Press.

The Central Committee of the Communist Party of China under the State Council. 2006. 'Certain Opinions Regarding Boosting the Construction of New Villages with Socialist Features.' [www.xinhuanet.com, 21 February.]

Chen, Shaohua and M. Ravallion. 1997. 'What Can New Survey Data Tell Us about Recent Changes in Distribution and Poverty?' *The World Bank Economic Review*, 11(2), pp. 357–382.

Chen, Shaohua and M. Ravallion. 2004. 'How have the world's poorest fared since the early 1980s?' Discussion paper (WPS3341). Washington, DC: The World Bank.

China Agricultural Development Bank. 1998. *Statistical Yearbook of China Agricultural Development Bank.* Beijing: China Statistics Press.

China Banking Regulatory Commission. 2006. Background information for a press conference on adjusting and loosening the policy governing financial institutions' entry into rural areas. www.cbrc.gov.cn/chinese/home/jsp/docView.jsp?docID=2925 (22 December 2007).

China Rural Technological Development Centre of the Ministry of Science and Technology. 2005. 'Government-guided boosting of technological innovation in poverty-stricken regions and enhancement of poverty-stricken regions' abilities in pursuing development on their own.' *Poverty Monitoring Report of Rural China.* Beijing: China Statistics Press.

Deaton, A. 2004. 'Measuring Poverty in a Growing World (Or Measuring Growth in a Poor World). The Review of Economics and Statistics Lecture, Harvard University, 15 April 2003.

de Brauw, A., J. Huang, S. Rozelle, Linxiu Zhang and Yigang Zhang. 2002. 'The Evolution of China's Rural Labor Markets during the Reforms.' *Journal of Comparative Economics*, 30, pp. 329–353.

De Ferranti, David, and others. 2004. *Inequality in Latin America: Breaking with History?* Washington, DC: The World Bank.

Deng Quheng. 2007. 'Education, Income Growth and Income Gap: Analysis of Proven Experience Gained in Rural Areas of China. A doctoral treatise.'

Department of Agricultural Economics, State Planning Commission. 1997. 'Work Relief for the Multitude's Good.'

Dercon, S., and P. Krishnan. 1998. 'Changes in Poverty in Rural Ethiopia 1989–1995: Measurement, Robustness Tests and Decomposition.' Working Paper Series (98–7). Oxford: University of Oxford, Centre for the Study of African Economies.

Division of Poverty Alleviation, China Disabled Persons' Federation. 1998. 'Conditions of Poverty-Stricken Disabled Persons in China.' www.cdpf.org.cn (18 June 2008).

Dollar, D., and A. Kraay. 2002. 'Growth is Good for the Poor.' *Journal of Economic Growth*, 7, pp. 195–225.

Drèze, J., and A. K. Sen. 1989. *Hunger and Public Action.* Oxford: Clarendon Press.

Du Ying. 2006. 'Basic Characteristics of the Circulating Rural Labourers in China for the Time Beijing and Analysis of Macroscopical Background.' In Cai Fang and Bai Nansheng, eds., *Flow of Labourers in China in a Transitional Period*, Social Sciences Documentation Press.

Duoji Cairang. 2001. *Research into and Implementation of China's Minimum Livelihood Security System.* Beijing: The People's Press.

Ellis, F., M. Kutengule and A. Nyasulu. 2003. 'Livelihoods and rural poverty reduction in Malawi.' *World Development*, 31 (9).

Faguet, J. P. 2000. *Does Decentralization Increase Responsiveness to Local Needs? Evidence from Bolivia.* London: London School of Economics.

Fajnzylber, P., D. Lederman and N. Loayza. 1998. 'Determinants of Crime Rates in Latin America and the World.' World Bank Latin American and Caribbean Studies Working Paper Series. Washington, DC: The World Bank.

Fajnzylber, P., D. Lederman and N. Loayza. 2000. 'Crime and Victimization: An Economic Perspective.' *Economia*, 1(1).

Fan Gang, Wang Xiaolu and Zhang Hongjun. 2005. 'Analysis of Proven Cases with Regard to the Influence Wielded by Transfer of Labourers upon the Income Gaps among Regions.' In *Income Distribution and Public Policies*, China Economic Reform and Research Foundation, Joint Experts Team of China Economic Restructuring Research Society, pp. 84–127. Shanghai: Shanghai Far East Press.

Fan, S., and C. Chan-Kang. 2005. *Road Development, Economic Growth, and Poverty Reduction in China.* International Food Policy Research Institute Research Report 138.

Fan Shenggen, Linxiu Zhang and Xiaobo Zhang. 2004. 'Reforms, Investment, and Poverty in Rural China.' *Economic Development and Cultural Change*, pp. 395–421.

Forbes, K. 2000. 'A Reassessment of the Relationship Between Inequality and Growth.' *American Economic Review*, 90, pp. 869–897.

Foreign Capital Project Management Center (Leading Group Office of Poverty Alleviation and Development, State Council of the People's Republic of China) and Center for Community Development Studies of Yunnan. 2001. *Reflecting Voice of the Poor: Participatory Poverty Assessment in Nayong County, Guizhou Province, P.R. China.* ADB RETA 5894-PRC. August 2001.

Gao Hongbin. 2001. *Research on Poverty Alleviation, Development and Planning.* Beijing: China Finance and Economics Press.

Gu Xin and Fang Liming. 2004. 'Somewhere Between Volunteer and Compulsory – Analysis of the Applicability and Sustainable Evolution of China's Rural Cooperative Medical System.' *Sociology Research*, 5.

Gustafsson, Bjorn, and Li Shi. 2004. 'Expenditures on education and health care and poverty in rural China.' *China Economic Review*, 15, pp. 292–301.

Hannum, Emily. 2003. 'Poverty and Basic Education in Rural China: Villages, Households, and Girls' and Boys' Enrollment.' *Comparative Education Review*, 47(2).

Health Economy Research Institute of the Ministry of Health. 2005. 'Research Report on China's Total Health Care Expenses.'

Heckman, James. 2003. 'China's Investment in Human Capital.' *Economic Development and Cultural Change*, pp. 795–804.

Hjorth P. 2003. 'Knowledge Development and Management of Urban Poverty Alleviation.' *Habitat International*, 27(3).

Huang Guoqing. 2002. 'Analysis of the Status Quo of the Urban Poverty-Stricken Population.' *Journal of Hubei University*, 1.

Huang Haili. 2007. 'New Characteristics of the Population in Financial Hardships – Analysis of Findings of the Sample Survey of the Population in Financial Hardships in Hefei City of Anhui Province'. Unpublished survey report.

Hussain, A. 2003. *Urban Poverty in China: Measurement, Patterns and Policies.* Geneva: International Labour Office.

International Labour Office (ILO). 2004. *Forum on the Pro-poor Delivery of Rural Infrastructure Services: The Challenge of Decentralization.* Bangkok: International Labour Office.

Jia Kang and Zhang Licheng. 2005. 'Suggestions for Improvement of the Fundraising Mode under the Policy with Regard to the New Type of Rural Cooperative Medical System.' *Finance Studies*, 3.

Karl, M. 2000. Monitoring and Evaluating Stakeholder Participation in Agriculture and Rural Development Project: a Literature Review.

Khan, Azizur. 1977. 'Basic Needs Targets: An Illustrative Exercise in Identification and Quantification.' In D. P. Ghai *et al.*, eds., *The Basic Needs Approach to Development*, Geneva: International Labour Organization.

Khan, Azizur. 2007. 'Growth, Inequality and Poverty: A Comparative Study of China's Experience in the Periods Before and After the Asian Crisis.' In Björn Gustafsson, Li Shi and Terry Sicular, eds., *Inequality and Public Policy in China*, Cambridge University Press (forthcoming).

Knight, John, Li Shi and Deng Quheng. 2006. 'Education and the Poverty Trap in Rural China.' Memo.

Kraay, A. 2005. 'When is Growth Pro-Poor? Evidence from a Panel of Countries.' *Journal of Development Economics* (forthcoming).

Kumar, N., N. Saxena, Y. Alagh and K. Mitra. 2000. 'India: Alleviating poverty through forest development.' Washington, DC: The World Bank www.worldbank.org (15 June 2001).

Kumar, S. 2002. 'Does "Participation" in Common Pool Resource Management Help the Poor? A Social Cost–Benefit Analysis of Joint Forest Management in Jharkhand, India.' *World Development*, 30(5).

Kwon, E. 2001. 'Infrastructure, growth, and poverty reduction in Indonesia: A cross-sectional analysis.' Mimeo. Manila: Asian Development Bank.

Leading Group for the 2nd National Sample Survey of Disabled Persons, National Bureau of Statistics of China. 2006. 'Gazette of Main Data Obtained from the 2nd National Sample Survey of Disabled Persons in 2006.' www.xinhuanet.com (1 December).

Li Jing, Yang Guotao and Meng Lingjie. 2006. 'Poverty Line: Theory, Application and Disputes.' *Agricultural Economics*, 7.

Li Shi. 2003. 'Status Quo of China's Urban Poverty Scene and Reasons Thereof.' *China Economy Times*, 27 February.

Li Shi. 2004: 'Deterioration of the Urban Poverty Scene in China in the Late 1990s and Reasons Thereof.' In Li Shi and Hiroshi Sato, eds., *Price of Economic Restructuring: A Study of Unemployment, Poverty and Income Gaps in Urban Areas of China*, China Finance and Economics Press.

Li Shi and Hiroshi Sato, eds. 2004. *Price of Economic Restructuring: A Study of Unemployment, Poverty and Income Gaps in Urban Areas of China.* China Finance and Economics Press.

Li Shi and John Knight. 2002. 'Three Types of Poverty in Urban Areas of China.' *Economic Studies*, 10.

Li Tianyou and Junsen Zhang. 1998. 'Returns to Education under Collective and Household Farming in China.' *Journal of Development Economics*, 56, pp. 307–335.

Li Wen and Wang Sangui. 2004. 'Distribution of the Central Government's Poverty Alleviation Funds and Analysis of Influencing Factors.' *China's Rural Economy*, 8.

Li Yaqin. 2004. 'Rural Elementary Schools: Redeployment Practices Urgently in Need of Standardization.' *Quanzhou Evening News*, 1 June.

Li Zhong. 2000. *Abstracted Discussions on Construction Work in One Decade in the Three Pilot Regions.* Lanzhou: Gansu People's Press.

Liu Chunbin. 2006. 'Re-discussion of Criteria for China's Poverty-stricken Population.' *Population Studies*, 6.

Li Shi and Bai Nansheng. 2005. *China Human Development Report 2005: Development with Equity.* Beijing: China Translation and Publishing Corporation.

Liu Yaqiao, Yang Jun and Cao Zijian. 2005. 'Review and Discussion of Development Modes of Poverty Alleviation in Gansu Province,' *Gansu Theoretical Journal*, 3.

Lopez, H. 2004. 'Pro-Poor-Pro-Growth: Is There a Trade Off?' Policy Research Working Paper (3378). Washington, DC: The World Bank.

Lundberg, M., and L. Squire. 2003. 'The Simultaneous Evolution of Growth and Inequality.' *The Economic Journal*, 113, pp. 326–344.

Mainsah, E., S. Heuer, A. Kalra and Q. Zhang. 2004. 'Grameen Bank: Taking capitalism to the poor.' *Chazen Web Journal of International Business*. New York: Columbia Business School, Columbia University.

Martinez-Vazquez, Jorge. 2005. 'The Current State of Decentralization Reform in Indonesia: A Postscript.' In James Alm, Jorge Martinez-Vazquez and Sri Mulyani Indrawati, eds., *Decentralization and the Rebuilding of Indonesia – The 'Big Bang' Program and Its Economic Consequences*, Cheltenham, United Kingdom and Northampton, United States: Edward Elgar Publishing.

Maurer, Klaus. 2004. 'Bank Rakyat Indonesia: Twenty Years of Large-Scale Microfinance.' In *Scaling Up Poverty Reduction: Case Studies in Microfinance*. Washington, DC: Consultative Group to Assist the Poor and The World Bank.

McKinnon, R. I. 1983. *Money and Capital in Economic Development*. Washington DC: The Brookings Institution.

Ministry of Civil Affairs. 2004. 'Descriptions of Social Succor Work in Rural Areas of China.'

Ministry of Civil Affairs. 2005a: Data from the 'Statistical Bulletin of the Civil Administration Cause in 2005.' http://admin.mca.gov.cn/mztj/yuebao0512.htm (18 June 2008).

Ministry of Civil Affairs. 2005b: 'Statistical Gazette of the Development of Labour and Social Security Cause in 2005.'

Ministry of Civil Affairs. 2005c. *China Statistical Yearbook of Civil Administration*. Beijing: China Statistics Press.

Ministry of Civil Affairs. 2006a. Data from the 'Statistical Bulletin of Civil Administration Cause in 2006.' http://admin.mca.gov.cn/mztj/yuebao0612.htm (18 June 2008).

Ministry of Civil Affairs. 2006b. *Quick Statistical Report on Civil Administration in 2006*. http://www.mca.gov.cn (18 June 2008).

Ministry of Civil Affairs. 2007. *China Statistical Yearbook of Civil Administration*. Beijing: China Statistics Press.

Ministry of Civil Affairs of the People's Republic of China. 2006. 'Monthly Statistical Report of the Civil Administration Cause.' November. www.mca.gov.cn (18 June 2008).

Ministry of Civil Affairs of the People's Republic of China. 2006b. 'China to Set up a Social Succor System for Rural and Urban Areas by 2010. www.mca.gov.cn/news/content/Media/20061124123537.htm (24 November 2007).

Ministry of Civil Affairs of the People's Republic of China. 2006c. *China Statistical Yearbook of Civil Administration*. Beijing: China Statistics Press.

Ministry of Civil Affairs of the People's Republic of China. 2007a. 'Statistical Gazette on the Development of China's Civil Administration Cause in 2006.' Website of the Ministry of Civil Affairs of the People's Republic of China.

Ministry of Civil Affairs of the People's Republic of China. 2007b, 'Implementation Details of the Minimum Livelihood Security System in Above-County Administration Units in Four Quarters of 2006.' Website of the Ministry of Civil Affairs of the People's Republic of China.

Ministry of Civil Affairs of the People's Republic of China. 2007c. 'The Minimum Livelihood Security Department of the State Ministry of Civil Affairs Replied to Medial Specialists' Questions about Their Concerns for Minimum Livelihood Security for Rural Areas.' www.mca.gov.cn/search/detail.asp?title=民政部最低生活保障司解答媒体关心的农村低保问题&Ftype=Acontent&keyword=农村最低生活保障。(18 June 2008).

Ministry of Communications. 2006. General descriptions of communications services. Website of the Ministry of Communications.

Ministry of Education. 2005. *Report on Development Conditions of China's Education Cause in 2004.*

Ministry of Finance and the World Bank. 2003. 'Intensify China's Management of Financial Funds for Poverty Alleviation Purposes.' March.

Ministry of Health of the People's Republic of China. 2006. *Statistical Yearbook of Health Care 2006.*

Ministry of Science and Technology. 2001. 'Poverty Alleviation via Scientific and Technological Advancement.' *Poverty Monitoring Report of Rural China.* Beijing: China Statistics Press.

Morduch, J. 1999. 'The microfinance promise.' *Journal of Economic Literature*, 37(4).

National Bureau of Statistics of China. 1999. *China Statistical Summary.* Beijing: China Statistics Press.

National Bureau of Statistics of China. 2001. *China Statistical Summary.* Beijing: China Statistics Press.

National Bureau of Statistics of China. 2002. *China Statistical Summary.* Beijing: China Statistics Press.

National Bureau of Statistics of China. 2003. *China Statistical Summary.* Beijing: China Statistics Press.

National Bureau of Statistics of China. 2004. *China Statistical Summary.* Beijing: China Statistics Press.

National Bureau of Statistics of China. 2005. *China Statistical Summary.* Beijing: China Statistics Press.

National Bureau of Statistics of China. 2006. *China Statistical Summary.* Beijing: China Statistics Press.

National Bureau of Statistics of China. 2007. 2006 *Statistical Gazette on the National Economy and Social Development.* Website of the National Bureau of Statistics of China.

National Information Centre. 2005. 'Estimated Labour Employment Climate in 2005.' www.lm.gov.cn (18 June 2008).

Park, A., and Changqing Ren. 2001. 'Microfinance with Chinese Characteristics.' *World Development*, 29.

Park, A., Changqing Ren and Sangui Wang. 2003. *Micro-Finance, Poverty Alleviation, and Financial Reform in China, Rural Financial and Credit Infrastructure in China.* Paris: Organisation for Economic Co-operation and Development.

Park, A., and Sangui Wang. 2006. 'Are China's Poor Able to Work?' Mimeo.

Park, A., Sangui Wang and Guobao Wu. 2002. 'Regional Poverty Targeting in China.' *Journal of Public Economics*, 86, pp. 123–153.

People's Daily. 2007. 'How the poverty-stricken rural population would be covered by the minimum livelihood security system.' Liu Rao, news reporter, overseas edition. 20 August.

Poverty Alleviation Leadership Group of the State Council. 1993. 'National Eight-Seven Poverty Alleviation Plan.'

Poverty Alleviation Leadership Group of the State Council. 2001. 'China Scheme of Rural Development for Poverty Alleviation (2001–2010).'

Poverty Alleviation Office of the State Council. 1989. *Schema of Economic Development in Poverty-Stricken Regions in China.* Beijing: Agricultural Press.

Poverty Alleviation Office of the State Council. 2005. List of the first batch of poverty-stricken villages where the poverty alleviation plan was implemented, in those major counties subject to poverty alleviation.

Press Office of the State Council. 2001. *White Book on China's Rural Development for Poverty Alleviation Purpose.*

Pretty, J., I. Guijt, J. Thompson and I. Scoones. 1995. *Participatory Learning and Action: A Trainer's Guide.* London: International Institute for Environment and Development.

Qin Hui. 2002. 'Globalization Process and China's Tertiary Sector after Her Accession to the WTO.' *Southern Weekend News*, 29 August.

Rao, M. Govinda. 2005. Fiscal Federalism in India: Emerging Challenges. Indian Country Roundtable on Fiscal Federalism, Global Dialogue Program on Federalism. New Delhi: Forum of Federations, National Institute of Public Finance and Policy.

Ravallion, M. 1994. *Poverty Comparisons.* Harwood Academic Publishers.

Ravallion, M. 2004. 'Pro-Poor Growth: A Primer.' Policy Research Working Paper (3242). Washington, DC: The World Bank.

Ravallion, M., and J. Jalan. 1999. 'China's Lagging Poor Areas.' *American Economic Review*, 89(2), pp. 301–305.

Riskin, C. 1994. 'Chinese Rural Poverty: Marginalized or Dispersed?' *American Economic Review*, 84(2), pp. 281–284.

Rowntree, S. 1901. *Poverty: A Study of Town Life.* London: Macmillan.

Rozelle, S., A. Park, V. Bezinger and Changqing Ren. 1998. 'Targeted Poverty Investments and Economic Growth in China.' World Development.

Rural Department of the National Bureau of Statistics of China. 2005. *China Yearbook of Rural Household Survey: 2005.* Beijing: China Statistics Press.

Rural Department of the National Bureau of Statistics of China. 2006a. *China Yearbook of Rural Household Survey: 2006.* Beijing: China Statistics Press.

Rural Department of the National Bureau of Statistics of China. 2006b. *Poverty Monitoring Report of Rural China.* Beijing: China Statistics Press.

Rural Survey Group of the National Bureau of Statistics of China. 2000. *Poverty Monitoring Report of Rural China: 2000.* Beijing: China Statistics Press.

Rural Survey Group of the National Bureau of Statistics of China. 2001. *Poverty Monitoring Report of Rural China: 2001.* Beijing: China Statistics Press.

Rural Survey Group of the National Bureau of Statistics of China. 2002a. *China Yearbook of Rural Household Survey: 2002.* Beijing: China Statistics Press.

Rural Survey Group of the National Bureau of Statistics of China. 2002b. *Poverty Monitoring Report of Rural China: 2002.* Beijing: China Statistics Press.

Rural Survey Group of the National Bureau of Statistics of China. 2003. *Poverty Monitoring Report of Rural China: 2003.* Beijing: China Statistics Press.

Rural Survey Group of the National Bureau of Statistics of China. 2004. *Poverty Monitoring Report of Rural China: 2004.* Beijing: China Statistics Press.

Rural Survey Group of the National Bureau of Statistics of China. 2005. *Poverty Monitoring Report of Rural China: 2005.* Beijing: China Statistics Press.

Rural Survey Group of the National Bureau of Statistics of China. 2006. *Poverty Monitoring Report of Rural China: 2006.* Beijing: China Statistics Press.

Sachs, J. 2006. *The End of Poverty – Economic Possibilities for Our Time.* The Penguin Press.

Sen, A. 1983. 'Poor, Relatively Speaking.' *Oxford Economic Papers*, New Series, 35(2), pp. 153–169.

Sen, A. 1999. *Development as Freedom*. Oxford University Press.

Shaw, E. S. 1973. *Financial Deepening in Economic Development*. New York, Oxford University Press

Sheng Laiyun. 2001. 'Research on the Rural Poverty Standard in the New Era.' In Xian Zude, ed., *Research on Eye-Catching Issues for Rural Areas of China in 2001*, Beijing: China Statistics Press.

Skoufias, E., and V. di Maro. 2006. 'Conditional Cash Transfers, Adult Work Incentives, and Poverty.' *World Bank Policy Research Working Paper* (3973).

State Council of the People's Republic of China. 2007. 'Notice of the State Council with Regard to Establishing a Minimum Livelihood Security System for Rural Areas throughout the Country.' 11 July.

State Forestry Administration. 2004. 'Conversion of Croplands into Forests' project. Website of the State Forestry Administration.

State Science Commission. 1995. Research on Poverty Alleviation Investments in China. A research report.

Statistical Information Centre of the Ministry of Health. 2004. *Survey and Research on China's Health Care Service: Analysis Report on the Third National Health Care Survey*. Beijing: Chinese Peking Union Medical College Press.

Sunderlin, W. D. 2006. 'Poverty alleviation through community forestry in Cambodia, Laos, and Vietnam: An assessment of the potential.' *Forest Policy and Economics*, 8.

Surveillance Centre of the China Labour Market Information Network. 2006. 'Analysis of the Supply–Demand Relations in the Labour Markets in Some Cities in the Second Quarter of 2006.' Website of the Ministry of Labour and Social Security.

Tang Jun, Sha Lin and Ren Zhenxing. 2003. *China Report on Urban Poverty and Anti-Poverty Measures*. Beijing: Huaxia Press.

Teaching and Research Division of Sociology, Party School of Beijing Municipal Party Committee. 2002. 'Report upon the Survey of the Poverty Scene among Urban Residents in Beijing.' *New Vista*, 1.

Territorial and Regional Department, State Planning Commission. 1991. *Guidance on Work Relief Practices*. Beijing: Science and Technology Documentation Press.

Topical Research Group of the Ministry of Labour and Social Security. 2006. 'Number and Features of Employment Mixture of Circulating Rural Labourers in Today's China.' [www.ccrs.org.cn/article_view.asp?ID=5651].

Topical Research Group of Nanjing Agricultural University. 2006. 'Study of Proven Cases of Food Safety and Sustainability of Conversion of Croplands into Forests with regard to Rural Families in Poverty-Stricken Regions.' A report for the China Development Research Foundation, 23.

Townsend, Peter. 1962. 'The Meaning of Poverty.' *The British Journal of Sociology*, 13(3), pp. 210–227.

Turk C. 2001. 'Linking participatory poverty assessments to policy and policy-making: experience from Vietnam.' World Bank Policy Research Working Papers. Washington, DC: The World Bank.

United Nations (UN). 2005. *The Millennium Development Goals Report 2005*. New York.

United Nations Educational, Scientific and Cultural Organization (UNESCO). 2005. 'Decentralization in Education: Policies and Practices.' Education Policies and Strategies Series (7). Paris.

Wang Rongdang. 2006. 'Measurement and Optimization of the Rural Poverty Line.' *East China Economic Management*, 3.

Wang Sangui, Albert Park, Shubham Chaudhuri and Gaurav Datt. 2006. 'Poverty Targeting of China's Integrated Village Development Program.' Mimeo.

Wang Sangui and Li Wen. 2005. *Research on China's Rural Poverty Scene*. Beijing: China Finance and Economics Press.

Wang Sangui, Li Wen and Li Yun. 2004. 'China's Investment of Poverty Alleviation Funds and Analysis of the Effect of Such Investment.' *Agricultural Technology Economy*, 5.

Wang Sangui, Li Zhou and Ren Yanshun. 2004. 'China's "Eight-Seven Poverty Alleviation Plan": National Strategies and Their Influences.' Report on country-specific data for the Shanghai International Conference on Poverty Alleviation.

Wang Sangui, Piao Zhishui and Wu Guobao. 1999. *Research on the Agricultural Economy and Sci-Tech Development. An appraisal of China's anti-poverty policies*. Beijing: China Agricultural Press.

Wang Xiaolu and Fan Gang. 2005. 'Variation Trend of and Factors Influencing the Income Distribution Gap in China.' In *Income Distribution and Public Policies, China Economic Reform Research Foundation and Joint Experts Team of China Economic Restructuring Research Society*, pp. 1–34. Shanghai: Shanghai Far East Press.

Wang Xiaoqiang and Bai Nanfeng. 1986. *Nominal Poverty*. Chengdu: Sichuan People's Press.

Wang Youjuan. 2005. 'Size and Characteristics of the Poverty-Stricken Urban Population in China in 2004.' Job treatise.

Wang Youjuan. 2006. 'Evaluations of the Implementation of the Policy of Minimum Livelihood Security for Urban Residents.' *Statistical Information of Civil Administration*, 10.

Wei Jinsheng. 2004. 'Research on the Poverty-Stricken Population in Major Chinese Cities.'

Wen Qiuliang. 2003. 'Poverty Alleviation Endeavours in Rural Areas of China and Adjustments to Poverty Alleviation Policies.' A research report.

World Bank. 1992. 'China's Strategy for Poverty Alleviation.'

World Bank. 2000. World Development Report 2000/2001: Attacking poverty. Washington, D.C.

World Bank. 2001. *China: Overcoming Rural Poverty*. Washington, D.C.

World Bank. 2002a. 'Have Trainings Helped China's Laid-off Workers and Staff Members Get Re-employed?' Cases from two cities (24161-CHA). Washington, DC.

World Bank. 2002b. 'World Bank's Project Management and Supervision Practices.'

World Bank. 2003. *China Country Economic Memorandum: Promoting Growth with Equity*. Washington, DC.

World Bank. 2004. *World Development Report 2005: A Better Investment Climate for Everyone*. Oxford University Press.

www.people.com.cn. 2006a. 'The State Food and Drug Administration Clarified Some Facts in Regard to Its Hearsay Approval of over 10,000 Kinds of New Drugs in a Year.' (31 March 2007).

www.people.com.cn. 2006b. 'Pour More Funds to Facilitate the Construction of New Rural Villages.' http://theory.people.com.cn/GB/40557/49139/49143/4588497.html (13 July 2007).

www.xinhuanet.com. 2007. 'Discussions on the Meeting of the Standing Committee of the State Council with Regard to Prosecution of Zheng Xiaoyu for His Lawbreaking Deeds' (24 January 2008).

Yang, Dennis Tao. 1997. 'Education in Production: Measuring Labor Quality and Management.' *American Journal of Agricultural Economics*, 79(3), 764–722.

Yangtze River Daily. 2006. 'Professor Zhong Nanshan Rapped Excessive Prices of Drugs and Appealed for a Drug Monopoly Sale System.' *Yangtze River Daily* (24 May 2007).

Yue Ximing, Terry Sicular, Li Shi and Björn Gustafsson. 2007. 'Explaining Incomes and Inequality in China.' In Bjorn Gustafsson, Li Shi and Terry Sicular, eds., *Inequality and Public Policy in China*, Cambridge University Press (forthcoming).

Zeng Yiyu. 2005. 'Survey on the Influence Wielded by the "Pool Resources for Good Education" Policy towards the Rural Basic Education Cause in Remote Poverty-Stricken Regions Populated by People of National Minorities in Guizhou Province.' *Education and Economy*, 1.

Zhang Deyuan. 2004. 'Overview of and Comments on the Evolution of China's Compulsory Education Cause.' *Guangming Observer*, 9 November.

Zhang Lu and Jiao Weidong. 2005. 'Status Quo, Analysis of Characteristics of, and Countermeasures for the Urban Poverty-Stricken Population in Xi'an.' www.gutx.com (1 January 2006).

Zhao Yaohui. 2006. 'Breakthrough: Decision on Migration of China's Rural Population into Rural Areas from Urban Areas.' In Cai Fang and Bai Nansheng, eds., *Flow of Labourers in China's Transitional Period*, Social Sciences Documentation Press.

Zhou Binbin. 1990. 'Retrospective on Basic Poverty Alleviation Policies During the 'Seventh Five-Year-Long National Development Programme'. *Economic Development Forum*, 12.

Zhou Binbin. 1991. 'Poverty Scene in the Era of People's Communes. *Economic Development Forum*, 3.

Zhou Binbin and Gao Hongbin. 1993. 'Research on Poverty and Summarization of Anti-Poverty Practices.' *Economic Development Forum*.

Zhou Furong. 2004. 'Experts with Asian Development Bank Reckon "Village-wide Implementation" Cannot Solve Problems Arising in Poverty Alleviation.' *Economic Reference News*, 8 October.

Zhou Haojie. 2005. 'New Type Rural Cooperative Medical System: Experience, Challenges and Countermeasures.' *China Health-Related Economy*, 1.

Zhu Ling. 2000. 'Medical Insurance and Medical Rescue in Rural Areas.' Website of the Chinese Academy of Social Sciences. www.cass.net.cn/chinese/s01_jjs/grxszl-suelingdao/zhuling/02.htm (18 June 2008).

BACKGROUND REPORTS

The following were prepared for the China Development Research Foundation for the China Development Report 2007.

Beijing De Sai Si Chuang Consultation Centre. 'Research on Parties Participating in the Formulation of the Budgets of County/Township-Level Governments.'

Cai Fang and Wang Meiyan. 2006. 'Laying-off, Unemployment, Reemployment and Urban Poverty.'

Du Yang. 2006. 'China's Urban Poverty Scene: Trends, Policies and New Problems.'

Gu Xin. 2006. 'Institutionalization of China's Social Succor System.'

Han Jun. 2006. 'Assessment of the Influence Wielded by Medicare Policies on Rural Poverty.'

He Ping. 'Influence Wielded by Minimum Livelihood Security Policies in Rural and Urban Areas on the Poverty Scene.'

Jin Lian. 2006. 'Assessment of the Influence Wielded by Rural Compulsory Education Policies on Rural Poverty.'

Li Wen. 2006. 'Assessment of the Poverty Alleviation Effect Generated by Training with Regard to Transfer of the Labour Force.'

Li Xiaoyun and Tang Lixia. 2006. 'Immigration and Poverty Alleviation.'

Li Zhou and Cao Jianhua. 'Assessment of Social Poverty Alleviation Endeavours and Their Influence.'

Li Zhou and Cao Jianhua. 'Report upon the Assessment of the Evolution of Industrialization Endeavours for Poverty Alleviation Purposes.'

Liu Minquan and Yu Jiantuo. 'International Theories and Practical Policies of Poverty Alleviation.'

Ma Guansheng. 'Nutrition and Health among Underprivileged Children and Related Governmental Policies.'

Ma Yongliang, Zhao Changbao and Wu Zhigang. 2006. 'Poverty issues in rural areas of China: An analysis of the findings of a survey among rural families.'

Rural Survey Department of the National Bureau of Statistics of China. China's Rural Poverty Scene and Conditions of the Low-income Population.'

Shanghai DataSea Marketing Research Co., Ltd. 'Rural Poverty Research Report.'

Topical Research Group. 'A generation living in a crevice in the city.'

Wang Sangui. 2006a 'Appraisal report upon the village-wide implementation work.'

Wang Sangui. 2006b. 'Structure of China's poverty alleviation work.'

Wang Zhenyao. 2006. 'Urban Poverty-Stricken Population and Population Covered by the Minimum Living Security System'.

Yue Ximing. 2006. 'The Child Poverty Scene in Rural Areas.'

Zhang Tao, Yi Cheng and Wang Tian. 'Research on Interest-Subsidized Loans for Poverty Alleviation Purposes.'

Zheng Feihu and Li Shi. 2006. 'Analysis of China's Urban Poverty-Stricken Population and Low-Income Population since 1995.'

Zuo Ting. 'Influence of Rural Policies on the Poverty-Stricken Population.'

Index